EARLY CHILDHOOD EDUCATION SERIES

AD
D

eney,
illo,
t

Supervision
2nd Ed.: A
JOSEPH J. C

The Early C
of Current I
CAROL SEI

Leadership
The Pathwa
JILLIAN RC

Inside a He
Developing
DEBORAH

Uncommor
Who Teach
JAMES R. K

Teaching ar
Multicultura
2nd Ed.
PATRICIA C

Windows or
Documentir
JUDY HAI
& KATHY

Bringing I
An Innovi
Early Chil
LOUISE B

Major Tre
Childhoo
Controvei
JOAN P. I
MARY RE

Master Pla
Learning f
GRETCHI

Understar
A Guide f
JILLIAN R

Understar
Research
WILLIAM

ractice

ES,
NSKY
l:
arly

LINSKI

, 2nd Ed.

ohn Dewey
om

hood

Eds.
nd

oung
entered

vent

n:
here in

ppropriate

Diversity in the Classroom:
New Approaches to the Education
of Young Children, 2nd Ed.
FRANCES E. KENDALL

BRUCE L. MALLORY & REBECCA S. NEW, EDS.

Understanding Assessment and Evaluation in
Early Childhood Education
DOMINIC F. GULLO

(Continued)

Supervision in Early Childhood Education

A DEVELOPMENTAL PERSPECTIVE

Second Edition

JOSEPH J. CARUSO
M. TEMPLE FAWCETT

Teachers College, Columbia University
New York and London

WITHDRAWN

Published by Teachers College Press, 1234 Amsterdam Avenue, New York, NY 10027

Library of Congress Cataloging-in-Publication Data

Caruso, Joseph J., 1943–
    Supervision in early childhood education : a developmental
 perspective / Joseph J. Caruso, M. Temple Fawcett. — 2nd ed.
        p.   cm. — (Early childhood education series)
    Includes bibliographical references (p.   ) and index.
    ISBN 0-8077-3852-2 (paper : alk. paper).
    1. School supervision—United States.   2. Early childhood
 education—United States.   3. Child development—United States.
 4. Educational surveys—United States.   I. Fawcett, M. Temple,
 1928–   . II. Title. III. Series: Early childhood education series
 (Teachers College Press)
 LB2822.7.C37   1999
 372.12—dc21   98-52823

ISBN 0-8077-3852-2 (paper)

Printed on acid-free paper
Manufactured in the United States of America

06   05   04   03   02   8   7   6   5   4   3

Contents

Preface

This book about supervising staff in early care and education addresses issues and methods pertinent to personnel working in a variety of public and private settings for young children, including programs for infants, toddlers, and preschoolers; school-age child care centers; kindergartens; and family child care homes. It is meant to fill a gap in the supervision and the early childhood literature, which is still only beginning to take into account the special needs of supervisors and staff in these programs.

Directors, educational coordinators, head teachers, consultants, or others currently working in programs for young children who recognize a need to expand and improve their supervisory skills should find this volume particularly relevant to their needs. College supervisors, administrators in public school systems, and those who may have limited experience with preschool programs and personnel will also find this book informative and useful. Instructors may wish to consider it as the principal text in courses preparing persons for early childhood supervisory, administrative, and leadership positions.

We believe that the personal and professional development of the adult is basic to formulating supervisory strategies. Through supervision, staff members can receive continuing support in their development as professionals and para-professionals, and thus become better providers of care and education for children. Although supervision may well encompass more than staff development, we have chosen to focus this book on that aspect of the role. We also stress the importance of the supervisor's ongoing development and learning.

The content of this volume is intended to be both descriptive and practical. We have administered surveys and conducted many interviews in order to incorporate the thoughts, feelings, dilemmas, and concerns of early childhood personnel into the text, and to clarify supervisor and supervisee roles and responsibilities. We provide the reader with specific suggestions for improving supervisory skills when working with individual staff members and with groups.

This volume has four major sections. In Part I, supervisory myths are challenged in order to ease the burden under which supervisors carry out their work. Then the various types of early childhood programs and the people who work in them are described from the perspective of the supervisor's role.

The development of supervisors and supervisees, their relationship to each other, and implications for planning supervisory approaches are explored in Part II. A new chapter, "Caring, Knowing, and Imagining," sets the context for this section in the second edition. Part III offers some basic information and suggestions for observing, holding conferences, and evaluating staff within the context of a clinical supervision approach. Several significant issues that affect staff morale and effectiveness are examined in Part IV, followed by suggestions for designing various types of staff development and training, and some specific tools for putting these plans into practice.

Throughout this book, we use the term *supervisor* to mean those persons who do supervision as part or all of their jobs. These may be administrators, supervisors, consultants, or teachers. The terms *teacher, staff member, caregiver,* and *supervisee* are generally used interchangeably.

Readers familiar with the first edition of *Supervision in Early Childhood Education: A Developmental Perspective* will notice that our new version reflects some of the notable changes that have taken place in the early childhood field since 1986, especially those significant efforts toward defining and improving quality and increasing professionalism initiated by the National Association for the Education of Young Children (NAEYC).

The NAEYC process for accrediting early childhood programs, for example, has become firmly established and has been followed by similar processes for family child care and school-age child care. We have included relevant standards for the NAEYC accreditation criteria at the end of several chapters. The training and publications of the National Institute for Early Childhood Professional Development of the NAEYC have contributed to our greater emphasis on career ladders and lattices.

In the period since 1986, increasing numbers of children from a wide variety of cultural and linguistic backgrounds are also receiving care and education in early childhood classrooms. At the same time, more information has become available that can assist supervisors and teachers whose backgrounds differ from those of staff and children. Diversity issues, therefore, have received greater emphasis in this edition, especially in Chapters 10, 12, and 13.

Finally, throughout this book we have made changes based on new understandings about effective supervisory and staff development approaches, particularly the importance of collaboration among staff, and between supervisors and staff members. We have included a number of promising new staff development and evaluation practices.

We hope this book contributes to the attainment of the goals reflected above, and to the common mission that brings early childhood professionals together—that is, to support the growth and development of young children and their families.

Part I

THE SUPERVISORY CONTEXT

1

Myths About Supervision

Myths influence and shape, and are often used to justify, behavior. Myths about supervision come from expectations supervisors have about their jobs and their past supervisory experiences, training, and education. Myths can also arise from the attitudes toward supervisors held by staff members and others. Some of these beliefs are simply not true. Others are partially true. Nevertheless, we have found that they can create internal stress for supervisors and bring about pressure from others.

What are some of the myths about supervision in programs for young children?

Almost anyone can be an early childhood supervisor.

If the individual hired to be a director, educational coordinator, or head teacher of an early childhood program has had children, is a nice person, and has taught in the classroom, then few other qualifications are thought necessary to be a good supervisor. After all, parents have raised children for years without formal training, so why would a director need any special skills or knowledge to supervise babysitters? And anyone who has taught understands teachers' problems and can, therefore, supervise teachers effectively.

This kind of thinking—perhaps more prevalent in the minds of the public at large than in the child care field—certainly contributes to the feelings many supervisors have that their work is not valued. Such thinking is based on a lack of knowledge about the process of working with adults and about the needs of young children and their cognitive, social, emotional, and physical development. It fails to recognize the importance of the environments in which children learn and of the interactions between children and adults in those environments.

Supervision cannot be carried out without careful thought, planning, and skill. Not all adults are competent to work with other adults or with children. Some who work well with children have to make many adjustments to work effectively with adults. Other adults work best alone, or with machines, or behind a desk. They may not have the stamina or sensitivity to interact with people daily in small settings.

Persons holding supervisory positions in early childhood programs usually have more than one role to fill and are responsible for working with all types of people. Those who strive to provide quality supervision to their staff members do so because they understand its positive effects on children. They carry on with conviction and determination, despite the perceptions people may have about the nature and importance of their work. The myth that anyone can supervise tends to be held by those unfamiliar with early childhood programs, not by those who work in them.

There is one best supervisory approach to use with everyone.

Life would be easy for supervisors if they could read a book or take a course that would guarantee them one workable method of supervision that would almost always succeed. Such a panacea can be appealing to supervisors who are frustrated by many problems and desperate for immediate solutions.

Supervisors work with people. The problem with adopting a "package" to solve one's supervisory dilemmas or clinging to a home-grown method is the human factor: Caregivers are unique. They have varying personal and professional needs and different levels of ability and skill, which require various supervisory strategies.

Experienced supervisors know that some supervisees need to be shown what to do and how to do it in a direct and detailed way. Yet others can develop their own solutions to problems or take the initiative to do what needs to be done without direction. Some people prefer to interact with authority figures with whom they can establish a personal relationship; that is, they prefer supervisors who are warm, expressive, and sensitive, and who model appropriate behaviors for them. Others object to overly attentive supervisors. They prefer to develop their own solutions to problems and appreciate a supervisor who is formal, serious, and impersonal.

The reasons supervisees respond to one approach or to another may have to do with cognitive style, cultural background, intelligence, personality, experience, developmental level, or other factors. Supervisors need flexibility when working with caregivers: The size of the settings, the number of supervisees for whom they are responsible, the individual differences among their supervisees, and their own personality and style all affect the supervisory strategies to be considered.

Supervision is a process involving the many variables of human behavior. Negating this process by looking at supervision with "tunnel vision" and adopting a single supervisory method will not resolve the complex problems supervisors face and will not help change caregiver behavior.

Supervisors have all the answers.

The myth that supervisors must have all the answers is one that creates continuous pressure on supervisors, who live in fear that someone might discover they don't have a solution to a problem or don't even know how to go about solving it. They fear that others will think less of them or will suggest that they are incompetent and shouldn't be in a leadership position if they cannot step in, take charge, and resolve a pressing problem in short order.

This assumption, based on the belief that supervisors are omnipotent, makes it difficult for supervisors to be honest with themselves and with their staff members. It fails to recognize that some organizational problems or people problems take time to resolve—sometimes several years. This myth also discourages collaborative problem-solving between a supervisor and a staff member, for a collaborative mode acknowledges that others have expertise, perhaps in areas in which a supervisor is weak. Through the dialogue, interaction, and give-and-take of the problem-solving process, supervisors and supervisees can grow professionally.

This myth is reflected in behavior in which supervisors feel obligated to tell caregivers how to resolve a problem or how to teach better. Supervisors may feel guilty if they cannot do so and may tend to react too quickly to a supervisee's questions or doubts by continually talking and offering solutions. The youthfulness of early childhood supervisors and the turnover rate among them may increase pressure on supervisors to prove themselves. Providing all the answers is, after all, what an expert, a supervisor, is expected to do.

Learning to listen to a staff member and to ask questions takes practice. By thinking through problems and developing solutions with a supervisor instead of simply being told answers, supervisees can be encouraged to move toward greater independence. By relieving themselves of the burden of having quick remedies to complex problems at their fingertips, supervisors can relax and explore the subtle circumstances and details of an event.

Supervisors are human. They have strengths and limitations. Although they have control over some of the variables affecting their programs, they have little influence and control over others. Supervisors who can be honest and realistic about themselves can create a group spirit in a program without losing supervisory credibility.

Direct confrontation with staff is nonsupportive.

Many supervisors, particularly those in the early childhood field, have great difficulty confronting employees about situations, behavior, and habits that may negatively affect a program. They are reluctant to "lay it on the line" with a caregiver who, for example, is always late or who is creating strife among staff members. A direct approach is deemed a nonsupportive one.

Avoiding explicit supervision, a supervisor may deal with a problem indirectly: by raising the issue in a delicate way during a conference, by hinting at possible new behaviors, or by manipulating other variables to reduce the tension a particular situation has created. These strategies make a supervisor feel better. After all, how can one be so petty as to confront a caregiver who is earning so little money or who really needs the job? Leveling with a supervisee seems so antihumanistic, so uncaring. The direct approach has not been given much credence in early childhood training.

Attempting to resolve a problem indirectly is often appropriate, but sometimes supervisees do not "hear" the message or do hear the message but choose to ignore it, so that problems continue to multiply. In situations such as these, stating the problem openly in a factual and honest way permits the issue to be acknowledged and dealt with.

Such a direct approach is exactly what some supervisees need. Although a caregiver may have recognized a problem, he or she may not have adequate self-discipline to solve it or the courage to go to a supervisor or other persons for help. On occasion, a teacher may not even be aware that he or she is not performing appropriately. Getting the concern out in the open can be revealing and cathartic, often laying the foundation for a trusting, supportive relationship.

Caregivers appreciate honesty in supervisors; they don't like "beating around the bush." They want to know what they are doing right and what they are doing wrong. Airing concerns in a straightforward, fair, and sincere manner prevents problems from deepening and feelings from intensifying. It allows supervisor and supervisee to start fresh without resentments from lingering unaddressed concerns. Evading issues will not improve relationships among people or increase program effectiveness. Problems create tension for supervisors, but confronting problems is part of the job and can actually relieve tension.

Skilled supervisors never engage in manipulation.

The notion of supervision as manipulation is a difficult one to discuss. No doubt there are supervisors who unfairly control staff members to satisfy their ego needs, to feel more powerful, or to serve their own purposes. Manipulation, for example, can take the form of paternalism on the part of supervisors who think they always know what's best for their supervisees and never permit them to voice opinions, feelings, or ideas about an issue. Such supervisors simply make major decisions about the work life of their teachers, "convincing" the staff and themselves that a particular action is best for a supervisee, even though sometimes it may really be best only for the supervisor. Often, issues of class, status, politics, and culture underlie this type of manipulative behavior.

Supervision as skilled management through which caregivers improve performance and grow professionally is distinct from that which is self-serving and paternalistic. Some supervisors fear that if they make use of skills that enable them to influence a supervisee's behavior, they are being manipulative. Concerned about disrespecting and controlling others, they question the ethics of using these techniques. Supervisory behaviors like praise might be considered manipulative in some situations, but such techniques that shape the behavior of staff members are often appropriate means for building self-confidence.

An example might be a beginning teacher who presents a lesson for the first time. The lesson has many flaws in it, but the teacher is fragile and insecure. In the follow-up conference, the supervisor's feedback may be positive, despite the many problems with the lesson, because the supervisor decides that the emotional state of the teacher requires positive feedback at this time so that he or she can gain confidence and continue to grow and develop professionally. In a sense, this is manipulation on the supervisor's part; yet the truth would have been damaging. In this case, the teacher was inexperienced and still in the process of developing teaching competencies. The supervisor's conscious means of guiding the teacher did not have a selfish motive, nor did it abuse supervisory power. If this had been an experienced teacher, the supervisor's strategy would have been straightforward. In critiquing the lesson with the teacher, most likely all of its flaws would have been openly discussed.

Let us acknowledge, then, that some supervisory situations can be interpreted to have manipulative overtones; however, assumptions that suggest that staff should not be trusted, that they must be constantly watched and controlled, need to have decisions made for them, or should be "used" to the advantage of the supervisor do not have validity as a basis for supervision.

Good teachers do not need supervision.

Supervisors sometimes assume that those staff members who perform their duties in an excellent fashion or who are very experienced in their roles require little or no supervision. This myth may allow problems to go unresolved, may diminish team spirit among staff members, and may cause excellent staff to feel neglected, undervalued, or excluded from the group.

Effective teachers, however experienced, require supervision. Like all staff members, they appreciate attention. They like to be recognized and to receive positive reinforcement. They want to know that supervisors are interested in their work and are knowledgeable about the scope of outstanding work. To do an excellent job without a supervisor's being aware of it can be discouraging and can create anxiety and stress.

Good teachers sometimes have work-related problems with other staff or with particular children. Their competence as teachers does not mean that they always have the right answer or the skills to resolve every problem. Often, they need someone else to validate their instincts about how to resolve a problem.

Some good teachers "burn out" over time and become bored with their work and eventually uninterested. They may be stimulated by a supervisor who can give them new ideas, allow them to take a new role within a program if there is one available, or encourage them to take leadership roles in the field outside the program.

Effective teachers also value criticism. They want constructive feedback. One reason for their excellence may be their ability to analyze their performance and to accept input about their work so that it constantly improves.

Good teachers have expertise that can be shared with a supervisor and others. A supervisor who neglects competent staff has lost a valuable resource. Excellent and motivated teachers can be a great help to supervisors by modeling behaviors for other staff, by teaching colleagues, and by providing ideas and suggestions to supervisors.

Directors who fail to supervise highly competent staff members risk losing the very people who provide strength to their programs.

Supervision is an objective process.

Supervising is a complex activity that cannot be totally objective. Supervisors come to the educational arena with "colored glasses." The ways in which they view their staff members are affected by their own childhood, their education, their life and work experience, and the philosophy and values they have developed. A supervisor's beliefs and values cannot easily be set aside as he or she works with staff members—nor should they be set aside. They should, however, be recognized.

If, for example, a teacher doesn't implement a lesson the way the supervisor would have, then the supervisor may question whether it was done correctly. But the lesson may have achieved its goals even though it did not reflect the supervisor's values. Supervisors are caught in a balancing act. They have their own goals, philosophy, and values, which they would like to see reflected in their programs; yet they wish to respect caregivers' values without being heavy-handed or forcing their personal styles or approaches on teachers.

It is perfectly legitimate for a supervisor to direct a program toward a particular philosophical orientation, but this does not mean that all staff members must think the way their supervisor thinks. It does suggest that supervisors who operate with a high level of consciousness about self can strive to be aware of the "tinted lenses" through which they view their programs and can recognize how their biases might affect the supervisory process.

The process of observing teachers is one that can become more objective through the use of various tools for gathering data. These instruments bring focus to an observation, generate information about teaching behavior, and raise questions of purpose and philosophy (see Chapter 11). Evaluation, however, is judgmental and therefore inherently subjective. Supervisors are expected to judge the competency of teachers in their programs as fairly as possible. Because they have expertise and experience, supervisors are qualified to judge and should not feel guilty for doing so.

Supervisors are always calm.

In writing about myths of teaching, Herbert Greenberg (1969) has described the myths of calmness and moderation. These myths apply to supervisors as well. Supervisors are expected to be model educators. Despite the many pressures they face—frustrations due to working conditions and feelings of impatience with staff members, parents, or government officials—they are always expected to be cool, calm, and collected. They are supposed to be able to respond to pressure in a low-keyed, logical, and emotionless manner. Greenberg notes that this belief is based on the assumption that the "mentally healthy" person does not experience strong feelings.

This myth can create a sense of fear and guilt in supervisors: fear that if they are caught off-guard and show emotion they will lose power and status and their supervisees will think less of them; guilt because they have demonstrated imperfection by losing control for a moment and revealed human weakness.

Supervisors who believe they must be "super" at all times carry a burden that rejects reality and denies their humanness. Teachers who see human qualities in their supervisors often gain greater respect for them. Supervisees respond to, empathize with, and demonstrate greater willingness and enthusiasm for following a leader when they realize that they share certain qualities with that leader.

EXERCISES

1. Discuss how one or more of these myths has affected your own view of supervision and your work as a supervisor.
2. Discuss how these myths might affect a staff member's expectations of the supervisory relationship.
3. Describe other myths that can affect the supervisory role or supervisor–supervisee relationships.

2

Early Childhood Programs and Their Implications for Supervision

The definition of early care and education that is used by the National Association for the Education of Young Children (NAEYC) is "any group program in a center, school, or other facility, that serves children from birth through age eight" (Bredekamp & Copple, 1997, p. 3). Within this scope there is a great diversity of programs: those for infants as young as a few months and for schoolchildren as old as third graders; settings designed for children who are present for a few hours a day, 2 or 3 days a week, and ones that serve those who come for many hours every day; large centers or schools where children are grouped by age, or homes with a few children of mixed ages. Goals may be limited to making social experiences available to children who have many advantages or may encompass a rich educational program together with health and social services for those who have very few advantages. And while many programs for young children are still found in traditional settings such as church parish houses, others are located on-site in businesses or public schools, or have facilities especially designed for young children.

Good supervisory practices do not change with the setting nor do basic staff needs. However, a program's administrative structure and such factors as size, hours, staffing patterns, regulatory agency, source of funds, children and families served, and educational goals do affect both staff needs and the ways a supervisor functions.

FULL-DAY PROGRAMS

Probably the most complex setting for young children is one that is available year round, for 8 or more hours a day, 5 days or more a week, while parents are working or in school. Because these programs act as a supplement to, and to some degree substitute for, parental home care, their quality is of special importance. The long operating hours in particular affect both program planning and the social-emotional needs of children and staff.

Center-based Child Care

Center-based programs are usually licensed to provide full-day care (more than 30 hours per week) for six to eight or more children. Although both the program goals and the client population have changed a good deal in recent years, there continues to be a public image of such centers as providing only custodial care for low-income children. In reality, center-based full-day, full-year programs are also now very common in middle- and upper-middle-income communities, and the number is rapidly increasing. In addition, developmental, educational, and caregiving goals are now all generally considered to be of great importance, although not equally emphasized in all programs. In general, the differences between these and other preschools are mainly influenced by the length of the day.

Centers that serve low-income families are almost always nonprofit, receiving federal funds administered through state social service departments in the form of direct grants or through vouchers for individual children, or from municipalities and states, churches, social service agencies, and the United Way. This funding supports children of families receiving public assistance who are in work or training programs and other families on a sliding fee scale. Children are also placed in centers for special services, as in cases of actual or potential abuse or neglect.

Small, individually owned centers are usually for-profit, with the "profit" principally being in the form of salary for the owner-director. The goals and policies of these programs depend almost entirely on the views of the individual owner.

Chains of child care centers are usually set up as corporations to be money-making enterprises. Although some are very large, with hundreds of individual centers, many have relatively few sites in a limited geographical area. These systems frequently have standardized buildings, equipment, and materials, and the goals, policies, and curriculum for each center are predetermined by the corporation, in some cases specified in great detail.

Full-day programs may also be sponsored by businesses, hospitals, or universities, designed specifically to serve the needs of the people working or studying at these institutions. Companies usually consider them an employee benefit, although fees are commonly charged.

Infant and Toddler Care. With more than 50% of parents of infants working outside the home (Carnegie Task Force on Meeting the Needs of Young Children, 1994), both the need for center-based infant and toddler care and the number of centers providing it have grown rapidly in recent years, and this trend will certainly continue.

Most centers for very young children are part of larger programs for older children. They may enroll children as young as 6 weeks, although some do not take babies younger than 5 or 6 months. The upper limit is 2 or 3 years, the age often influenced by licensing standards. Because the children are so young, group sizes must be smaller, and larger numbers of staff are needed to maintain desirable adult-to-child ratios. The NAEYC accreditation criteria recommend a maximum group size of 6 to 8 and a staff-child ratio of 1:3 or 1:4 for infants, and 6 to 12 and 1:3 to 1:6 respectively for toddlers (12 to 30 months), with the higher ratios where groups are smaller (National Association for the Education of Young Children, 1998, p. 41).

School-age Child Care. These programs provide a place before and/or after the school day for children of working parents. The children may take part in a varied program on a 5-day-a-week basis for as few as 2 hours or, for kindergarteners in half-day programs, as many as 8 hours per day. Some programs also provide services for school holidays and vacations. Care may take place in family child care homes, but much is organized by, or at least housed in, public or independent schools, child care centers, religious institutions, or Ys. About one-third of the programs are operated for profit (Seppanen, deVries, & Seligson, 1993).

The age range of children in extended-day programs is from 5 to around 13, although the majority of children are younger. With such an age span, it is not unusual to have several children from the same family in a program, and children may attend the same center year after year.

Implications for Supervision

With their long days and year-round calendar, full-day programs present great challenges for supervisors. Because centers must be staffed for 10, 12, or more hours a day, staff members must work on staggered shifts, making it difficult for supervisors to find time for meetings. They often take place during nap-time, thus excluding some people, or in the evening, creating extra burdens on caregivers. There is much evidence that feelings of continuity and cohesiveness among staff members are not easily reached when they are not able to meet together to work on common goals.

Routines such as eating, napping, tooth-brushing, and toileting can take a prominent place during the day, making it more difficult to create individual and family-like activities along with age-appropriate educational experiences. We believe that private time for both staff and children is especially important, but privacy and individual attention require flexibility, and there is not always enough staff available to achieve these goals. Communication with parents, of great importance in such centers, is also not easy to establish, since most parents are at work during the time their children are being cared for.

When a child care center is part of a larger system, such as a social agency, a business, or a multicenter operation, decisions that are made at a central office may reflect an order of priorities different from those of the local center. Administrators or boards even of social agencies may not understand the developmental goals or space and equipment needs of early care and education. Or the goal that a child-care-center chain maintain a uniform curriculum may stand in the way of flexibility or creative programing. On the other hand, central administrators can become sources of support and backup because of the resources at their disposal.

Nonprofit centers have available to them supplemental employees from a number of government-funded sources, such as job training programs, the Foster Grandparents Program, and people fulfilling welfare-to-work requirements. These additional staff members must be integrated into classroom teams and offered training and support directed toward their special needs. In large day care programs, administrators are also likely to have responsibility for support staff including cooks, custodians, and health and social service personnel, calling for greater diversity of supervisory skills.

Another challenge for supervisors is to assist staff in recognizing the strengths as well as the needs of low-income or at-risk children, those with disabilities, or those who are culturally or linguistically different from the mainstream population. Although in many ways they do not differ from all young children, there are issues that are special to these populations. (See Appendix A.)

In *infant and toddler centers*, the issues confronting supervisors and staff are directly related to the developmental needs of very young children, about which supervisors themselves may have limited knowledge. With the demands of babies' cycles of sleeping and being fed and changed, caregivers may not easily see that their role has dimensions beyond that of responding to physical needs. The brain research publicized in the late 1990s has shown how neurological systems are rapidly being shaped by the quality of care in the earliest weeks and months of a child's life, making them critical "windows of opportunity" that have long-term consequences for children's development. Language, sensory, and social interactions with both adults and children, along with warm, loving, and consistent care, are the keys to making it possible for children to form secure attachments to those who care for them and to grow into curious, confident, competent learners. These factors are especially crucial for children who are from unresponsive or chaotic homes or who have experienced loss of or long-term separation from their mothers (Newberger, 1997; Shore, 1997).

Training and mentoring can help caregivers to be able to see each baby as unique and to learn to respond to subtle differences in a child's need for stimulation versus comfort, and to sleeping, eating, and other developmental patterns (Lally, Young-Holt, & Mangione, 1994). Providing a primary caregiver to each child over relatively long periods of time, though difficult, is another way that supervisors can respond to this research information.

Toddlers, of course, are extremely active. They need both freedom to explore and limits, along with help in negotiating social exchanges with their peers and developing control over elimination. Staff often need help in dealing with their own feelings about discipline and about appropriate times and methods for toilet training.

As in all center-based programs, the group situation can obscure a young child's individuality. It can make it difficult to provide for the stimulation and active exploration that very young children require. We hold that course work in infant and toddler development, even though many states do not require it for licensing, is essential in equipping caregivers to provide an appropriate environment for their growth. Developing observation and recording skills also helps them be able to see and appreciate the differences in children and the ways they change in this period of fast growth.

Relationships between caregivers and parents is an issue that is important at any age, but may require even more nurturing by supervisors of infant/toddler center staff. Validation of a family's culture, language, and values is important even at this early age. Staff members are not immune to the feeling that parents should not place very young children in day care, especially if they believe the mother can afford to stay home with her child, and may play on the guilt often felt by parents.

The caregiver-parent relationship becomes particularly critical as a child grows toward toddlerhood and acquires greater self-control. Parents will have strong feelings about feeding, toilet training, and discipline, which become more important at this time. Supervisors may have to spend both individual and group staff development time helping caregivers to deal with their feelings and to find ways to develop a partnership, rather than a rivalry, with parents. Staff members who have developed skill in communicating with parents will be able to discuss such matters in an atmosphere of mutual respect, which encourages an exchange of ideas, feelings, and expertise about what the child is doing.

Among the important issues in *school-age care* are the range in age of the children served and the fact that the children have been (or will be) in a school setting for a good part of the day. In addition, split shifts for staff, using shared and often inadequate space, can create stress (Neugebauer, 1993). Creative accommodation to the different social, emotional, and intellectual needs of 5-, 8-, and 12-year-olds, as they become more autonomous and independent and as their peer relationship needs and skills increase, is a major goal of staff. School-age child care may be one of the few planned situations in today's world in which children can interact with others of different ages, so planning both same-age and multi-age activities can be appropriate (Genser & Baden, 1983).

Helping staff organize for and feel comfortable with a program that is flexible enough to provide contrast to the structured school day is another issue for supervisors. A staff with many abilities is required for a program that includes recreational and arts activities, field trips and neighborhood excursions, along with homework assistance, tutoring, and language help for bilingual children. Special training is often necessary to help staff see the *overall* goals of a program for out-of-school time as a place to enhance children's socialization, relaxation, and informal learning, and to understand the developmental needs of school-age children. We recommend that staff time be built in to meet and discuss the special needs of all the children cared for during these important periods of the day.

Teachers and directors, who usually work part time, are likely to be young, come from a variety of backgrounds, and have little experience in the field. They frequently come to school-age care "by default rather than design, on the way to or from another career" (O'Connor, 1994, p.123). Since many programs are small, directors may also serve as teachers, working as colleagues alongside the staff for whom they are responsible. They may not have much contact with other school-age program administrators, and those whose programs are housed in school buildings frequently have little support from the regular school staff. There is still no systematic training available for staff in school-age programs, academic or otherwise, resulting in a field that lacks a common body of knowledge (O'Connor, 1994).

As school-age care becomes more professionalized, more staff may see it as a place for long-term employment. It is a place where staff members can develop interesting, long-term relationships with children who come back year after year, and where creative programming can flourish. We have found that supervisors who use a team approach among staff and search out colleagues in nearby programs or communities as a support system can grow professionally while developing exciting programs for children.

Family Child Care

Family child care takes place in the home of a nonrelative for up to 12 hours a day, 5 or more days a week. In most states where such care is regulated, the number of children in one home is limited to about six to eight, usually including the provider's own children. In some states group home care for up to 12 children is allowed with an assistant. Subsidies are available from the Child Care Food Program and to licensed providers who take care of children of parents on government assistance who work or attend school, and abused or neglected children.

Although most states now license child care homes or have a required or voluntary registration process, many homes are not licensed. Providers are often reluctant to go through the process of becoming licensed because of the limits imposed by the regulations or through fear of intrusion. However, the Study of Family Care and Relative Care found that being regulated has the strongest relationship of any factor to quality care (Kontos, Howes, Shinn, & Galinsky, 1995).

The ages of children cared for in home settings range from infants to elementary school children, although most are younger than school age. Infants and toddlers are more likely to be cared for in family child care, because center-based care for very young children is not widespread, and because many parents value a homelike atmosphere.

Family child care providers have many different backgrounds, income levels, and reasons for involvement. Almost all are women, 75% are married, and their median age is about 41. The U.S. Department of Education (USDOE) reported in 1990 that about 12% had a college degree, while 11% had not graduated from high school. However, Kontos and her colleagues (1995) found far higher levels of education, with 33% of all providers having a college degree, and nearly half in programs that were licensed or registered.

The average pay of family child care providers is less than half of those in most types of center-based programs (USDOE, 1990). For many this income is mainly a supplement to the family income, since it is difficult to earn a living this way without taking in more children than the law allows (Kontos, 1992).

Implications for Supervision

Because of the isolation of family child care providers together with licensing requirements that are generally less stringent than those for center-based caregivers, there are still many who have had little or no specialized training in child care. National studies have reported that 64% of regulated providers and 34% of nonregulated have had such training, although many more have probably attended some informal workshops (Kontos et al., 1995). It is probable, however, that a much lower percentage have had on-site supervision.

About half of regulated caregivers meet regularly with other caregivers, and one-fourth are sponsored by an agency or system that helps with recruiting and training (USDOE, 1990). When training exists, it is usually provided by such systems, or through the federal Child Care Food Program, resource and referral agencies, or licensing or other state training agencies. Formal and informal associations, including affiliates of the National Association for Family Child Care (see Appendix B), are becoming more common as vehicles for providing caregivers with support and self-help, as well as assistance and training from professionals.

The supervisory role in family child care is most likely to grow out of some form of group training. Workshop or course instructors can build in on-site visits to get a sense of the physical environment of the homes, the kinds of children enrolled, and the caregivers' interactions with the children. This helps trainers to become trouble-shooters and supporters for individual providers and to build more meaningful content into their workshop or course sessions. It is essential that these supervisors be knowledgeable about the special characteristics of home-based care.

All caregivers should have knowledge of child development and how to provide programs appropriate to the age and development of children, but family child care providers have some unique additional needs. First, they are probably the most susceptible of early childhood caregivers to society's view that child care is "only babysitting." Thus a major priority for some providers is to improve their self-image, so they can begin to see themselves as professionals who do indeed have, and can further develop, special skills for working with children and parents, and who are carrying out a socially valued job.

Other provider needs are related to the fact that care is given in the provider's own home. The intimacy of the setting may affect parents' and caregivers' expectations about care. For example, a major area of need is to become aware of the importance of planning for the children's day (Kontos et al., 1995). Misunderstandings between parents and providers can develop, especially where there are differences in culture, standards, or values, unless open communication systems have been developed. In fact, the parent-caregiver relationship is one of the most commonly reported areas of dissatisfaction and stress among family child care providers (Kontos, 1992). Relationships with the provider's spouse and own children, too, can be strained by the presence of day care children.

Other issues not encountered by center-based caregivers include developing effective learning environments within the limitations of the physical layouts of their homes, planning and choosing appropriate materials for a span of ages, home safety, meal planning, handling finances, and using community resources.

Because of the large number of day care homes and the difficulties involved in setting up monitoring systems, supervisors will find a great deal of variation in the quality of care provided. Even when their level of education and training is not high, however, most providers are people who have great potential. Training is particularly important prior to and during providers' first year, when they are especially vulnerable to failure (Kontos, 1992). Baker (1997) found great success with low-income caregivers through home visits by other providers. Sensitively run training sessions with other providers also give them opportunities to share personal and professional concerns while improving their skills.

HEAD START

Head Start is a national program, funded to local agencies through the federal government. It provides comprehensive developmental services to low-income preschool children and their families, focusing on education, socio-emotional development, physical and mental health, and nutrition. Although direct services to children have always been a major goal, health and nutrition, social services, and parent involvement all receive equal emphases in program goals and implementation.

Most Head Start children take part in a center-based preschool program for 3- to 5-year-olds, 5 hours per day, 4 or 5 days per week. A home-based option that provides comprehensive services to children in their own homes is usually available. Other Head Start options include full-day/school-year, full-day/full-year, Early Head Start (which serves low-income pregnant women and families with children from birth through 3 years of age), and Parent and Child Centers. At least 10% of the enrollment in Head Start must be children with disabilities. They receive both regular Head Start services and individualized special services.

One of the most important premises of Head Start is the significance placed on the role of parents, who must be included as paid workers or as volunteers in classrooms. They are also to be given opportunities to participate in program decisions through committees and the policy council or committee, which is the governing board of each Head Start program. Staff members are required to communicate with parents frequently, including making home visits.

Current Head Start Performance Standards have put a strong emphasis on staff supervision and support, buttressing the importance that Head Start has always placed on staff training. Individual training needs are to be assessed, and in-service training and college-based course work made available. All staff are encouraged to develop competencies that enable them to move vertically (e.g., from aide to teacher) or horizontally (e.g., from social service to education) within the program.

Another distinctive feature of Head Start is its built-in system for ensuring that services based on Head Start goals are actually being delivered by each local program, while allowing for flexibility at the local level. Two procedures assist this effort:

1. The Head Start Performance Standards, which clearly define minimum performance expectations for all Head Start programs, reflecting "a combination of sound practice, research, and a focus on quality in working to enhance children's development" (U.S. Department of Health & Human Services, n.d., p. 5).

2. A mandated system through which grantees are required to evaluate their performance in relation to the Performance Standards. This yearly self-assessment, which includes parents, staff, and community representatives, uses the On-Site Program Review Instrument (OSPRI). Every 3 years this includes a week-long on-site visit from an outside team. The local program's own self-assessment is "validated," and where it is found to be out of compliance with the Performance Standards, it is given from 3 months to a year to correct the deficiencies.

Implications for Supervision

Each of the elements discussed above has an impact on the supervisory process, both for program directors and for educational coordinators. First, administrators will find that program goals that are mandated and closely monitored by the funding source (in this case, the federal government) can have both advantages and disadvantages. Accountability through various levels of bureaucracy can be confusing and frustrating. Newcomers to Head Start are confronted with a dizzying array of terminology and acronyms. Paperwork can seem endless. Policies or their interpretation may change with little time for staff preparation, and questions about whether the local program is in compliance with the Performance Standards are not always easily answered. These concerns can be especially unnerving when it comes time for an OSPRI review.

On the other hand, the structures that Head Start has created provide supports within the system that can be very helpful to supervisors. The Performance Standards, which serve as the basis for all program decisions, provide clear goals within a developmental early childhood perspective. They serve as common reference points for all staff, from aides and volunteers through the director. Supervision, training, and curriculum development all start from this point, but enough flexibility is allowed so that staff and parent input can make a difference. In addition, the OSPRI, in spite of the tremendous amount of work it requires, furnishes valuable information on strengths and weaknesses on which to build for the future.

Other supports built into the Head Start system are funds for training and technical assistance and for college courses and Child Development Associate (CDA) training; state and regional organizations of Head Start directors and supervisors; and regional office personnel.

The emphasis on the involvement of parents has a number of implications for supervision and training. Staff members—and supervisors themselves—may find it difficult to adjust to untrained parents as decision makers or to find ways to work through differences of opinion on important issues. Staff development that emphasizes communication skills, cultural competence, and an understanding of the concerns and strengths of low-income parents can help teachers to work sensitively with parents in the classroom, in conferences, and in home visits. Effective orientation and training programs for parent aides and volunteers also contribute to staff-parent understanding.

Finally, in any program with a predominantly low-income clientele, some staff members may find it difficult to deal with the very real problems facing some children, parents, and even other staff members. Racial, class, linguistic, and cultural differences can sometimes create barriers to communication and understanding. Young middle-class teachers with little or no experience with low-income or culturally different children may especially need training and supervisory assistance.

PART-DAY PROGRAMS

Half-day school-year programs for 3- and 4-year-olds have until recently, except for kindergartens, been the most widespread type of early childhood program. Nursery schools (now often called preschools or child development centers) are characterized by small size, attendance by different children and teachers in mornings and afternoons, and alternate-day attendance options. A number also include kindergartens. Full-day or school-day options for children of working parents are becoming more common.

Nursery schools are almost always either privately owned or sponsored by a church, synagogue, YM or YWCA, or similar organization, or are part of a private school, rather than being publicly funded. An individual school may be an independent enterprise for an owner-director, or it may be parent sponsored and managed.

Formally organized *parent cooperatives* usually are nursery schools where there is a paid director, who most likely teaches, and sometimes one or more paid teachers. A large part of the responsibility for the teaching and care of the children, along with secretarial, maintenance, or other needed work around the school, is carried by the parents. In most coops parents both govern and manage the school as well.

A *laboratory school* that is associated with a high school, vocational school, college, or university is established primarily as a place for students to observe and practice working with children as part of early childhood training, and generally has a part-day format. Day care programs, increasingly available in colleges to provide care for children of faculty, staff, or students, may also be used as a laboratory setting, but usually training is a secondary rather than a primary objective of these programs. In both types of centers, major teaching responsibilities are borne by the students in training or by work-study students who serve as paid assistants. Child care centers that are part of teen-parenting programs in high schools have some of the same characteristics as lab schools.

Implications for Supervision

Traditionally nursery schools were thought of mainly as places for children to develop social skills. Today there is often at least an equal emphasis on providing a more comprehensive developmental and educational program. Pressure from parents to train children in academic skills sometimes makes it difficult for teachers to resist the inclusion of activities that are inappropriate for preschool children.

The small size of most nursery schools makes supervision an informal process. Directors may find it difficult to even think about "supervising" an assistant or a teacher whom they think of as a colleague or friend. In this intimate atmosphere, problems can be hard to deal with. It is also difficult for teacher-directors who have responsibility for a group of children to find ways to observe teachers who work in adjacent rooms. Even in small programs, however, staff members can benefit from opportunities for peer evaluation and from assistance in improving their teaching.

Since it is common for different teachers to work in the morning and in the afternoon, staff in nursery schools often have difficulty finding time when all can meet together. Supervisors may find it hard to convince owners or boards that it makes sense to pay teachers, or sometimes even the director, for time to attend staff and parent meetings, to set up classrooms before the school year officially begins, and to participate in staff development during the year. When funds must come out of an owner-director's own pocket, obtaining money for such "extra" time may be even more challenging.

In *parent coops*, training and coordination are major issues for supervisors. Not only are there likely to be many different individuals working with the children over the course of each week, even in a small school, but there also may be an almost entirely new group of parent-staff as well as board members each year, frequently with little or no training in early care and education. A clear understanding that staff development sessions are part of the parents' responsibilities helps to set a positive climate for such training.

Differences in philosophy about discipline and about curriculum and methods are bound to arise from time to time between parents and staff. As in Head Start programs, one of the supervisor's tasks is to work out processes for resolving such differences. Where parents are the owners and managers, it may be especially difficult to integrate parents' ideas about curriculum and other issues with the professional knowledge of the staff.

In a *lab school* setting, one of the most important supervisory issues is creating real learning situations and support for education students while at the same time ensuring that the children receive skilled care and teaching. Supervisors may find that their attention—and loyalty—is divided among children, students, and paid staff. Settings for the children of teen parents have the added issue of the need to nurture parenting skills while dealing with self-esteem and normal adolescent concerns.

Because lab schools are a part of a larger institution whose goals mainly focus on a different age group, sometimes support for funding and resources is difficult to obtain. Maintaining good communication and coordination with all those who teach and supervise students is more complicated when course instruction is the responsibility of a separate faculty, when a supervising teacher is not directly involved with the children, or when lab school staff do not have faculty status.

Ensuring adequate staff coverage can be another problem for supervisors. Sometimes children may be overwhelmed by too many caregivers. At other times, class schedules of education students may conflict with periods when staff are needed the most, or students may want time off during exam weeks, even though student and faculty parents still need care for their children. Helping education students understand the importance of their presence to children's well-being, therefore, becomes a key task for the supervisor.

SCHOOL-BASED KINDERGARTENS
AND PRESCHOOLS

Although kindergartens may be part of a nursery school or day care program, most are based in public, private, or parochial schools. Half-day, 5-day-a-week schedules have been the norm for many years, but full-day kindergartens are becoming more prevalent. By 1994 about half of kindergarten children were in full-day classes (Rothenberg, 1995). Some kindergartens have extended-day programs, with a nonacademic focus for that portion of the day, or children of working parents may be transported to or from child care centers for before- and after-school care.

Teachers in public school kindergartens (and in some states, independent schools) must be state certified with bachelor's degrees and specific teacher training experiences. This training may or may not be at the early childhood level.

Many communities allow more children per class in kindergarten than they do in preschools, some permitting 30 students or more. Often a paraprofessional is assigned when a class reaches a certain size. In contrast to many nursery schools, the same teacher usually teaches both morning and afternoon sessions of half-day programs so that a teacher may be responsible for 60 or more children per day. However, as of 1989, two-thirds of the states with state-funded kindergartens limit group size to 20 or fewer and staffing ratios to 1:10 (Mitchell & Modigliani, 1989), a trend that is growing.

There is a great deal of variation in kindergarten goals and curriculum, even in public school systems. Some use a developmental, emerging-literacy model in which child-initiated experiences and play are considered major means of learning. Others are group-oriented and tightly scheduled, and focus on readiness activities, especially in reading, that begin early in the year. They may include using workbooks as a daily routine, and play is usually not seen as a major vehicle for learning.

Most kindergartens probably combine elements of both of these models, with some systems allowing greater flexibility than others. However, teachers are likely to feel considerable pressure to "get children ready for first grade," pushing them toward more academically oriented curricula and methodology, which may be prescribed, or at least recommended.

Early childhood programs at the prekindergarten level are becoming more common in public as well as nonpublic schools. More than half of the states and some local communities support such programs (Mitchell & Modigliani, 1989). Many of these are part-day classes for at-risk 4-year-olds, some funded through Title I and Head Start. School systems may also have bilingual pre-schools or programs for special-needs children, and some have full-day care supported through various sources including parent fees.

Implications for Supervision

Teachers and aides in kindergartens in public schools always come under the jurisdiction of their school principal. Preschool staff members, on the other hand, may be supervised by a principal or by a system-wide early childhood supervisor, an in-house director, or, in the case of Head Start, by the director or educational coordinator of an area-wide Head Start program.

When elementary school principals do not have training or experience in teaching young children, they may be uncomfortable about supervising teachers at these levels. Some may have unrealistic scheduling or curricular requirements for kindergartens, especially centering on the early formal teaching of reading and math, or they may not understand such things as the appropriateness of play in young children's education.

Principals are, however, becoming more knowledgeable about the needs of children and teachers at the early childhood level. The burgeoning preschools in public systems, the development of "early childhood centers" housing pre-schools through grades 2 or 3, and the greater number of states with special early childhood teacher certification, along with the widespread availability of such sources as the National Association for the Education of Young Children's (NAEYC) *Developmentally Appropriate Practice in Early Childhood Programs* (Bredekamp & Copple, 1997), have contributed to this trend.

System-wide early childhood supervisors or preschool directors usually have an early childhood background and have a good understanding of the developmental needs of children at these ages. With this knowledge they can directly develop and support teachers' efforts to lay conceptual foundations before moving on to specific skills, and to focus on child-initiated learning. These supervisors are also in a position to establish or support the continuation of the strong parent-teacher relationships that may have been established at the preschool level. On the other hand, they may need to spend a lot of time and energy interpreting and advocating such goals to other administrators, teachers at other grade levels, school boards, and parents. Mitchell and Modigliani (1989) found that having supervisors who are not only well grounded in early childhood education/child development but who also become skilled in communicating with other school personnel at all levels can make a great difference in the quality of programs for young children in public schools.

To help those who do not have this background to understand the issues, *Developmentally Appropriate Practice* (Bredekamp & Copple, 1997) can be especially helpful. Two other sources that can help in understanding early childhood principles from different perspectives are *The Creative Curriculum for Early Childhood* (Dodge & Colker, 1992) (also available in Spanish and for family child care) and *Educating Young Children* (Hohmann & Weikart, 1995).

ACCREDITATION

A voluntary procedure through which early care and education center– and school-based programs, including kindergartens, can become accredited in accordance with the criteria for high-quality programs has been developed by the NAEYC (1998). One of the goals for this process is to "help early childhood program personnel become involved in a process that will facilitate real and lasting improvements in the quality of the program" (p. 1).

At the end of several of the chapters that follow you will find listings of the specific criteria that apply to the issues that have been discussed in the chapter. We encourage you, as a supervisor, to consider these criteria in the development and ongoing assessment of your own program and to become accredited through this system or that of the National Association for Family Child Care or the National Institute for Out-of-School Time (formerly School Age Child Care Project). See Appendix B for addresses.

CONCLUSION

The programs we have described in this chapter are the broad categories that supervisors of early childhood staff are most likely to encounter. Program differences affect the way supervisors function because they form the context within which supervision takes place. Nevertheless, when it comes to the needs of children and staff members, the similarities are greater than the differences, for it is individuals who are being supervised, and appropriate practices within each context that are the goals.

EXERCISES

1. Using the specific program in which you work, or one in which you are interested, describe characteristics that affect supervision of the staff. Include all the factors that (a) give clues to the kinds of areas where staff are most likely to need help, and (b) might have a positive effect on or make more difficult your ability to carry out effective supervision and staff development. Interview the director and other supervisory staff to obtain as broad a view of these issues as possible.
2. Compare and contrast your perceptions with those of a group of teachers or supervisors from similar and different programs than the one you have chosen. Discuss ways that problem areas might be alleviated.

3

Supervisors and Staff: Roles and Responsibilities

The roles and duties of persons in supervisory positions and of those whom they supervise are as varied as the early childhood programs described in the previous chapter. Our purpose in this chapter is to describe the most common positions supervisors occupy, the responsibilities associated with these positions, and the roles and duties of the people they supervise.

SUPERVISORS

Practitioners with supervisory responsibilities range from executive directors in central administrative offices of large agencies to those whose main responsibility is to teach children but who also supervise other teachers, aides, and volunteers.

Representative Job Titles and Descriptions

Some of the most common positions involving supervision are executive director, program director, educational coordinator, head teacher, teacher, college supervisor, and consultant.

Executive Director

The executive director is usually the chief administrator of a large child care agency and reports directly to a board of directors. Although the organizational charts of such agencies vary, the executive director may supervise an assistant, the coordinators of several social service programs within the agency, program directors at various sites, and all other employees through a central chain of command. Supervision is usually one aspect of an executive director's responsibilities, along with administrative and fiscal duties. The executive director is likely to supervise upper-level staff directly but may have little personal

26

contact with the staff who are responsible for children in the agency's various centers.

Program Director

Program directors are administrators who are responsible for running a program. In large child care agencies, they work within the larger organization but do not administer the organization as a whole. Most Head Start directors and public school principals are in this category since a program or a school is one of several in the organization. In small, private, or nonprofit independent child care centers or nursery schools, directors manage programs that are somewhat more autonomous. Some program directors administer more than one center.

The responsibilities of program directors usually include administration, supervision, board relationships, and community relationships, and, for many, teaching as well. Among their duties are maintaining compliance with applicable laws, recruiting staff and children, budgeting and fund raising, supervising and evaluating staff, conducting annual program evaluations, working with parents and outside agencies and institutions, planning curriculum, reporting to and working with a board, overseeing the maintenance of the facility and of equipment, and planning meals with the cook.

Because program directors are on site and work directly with classroom and nonclassroom staff, supervision is a larger part of the job than it is for executive directors. Program administration or teaching can take up much of their time, however, and can overshadow supervisory duties.

Directors come in regular contact with a host of people, each of whom has a set of expectations about what the director should do and how he or she should do it. These include the director's supervisor, employees, and others with whom the director works closely. Together these people make up what sociologists (Katz & Kahn, 1966) call a *role set* (see Figure 3.1).

Members of a role set communicate their expectations to the director, who responds in certain ways based on his or her understandings and perceptions of the messages received. For example, representatives of community service agencies may believe that the program director should be more active in dealing with families with serious problems. Or the executive director may think that the director should do a better job of linking with coordinators and other program directors, and in completing paperwork on time. Teachers may feel that the director should give them more help in working with hard-to-manage children. And the cook may be unhappy because the director is too involved in weekly menu planning.

Thus, members of the director's role set "push" and "pull" the director, competing for time and attention and creating multiple demands. This pres-

Figure 3.1 Role Set of a Program Director

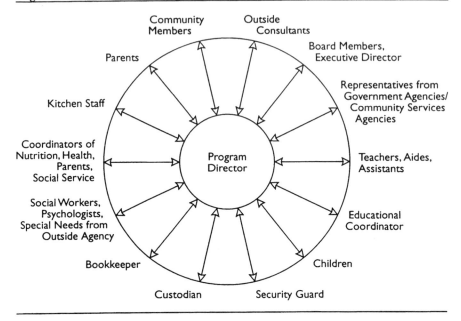

sure may be more intense when the administrator fills more than one official role, a common occurrence. Program directors with clear priorities, goals, and philosophy of education will be better able to formulate realistic expectations for the job and for supervision.

As Figure 3.1 indicates, the program director is also a member of the role set of teachers, children, kitchen staff, and others, and has a responsibility to them. In reality, however, teachers may relate more often and sometimes more immediately to social service or other staff than to the director.

Educational Coordinator

The educational coordinator's role is narrower and more focused than the program director's. The coordinator's responsibility is to oversee the educational component of an agency or program to ensure that classrooms and staff are functioning according to the program's guidelines for the greatest benefit to children. The educational coordinator works in the areas of staff development, training, and curriculum, with time allotted for these purposes.

Supervision forms a large part of educational coordinators' work. In smaller programs, educational coordinators supervise staff who work directly with children and are supervised by the program director. In large day care or Head Start agencies, educational coordinators provide emotional and technical support to program directors, as well as to classroom staff, often traveling to various program sites. The coordinator's duties may include observing teachers and children; planning and conducting staff training; conferring with staff; developing curriculum; serving as a liaison with health, nutrition, special-needs, and social service coordinators; modeling good teaching behavior; ordering classroom supplies and equipment; working with psychologists; and providing directors with guidance and support.

Coordinators, too, have a role set (see Figure 3.2). Those working in multiple settings are particularly susceptible to situations involving interpersonal conflicts. With their time divided between central office and various sites, they may not have the opportunity to build relationships to the extent they would like or to engage with staff in the process of clarifying and defining each other's roles and responsibilities.

Educational coordinators are usually free from a daily routine and have some flexibility in organizing their day's work. The job of coordinator can be a lonely one, however, as there is usually no one else in the organization with the same role to share common problems and successes.

Figure 3.2 Role Set of an Educational Coordinator

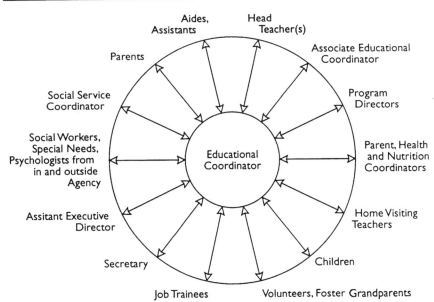

Head Teacher

Unlike program directors and educational coordinators, who work mostly with adults, head teachers have a primary responsibility for working with children. Usually because of experience, education, training, and/or demonstrated expertise, classroom teachers become head or lead teachers. Head teachers usually oversee the functioning of several classrooms and, in some cases, even small centers. They supervise other teachers, and are supervised by the educational coordinator or program director (see Figure 3.3). As head teachers attempt to meet the dual responsibilities of teaching and supervising, they are likely to experience a certain degree of role conflict.

Among the specific duties of a head teacher are arriving before class to prepare and arrange materials for the day's activities, keeping daily attendance and observation records of children, assisting in planning parent programs, attending evaluation meetings with social service agency representatives, arranging yearly conferences with each parent, making special referrals, supervising other team members, teaching children, and planning and leading team meetings.

Figure 3.3 Role Set of a Head Teacher

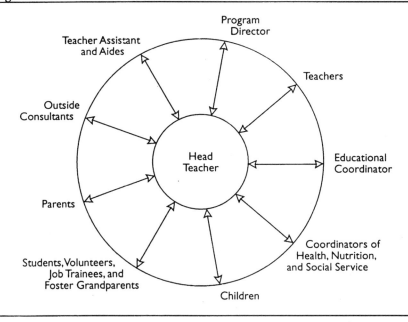

Teacher

Unlike public school teachers, who rarely supervise other adults in the classroom, preschool teachers often supervise an assistant, paid or volunteer, in addition to educating and caring for young children. Teachers are usually supervised by a head teacher, coordinator, and/or program director.

College Supervisor

The college supervisor is a faculty member of a college or university who is responsible for training and supervising those individuals aspiring to work in early childhood programs. Sometimes they supervise experienced caregivers who are working in a special program or for an advanced degree. More often, they supervise undergraduates who plan to work with young children.

Child Development Associate (CDA) Advisor

The CDA advisor may be part of a Child Development Associate training program or may work on a free-lance basis with classroom staff who are preparing to be assessed for the CDA credential. A CDA advisor is often associated with a college, university, or resource and referral or training agency but may be a staff member from their own or another preschool. (See Chapter 14 for a description of CDA.)

Consultant

Consultants from training agencies, resource and referral programs, and cooperating colleges and universities, or who advise independently, sometimes work on site with a program as a whole or with individual teachers. They may work with staff members through one-to-one or group supervision. This is a typical form of supervision for family child care.

These positions are the most common ones in the early childhood field with important supervisory responsibility. These jobs, however, have many titles. Individuals in them often have more than one major role to perform. Rarely is supervision the sole component of their work. Positions that carry multiple roles and responsibilities, such as owner-manager, director-teacher, or supervisor-bookkeeper, create consequences not always foreseen. Supervisors may experience role ambiguity; conflicting expectations from staff members; and overload, stress, and disenchantment with their jobs as they discover that they do not have the time or the resources for all their roles.

Training and Experience

Many supervisors come into their roles directly from the classroom ranks. Some, particularly those in Head Start or other community-based programs, may have begun work as aides. After receiving on-the-job training, a high school equivalency degree, a Child Development Associate credential, or even an associate's or bachelor's degree while working in a program, they are good candidates for supervisory positions because of their understanding of the needs of children and families and their experiences in early childhood education.

Others, initially hired as teachers or even aides, move into coordinator's or director's roles because of their exceptional skills in working with children or sometimes because they are the only staff members with a degree in early childhood education or specific training in supervision. There are also early childhood supervisors with backgrounds in elementary or special education, or such related fields as counseling, nursing, social services, and recreation; still others have job experience in completely unrelated occupations.

Relatively few supervisors have had formal preparation in supervision; of those who have, the great majority have had minimal amounts in the form of workshops and college-level course work. In fact, very few states require course work in administration and supervision for the licensure of directors and others in supervisory roles (Morgan, 1997; Morgan et al., 1993). Thus, for many, their work with children and the model provided them by their own supervisors are the most helpful experiences in preparing them for their jobs.

Data describing the education and training levels of those in supervisory roles, as separate from child care workers as a whole, continue to be scarce; however, we do have some information about experience levels. Bloom (1989) revealed that Illinois directors averaged more than 10 years of experience in the early childhood field, 5 years in their present positions. The National Child Care Staffing Study (Whitebook, Howes, & Phillips, 1989) reported that the average length of tenure for directors in a program was 5.5 years in 1988. In their follow-up study published 4 years later, Whitebook, Phillips, and Howes (1993) noted that 60% of the directors remained in their jobs and that lead teachers and teacher-directors had lower turnover rates (64%) than did teachers and aides (77%).

A relatively new phenomenon that is rapidly spreading across the country is the idea of credentialing directors. Morgan (1997) reports that there are currently national, state, and private groups that offer director credentials and that numerous additional efforts are under way; however, there is a wide range of differences in the number of hours or credits that these groups require as well as in their relationships with higher education, state licensing, and state early childhood career development initiatives.

The multiplicity of supervisory roles; the variability of background, experience, education, and training among supervisors, as well as differences in state licensing requirements for those in supervisory positions; and the necessity of fulfilling duties outside of supervision are in a very real sense indicators of the evolving nature of early care and education. As early childhood professionals upgrade their skills and strive to make the field more professional, job qualifications, competencies, titles, and responsibilities are likely to become more uniform. With less ambiguity, some of the sources of stress may be removed, enabling supervisors to attain greater satisfaction from the job.

STAFF

Early childhood supervisors work with staff employed in a variety of jobs. These include providers of direct care, education, or services to children in classrooms, as well as nonclassroom staff who help the program run smoothly and/or support children by working with families or outside agencies. Program settings, the age levels of the children served, and the range of services provided influence the names we use to identify early childhood staff.

Historically, practitioners have made a distinction between teacher and caregiver and between those in professional and auxiliary roles. Nursery schools have been viewed as serving mainly an educational function, while day care has been seen as having a caregiving/nurturing function. Thus, practitioners in nursery schools have been thought of as teachers and those in day care centers as caregivers. Supervisors and teachers were considered professionals. Teacher aides, volunteers, and assistants have been viewed as auxiliaries (Spodek & Saracho, 1982). Today, as more is understood about the developmental, educational, and care needs of young children, many have come to refer to the early childhood field as "early care and education" and the terms *teacher* and *caregiver* have become more or less interchangeable.

Representative Job Titles and Descriptions

Classroom staff have a major responsibility for working with children and often have secondary obligations in other areas. Marcy Whitebook (1989) and her colleagues found that head teacher-directors, teachers, and aides all have the same range of duties, although head teacher-directors spent more time on parent communication and clerical and administrative work. All did curriculum planning and implementation, meal preparation, and maintenance.

Classroom Teachers

Responsibilities of all teachers usually include planning and carrying out the program for children indoors and outdoors, arranging classroom space for play and group activities, observing and recording children's growth in various skill areas, and preparing for snack and lunch. Those working with infants and toddlers spend a larger amount of their time feeding, changing, playing with, and observing children. Part of a caregiver's day also includes communicating with parents about the psychological well-being of their children, not only at the center but often in home visits. Sharing information and ideas with speech or physical therapists, nurses, social workers, and others is also a typical part of the regular routine when these specialists are available.

Although teachers may be supervised by a head teacher, director, or coordinator, as we noted earlier, they have supervisory responsibilities themselves. They usually have at least one aide or assistant, and many programs have parent and other volunteers, student teachers, foster grandparents, and job trainees. Classroom staff also informally supervise peers who are new to a program, providing emotional support and suggestions. Although the latter form of supervision often happens spontaneously, supervisors can support and train caregivers to work with other classroom staff who have little or no training.

Classroom Aides and Assistants

The job of aide or assistant in a classroom is also important but can be misused. The terms *aide* and *assistant* usually describe the same job, though there are sometimes both positions in a program. In general, the position of aide is an entry-level job with few qualifications other than sensitivity to children and willingness to learn. In some programs, especially those for low-income families, aides may not be required to have a high school diploma, often beginning work as volunteers and later advancing to paid positions.

Aides assist the classroom teacher in carrying out such duties as teaching, performing clerical or housekeeping chores, preparing for snack time, and ensuring that the environment is sanitary and healthful. They are usually expected to attend staff meetings, training sessions, meetings with other professionals, and meetings with parents. Aides also provide general supportive help in family child care homes, allowing caregivers time for other duties.

Nonclassroom Staff

Sometimes taken for granted, nonclassroom staff are central to a program's efficiency and success. Nonclassroom staff come into contact with children and support and serve them and the program in peripheral yet important ways, but their responsibilities do not encompass the direct and ongoing care and education of children.

While some nonclassroom staff assist with the daily operation of a center, others support staff, families, and children. Cleaners, painters, and landscapers perform maintenance functions. Secretaries, bookkeepers, file clerks, purchasers, and office assistants are primarily involved with paperwork and administrative tasks. Cooks, custodians, and bus drivers may have more opportunities to interact with children, while community developers and outreach workers may get to know families. Some individuals, such as health coordinators, have supervisory functions with adults. Professionals who work on behalf of children and families on a consultant basis, for example, social workers, speech therapists, and psychologists, might also be considered part of the nonclassroom staff of a center, as well as individuals who are affiliated with centers but who spend most of their time working with children and families in their homes. As with supervisors and classroom staff, nonclassroom staff may be expected to carry out more than one role.

Nonclassroom staff members can be indispensable to supervisors and caregivers. They may orient a new director or teacher to a program, "be there" for a director to lean on when there is no one else with whom to discuss pressing problems, or fill in during an emergency. Nonclassroom staff should be considered integral members of the program "family."

Training and Experience

Child care staff education levels may range from a high school education to graduate degrees. By and large, however, child care staff are well educated. More than half of assistant teachers and almost three-quarters of teachers represented in the 227 centers examined in the National Child Care Staffing Study (Whitebook et al., 1989) had some college background, while Kisker, Hofferth, Phillips, and Farquhar (1991) found in their large national sample that almost half (47%) of all teachers in center-based early childhood programs had completed college. An additional 13% possessed a 2-year college degree. Fully 93% of preschool teachers in center-based programs in their study also had some specialized training in child care or early education, particularly those in Head Start and public school–based programs.

Although there continues to be a high turnover rate among child care staff, 19% of teachers and assistant teachers in the National Child Care Staffing Study (Whitebook et al., 1989) had been working in child care for 10 years or more in 1988 compared with only 5% of those in the National Day Care Study (Ruoop, Travers, Glantz, & Coelen, 1979) completed almost a decade earlier. Kisker et al. (1991) report that, on average, teachers in center-based early education and care programs have 8 years of experience, 5 years of which are in their current program. Half of them, however, have 6 or fewer years of experience.

The lack of long-term stability is still a serious problem. The sample in the study by Kisker et al. (1991), which included part-day Head Start and school-based programs, showed an annual turnover rate of 25%. Whitebook et al. (1993)

found an average annual short-term turnover rate of 26% between 1991 and 1992, a lower figure than the 41% reported by directors in their original study (Whitebook et al., 1989). Unfortunately, however, these figures are still significantly higher, they note, than the 5.6% turnover rate reported for public school teachers and the 9.6% reported by all companies in the United States.

The education and experience levels of prospective staff members as well as their training in early childhood education are important criteria to consider when filling staff positions. It is interesting to note that while the National Day Care Study (Ruopp et al., 1979) found that individuals specifically educated and trained to work with young children raised the standard of care, the more recent National Child Care Staffing Study (Whitebook et al., 1989) reported that the strongest predictor of appropriate caregiving is a teacher's amount of formal education. Specialized child-related training, however, emerged as a predictor in infant classrooms. In their further examination of the role of formal education and specialized training, Whitebook et al. (1989) found that either a bachelor's degree or specialized training at the college level, rather than at the high school or vocational level, was associated with higher program quality. In their study, child care experience emerged as a poor predictor of teacher behavior toward children. The Cost, Quality, and Child Outcomes Study Team (1995) also found that high levels of general education were important.

In reviewing the contradictory nature of these findings, Kagan and Neuman (1996) make several suggestions to directors. First, they recommend that directors hire staff who have a range of skill and ability levels, with most staff having some experience in early childhood programs, as well as high levels of general education or early childhood related training/education. Second, since more training/education does improve quality, a commitment by directors to professional development for all staff is critical. Finally, directors need to provide a range of professional development options for staff based on their individual needs and their levels of experience and training.

Certification and Licensing Requirements

Teacher *certification* is a process by which states certify individuals for teaching positions for public schools. *Licensing* regulates nonpublic programs. All states have some kind of licensing regulations for child care and education programs. The two processes, certification and licensing, are quite separate, with no bridges between them (Morgan et al., 1993).

In *Making a Career of It*, Morgan et al. (1993) found that many practitioners are not required to have any training at all. While most licensing regulations include qualifications for teaching staff, there are great variations in the amounts and types of training required. Licensing rules tend to favor experience over course work, making employment more accessible, while certification tends to value academic pre-service preparation at the expense of early access to the profession. Neither licensing policies nor teacher certification requirements facilitate career mobility for early childhood practitioners.

CAREER LATTICES AND LADDERS

In 1991, the National Association for the Education for Young Children (NAEYC) established the National Institute for Early Childhood Professional Development. As part of its main goal that all programs for young children provide high-quality early childhood education, the institute embraced a framework for professional development based on the concept of the early childhood career lattice, which was edited by Barbara Willer and Sue Bredekamp and adopted by NAEYC's governing board in 1993 (Willer, 1994).

In developing this notion, Bredekamp and Willer (1992) looked at the early childhood field and the early childhood profession in a broad way, taking into account the diversity of early childhood care and education programs and the variability of the education, training, and experience levels of early childhood professionals. Their concept provides a structure that encourages professional development for individuals, regardless of level of professionalism, role, or setting.

This structure is that of a career lattice that forms a "net" or network of strands connecting the range of sectors, programs, and settings within the early childhood profession as well as intersecting career ladders within that network. Career ladders represent steps of increased responsibility, based on increased qualifications and preparation that result in higher compensation. Early childhood professionals, then, have the potential to move up the career ladder within a setting or horizontally across the career lattice to another sector within the early childhood profession to a compatible position of responsibility and compensation. Figure 3.4 reflects a continuum of six levels of professional development that is at the heart of the career-lattice and career-ladder concepts (Willer, 1994).

For an individual early childhood program, the career-ladder concept is critical to the recruitment, retention, development, and assessment of staff members. We recommend that supervisors incorporate this concept within a program's personnel policies and professional development plan.

A good career-ladder plan provides clear job descriptions so that workers know what is expected of them, rewards teachers who are effective, and offers incentives for those who need to improve. It also provides a hierarchy of roles that makes use of the special expertise of teachers and provides incentives for staff members who are at different stages of development (Bloom, Sheerer, & Britz, 1991).

Figure 3.4 Definitions of Early Childhood Professional Categories

This figure is designed to reflect a continuum of professional development, identifying levels of preparation programs for which standards have been established nationally.

Early Childhood Professional Level VI
- Successful completion of a Ph.D. or Ed.D. in a program conforming to NAEYC guidelines; OR
- Successful demonstration of the knowledge, performance, and dispositions expected as outcomes of a doctoral degree program conforming to NAEYC guidelines.

Early Childhood Professional Level V
- Successful completion of a master's degree in a program that conforms to NAEYC guidelines; OR
- Successful demonstration of the knowledge, performance, and dispositions expected as outcomes of a master's degree program conforming to NAEYC guidelines.

Early Childhood Professional Level IV
- Successful completion of a baccalaureate degree from a program conforming to NAEYC guidelines; OR
- State certificate meeting NAEYC certification guidelines; OR
- Successful completion of a baccalaureate degree in another field with more than 30 professional units in early childhood development/education including 300 hours of supervised teaching experience, including 150 hours each for two of the following three age groups: infants and toddlers, 3- to 5-yeor-olds, or the primary grades; OR
- Successful demonstration of the knowledge, performance, and dispositions expected as outcomes of a baccalaureate degree program conforming to NAEYC guidelines.

Early Childhood Professional Level III
- Successful completion of an associate degree from a program conforming to NAEYC guidelines; OR
- Successful completion of an associate degree in a related field, plus 30 units of professional studies in early childhood development/education including 300 hours of supervised teaching experience in an early childhood program; OR
- Successful demonstration of the knowledge, performance, and dispositions expected as outcomes of an associate degree program conforming to NAEYC guidelines.

Early Childhood Professional Level II
- II. B. Successful completion of a one-year early childhood certificate program.
- II. A. Successful completion of the CDA Professional Preparation Program OR
- Completion of a systematic, comprehensive training program that prepares an individual to successfully acquire the CDA Credential through direct assessment.

Early Childhood Professional Level I
- Individuals who are employed in an early childhood professional role working under supervision or with support (e.g., linkages with provider association or network or enrollment in supervised practicum) and participating in training designed to lead to the assessment of individual competencies or acquisition of a degree.

Note: Reprinted with permission from the National Association for the Education of Young Children.

Ideally, a center should have a mix of classroom staff in different roles at different levels: some at entry-level positions that require little training, some who are academically prepared but with little experience, others who are very experienced and prepared, and still others who have had leadership and administrative training (Morgan et al., 1993).

In designing a career ladder, a program director and staff members might begin by identifying several levels of professionalism within a program that form the basis of a hierarchy. The ladder might begin with a precredential level that requires entry-level qualifications such as those of teacher aide and then move up to professional roles held by those with specialized training such as teachers and assistant teachers. Professional levels for staff members who have training beyond a bachelor's degree and who are more experienced, and specialty roles such as that of educational coordinator, might form the upper levels of the ladder (Bloom et al., 1991). For each professional level, clear job descriptions will have to be written that describe the role, outline qualifications, and designate salaries and benefits.

A description of how a staff member can move up a program's career ladder, including staff development opportunities and ways that staff members are assessed and rewarded, should be available to staff in an orientation booklet when they enter a program. Prospective staff members therefore understand that they are joining a program that has a thoughtful plan that encourages and expects professional growth and development and that they will be working within a professional culture.

CONCLUSION

Supervisors and administrators in early childhood programs often have more than one significant role associated with their jobs. Their preparation for supervision varies greatly as do the competency levels, ages, and stages of professional development of the staff members they supervise.

Because of the many demands for supervisor time, attention, and energy, and because of possible insecurity about supervising, sometimes supervision may not take place at all unless it becomes a conscious goal with time set aside to confer with and observe staff on a regular basis. This is a point we would like to underscore.

Individuals who prefer certainty, predictable routines, and clarity of expectations may find the fluidity and complexity of early childhood settings overwhelming, in comparison with those persons who are more adaptable and enjoy challenges. Knowledge of early childhood development as well as an understanding of how adults grow and develop can make supervision more satisfying.

Lastly, those who can analyze themselves in relation to their settings and who are realistic about what can be accomplished are likely to be more successful as early childhood supervisors.

PROGRAM ACCREDITATION

In its *Guide to Accreditation,* the National Academy of Early Childhood Programs (*Guide to Accreditation*, 1998) includes the following criteria related to staff roles, qualifications, and responsibilities:

D-1 a. Staff who work directly with children are 18 years of age or older and demonstrate the appropriate personal characteristics for working with children as exemplified in the criteria for Interactions among Teachers and Children and Curriculum.

D-1 b. Early Childhood Teacher Assistants (staff who implement program activities under direct supervision) are high school graduates or the equivalent, have been trained in early childhood education/child development, and/or participate in ongoing professional development programs.

D-1 c. Early Childhood Teachers (staff who are responsible for the care and education of a group of children from birth through age 5) have at least a CDA Credential or an A.A. degree in Early Childhood/Child Development or equivalent, preferably teachers have baccalaureate degrees in early childhood education/development.

D-1 d. Staff working with school-age children have training in child development, early childhood education, elementary education, recreation, or a related field.

D-2 a. The administrator has expertise (acquired through formal education and experience) in both early childhood education/child development and administration such as human resource and financial management.

D-2 b. In programs serving infants, toddlers, preschoolers, and/or kindergartners, an Early Childhood Specialist (an individual with a bachelor's degree in early childhood education/child development and at least three years of full-time teaching experiences with young children and/or a graduate degree in ECE/CD) is employed to direct the educational program (may be the director or other appropriate person). In public schools, the individual who provides support to prekindergarten and kindergarten teachers and/or who is responsible for program development is a qualified Early Childhood Specialist.

D-2 c. In programs serving only school-age children, the educational program is directed by a school-age specialist with a bachelor's degree in elementary education, recreation, or related field and at least three years of experience working with school-age children.

E-1 b. The annual program evaluation examines the adequacy of staff compensation and benefits and rate of staff turnover, and a plan is developed to increase salaries and benefits to ensure recruitment and retention of qualified staff and continuity of relationships.

E-3 a. The program has written personnel policies, including job descriptions; salary scales with increments based on professional qualifications, length of employment, and performance; benefits; resignation and termination; and grievance procedures.

E-3 b. Hiring practices are nondiscriminatory.

E-3 c. Every effort is made to hire staff who reflect diverse cultural, racial, and linguistic characteristics as needed to communicate with the children and families served.

E-4. Benefits packages for full-time staff include paid leave (annual, sick and/or personal), medical insurance, and retirement. Other benefits such as subsidized child care or continued education may be negotiated as unique to the situation. Benefits for part-time staff who are employed at least half-time are available on a prorated basis.

E-5 b. Confidential personnel files are kept including resumes with record of experience, transcripts of education, documentation of ongong professional development, and results of performance evaluation. (See criterion J-1.)

E-6 a. In cases where the program is governed by a board of directors, the program has written policies defining roles and responsibilities of board members and staff. (pp. 63–67)

Reprinted with permission from the National Association for the Education of Young Children

EXERCISES

1. Write a job description for your present supervisory position.
2. Given the nature of supervisory jobs in early childhood education, what qualities and competencies should early childhood supervisors possess?
3. Who are the members of your role set? What expectations do they have of you?
4. Work with staff members to develop a career-ladder plan for your program. Use the headings below to work out a plan as you read the remainder of this text: job title, description, and qualifications; salaries and benefits; required professional development; optional professional development; and staff evaluation options.

Part II

A DEVELOPMENTAL PERSPECTIVE

4

Caring, Knowing, and Imagining

Caring, knowing, and imagining are key and interrelated concepts associated with the notion of supervision as development. In this chapter, we explore supervisory issues related to these ideas as well as the roles of supervisors as caregivers, as helpers of others to become knowers, and as those who nurture imagination.

CARING

The word *care* is embedded in the names that we give to those who work with young children—*care*givers and child *care* providers—and to those places that house programs for young children—child *care* centers. If we consider various dictionary definitions of care, caregivers may be thought of as individuals who are in charge of the welfare of children and child care centers as places where children are attended to, protected, and entrusted in care.

Noddings (1992) has proposed that education be organized around centers of care. Thinking of early childhood programs as centers of care might enable us to imagine them in different ways and to broaden our conceptions of caring. Centers of caring place an emphasis on caring for children, for adults who work with children, for other adults who enable centers to function, and for families who are associated with them. In addition to caring for people, educators in such centers also care for ideas, particulary about pedagogy and ways to support and nurture the growth of young children and their families and about principles and ideals, especially principles of social justice and policies that can put those principles into law and action.

But this is a book about supervision. What does supervision have to do with caring? Are those in supervisory positions caregivers? Can those who bear so much responsibility afford the risk of caring?

We believe that supervision is a caring process. Supervisors as caregivers strive to develop in programs a culture of caring, a place where staff members and children grow in their capacity to care. Supervisors are also advocates for policies based on attitudes of caring.

45

A starting point for our discussion of supervision as caring behavior can be found in the following definition of caring:

> To care for another person, in the most significant sense, is to help him grow and actualize himself. . . . Caring, as helping another grow and actualize himself, is a process, a way of relating to someone that involves development. (Mayeroff, 1971, p. 1)

Mayeroff (1971) describes eight major ingredients of caring that have relevance for supervisors. The first of these is *knowing*. Caregivers, including supervisors, have to know themselves and those cared for, their needs, interests, and concerns, and they also have to *know-how* to respond to them.

Caring also involves the use of *alternating rhythms*. This concept involves reflecting on, learning from, and changing caring behavior. Caring may mean standing back sometimes and taking action at other times. The caregiver may address or ignore a specific incident or examine the larger context before modifying caring behavior. In many ways, using alternating rhythms is much like developmental supervision in which the supervisor employs a range of strategies on a continuum, depending on the developmental characteristics of the supervisee, a concept we discuss in Chapter 5.

Mayeroff (1971) includes *patience* as a key ingredient in caring, patience as giving time for the other to grow, yet not waiting passively for something to happen. Caregivers must also be patient with themselves and give themselves a chance to care. *Honesty* and *trust* are also elements of caring—honesty in the sense of confronting and being open to oneself and trust as encouraging the independence of another. A lack of trust is sometimes exhibited through dominance of the other or through overprotection. *Humility* is present in caring as we learn from the cared-for, as is *hope*, that is, excitement with a sense of the possible. Finally, as caregivers and the cared-for do not know where their journey will take them, they need *courage*.

Noddings (1984) believes that Mayeroff's (1971) definition of caring overemphasizes the actualization of the other, and that it is the relation between the cared-for and the one-caring that is essential, rather than personal attributes. She views a basic caring relation as an encounter in which there is genuine reciprocity. The one-caring cares for the other. The other, the cared-for, recognizes and receives the caring and reacts in a way that shows it.

In Chapter 5, we emphasize the dynamic relationship between supervisor and supervisee because we want to underscore that staff members are not the object of supervision, but play an active role in the process and that supervisors learn, change, and grow as a result of the process too. Caring as relation and reciprocity means that supervisors and staff members as caregivers and carereceivers are participants in and contributors to acts of caring.

Noddings (1992) makes the important point that teachers, mothers, and other caregivers lose energy when there is no response to their caring. Supervisors and administrators as caregivers of staff and children need a response too, for much of their work involves attending to others while seeing things as others see them.

Some staff members, so engrossed in their own survival, may be less able to respond because they cannot "get out of themselves," but some response is necessary in order for caring to be complete. A teacher's response to a supervisor may take the form of showing natural excitement for an accomplishment, following through on a suggestion made by a supervisor, thinking out loud with a supervisor, revealing one's true thoughts and feelings with a supervisor, asking for advice, or simply letting one's supervisor know how things are progressing. In some cases, with supervisees who are at advanced stages of development, a response might take the form of a role reversal by attending to the needs of their supervisors.

In her discussion of moral education from the perspective of an ethic of care, Noddings (1992) describes four essential components that might be considered by supervisors who wish to create environments where caring can thrive. The first of these is *modeling*. Just as teachers need to model for children, we have to show staff members how to care by fostering caring relations with them. As Noddings reminds us, the capacity to care may be dependent on having adequate experience in being cared for.

A second component is *dialogue*—dialogue in an open sense, without predetermined outcomes. Dialogue connects individuals to each other and develops, in people, the habit of acquiring information before making decisions. And as Freire (1972) points out, only dialogue, "which requires critical thinking, is capable of generating critical thinking. Without dialogue, there is no communication, and without communication there can be no true education" (p. 81).

Dialogue is really the heart of the supervisory process, yet sometimes honest dialogue is hard to achieve because of contextual issues, role definitions, or some of the personal background characteristics noted in Chapter 5 such as perceptions of authority figures and cultural values. The stage of development of supervisees and the skill levels of supervisors may also have an effect on the extent to which genuine dialogue is achieved. However, without dialogue there is no supervision. Caring between supervisors and staff will bring about more trust, which is the basis for honest and open dialogue.

Practice is a third component of moral education in which staff and children have experiences in acquiring skills in caregiving and in developing caring attitudes. We agree with Noddings (1992) that practice in caring will transform schools and eventually the society in which we live. Lastly, a person working toward a better self needs *confirmation*. This is an act of affirming and encouraging the best in others.

Supervisors, who spend a great deal of time encouraging staff, helping them to feel valued, and letting them know that their contributions are appreciated, also need to care for and nurture themselves. Caring can be exhausting. Sometimes we care too much and/or feel guilty if caring seems to fail or if we don't want to care anymore. However, it is critical for supervisors to maintain their inner resources and to focus on their abilities in other areas, particularly outside the profession. Preserving oneself may take the form of participating in physical, intellectual, spiritual, and/or artistic pursuits that bring one into contact with new experiences and people outside the work setting and that permit one to be absorbed in creative or intellectual endeavors that actually can have the effect of restoring the energy that one needs for caring in the workplace each day.

KNOWING

A second objective in broadening our conceptions of early care and education programs is to facilitate knowing. Children and staff come to child care centers at different stages in perceiving themselves and in having confidence in themselves as knowers. It is not unusual for women with mothering skills, for example, to begin work as teacher aides and, with education and training, to move up the career ladder professionally. They blossom as individuals as they see themselves and gain confidence in themselves as knowers. Child care centers can be liberating learning environments for staff as well as for children. In their classic book *Women's Ways of Knowing*, Belenky, Clinchy, Goldberger, and Tarule (1997) offer a framework of five categories of knowing that is a particularly helpful construct for supervisors and other facilitators as they think about their work in supporting the development of staff.

The first category of knowing identified by Belenky at al. (1997) is *silence*. In their study, silent women viewed themselves as "deaf and dumb." They felt voiceless. As they were disconnected and isolated from others, they rarely had any dialogue with others. Growing up without experience in conversing and playing, they had difficulty understanding and using metaphors and symbol systems. They had little formal schooling and their experiences with schooling were negative; as a result, they had little confidence in their ability to learn. They tended to be passive, obedient, and subdued.

Silent women tended to blindly obey authority figures whom they saw as knowers. For some, a profound event, like the birth of a child and the responsibilities associated with mothering, forced them into the next category, *received knowledge*. Received knowers, who may also be educated, learn by listening to others. They are aware of the power of words, but keep their voices still in order to listen to others for direction and wisdom, for the "right answers." Unlike silent women, they see themselves as having the ability to absorb knowledge, and even to reproduce it, but not as sources of knowledge (Belenky et al., 1997).

Received knowers become *subjective knowers*, sometimes because of changes in their personal lives and/or crises of trust with authority figures. They become aware of their inner resources, perhaps out of protest, and take actions on behalf of themselves such as moving out of their present circumstances or returning to school. As a small inner voice begins to emerge in them, they rely on intuition, feeling, and first-hand experiences as sources of knowledge.

The last two categories in women's perspectives on knowing developed by Belenky et al. (1997) are *procedural knowledge* and *constructed knowledge*.

Procedural knowers are invested in learning. With their old ways of thinking challenged, procedural knowers move away from the personal and become more objective. They begin to learn in more formal and systematic ways. They carefully observe, learn to read between the lines, take another's perspective, and consider the opinions and expertise of others. They begin to become critical thinkers. The comments below by a Head Start teacher we interviewed reflect some of the characteristics of knowers in this category, as well as those who are constructivists.

> I'm fairly open minded. I listen, see both sides. I like that I have my own set of beliefs that I have come to, that I can stand on. And if new information comes to me, I can turn it around and look at it in many different ways and hold it against my beliefs and see if I can make it fit, or disregard it if it doesn't and know why because of my beliefs. I can respect others because they've done the same kind of searching, but I can still disagree. . . . I like to sit and contemplate on what I've heard or read and run it through my mind and shadow wrestle with myself, take sides. I like to take what I've heard and put it into some sort of relevance, a real situation, relate it to some sort of experience I've had or have seen others have.

Constructivists are passionate knowers who have found their voices. They carefully listen to and speak with others, and also listen to themselves. They believe that their own ways of knowing matter and that they can create knowledge. They pay attention to situation and context. Through empathy, they connect with what they are trying to understand. They wish to empower others and to integrate feeling and care into their work (Belenky et al., 1997).

How can we as facilitators assist staff in finding their voices so that they can engage in dialogue with us, which is so central to coming to know and to growth and change? As Freire (1972) reminds us, through dialogue, the "teacher is no longer merely the-one-who-teaches, but one who is himself taught in dialogue with the students, who in turn while being taught also teach. They become jointly responsible for a process in which all grow" (p. 67).

In helping those who have been denied voice because of race, gender, social class, or culture to think of themselves as learners and knowers, relationship building is key, but this must be a relationship between two human beings that stresses a mutuality of trust, respect, and learning. Drawing out the concerns, questions, and ideas of those silenced can be achieved only if trust is developed.

As Child Development Associate (CDA) advisors in Native American Head Start programs, Katherine Greenough (1993) and David Beers (1993) encountered women who did not perceive themselves as knowers. Native Americans in particular were denied voice when government education policies replaced the use of their native languages with English in schools. Greenough and Beers helped these women come out of silence by building trusting relationships with them and in several other ways as well. They were good listeners and invited speech by encouraging the women to tell stories about their work with children, which eventually became the basis of training materials written in their own words rather than in the words of outside authorities. The CDA candidates also told their own life stories as autobiographical portfolio entries. Advisors encouraged one-on-one dialogue about observations of children and created opportunities for group problem-solving. And they emphasized the strengths and competencies teachers already had. Gradually, these Native American teachers gained competence and confidence.

Teachers who are procedural and constructivist knowers also require support. They need to continually engage in dialogue with supervisors and colleagues as the challenge of dialogue, problem-posing, and problem-solving has the potential to push their thinking to new levels. Formal staff development in which they are confronted with new ideas to explore, reflect on, and critique can also have a major impact on their growth.

Persons come to know and to express what they know in different ways. Early care and education programs as centers of knowing are places where these differences are valued and fostered. Howard Gardner's (1983) theory of multiple intelligences has implications for supervisors as it helps us to think of the varied abilities people have. He has identified seven types of intelligence: linguistic, logical-mathematical, musical, spatial, kinesthetic, interpersonal, and intrapersonal. Daniel Goleman (1995) has added to this list with his work on emotional intelligence. We can strive to help staff to develop their particular intelligences and to use them in working with children by seeing staff members as unique and by making opportunities for them to display the different ways that they know. This is really an act of caring.

IMAGINING

Preschools and infant and toddler centers in the city of Reggio Emilia, Italy, are places where young children have opportunities to explore and to communicate with the world through their strengths, with different "languages" or intelligences.

These schools have captured the attention of educators the world over because those who created them have imagined schools differently. Reggio Emilia educators have broken down the barriers of traditional pedagogy by creating liberating environments in which children's imaginations can flourish.

Children are encouraged to use their creativity in representing what they know or what they imagine. They represent their ideas in many ways, sometimes by constructing objects in clay or in paper, and/or by drawing them or building with blocks. A fascination with bridges, for example, may result in constructions of bridges in all of these media and then studying them from different perspectives and profiles. Shadow screens are often used so children can see images of subjects in a completely different light; they gain a "fresh eye." Observing the ordinary in a new way creates a sense of enchantment and wonder.

Constructing in various materials requires that particular problems be solved based on the medium used. Building a bridge with clay, for example, poses problems of equilibrium. Studying creations from multiple perspectives as part of a process of encouraging new ways of looking and representing is problem-solving, too. Reggio educators describe this process as expressive research (Vecchi, 1997).

The physical environment fosters an aesthetic atmosphere. Many kinds of materials and tools are available to children. The role of teachers is to encourage risk-taking. Error is viewed as a natural part of the knowledge-building process. Children's courage is appreciated, sustained, and admired. Teachers observe, listen, and support exploration and encounter. Children work in groups where they discuss what they have seen or have constructed in common. They learn to listen, to respect each other, to take turns, to plan together, and to give suggestions and ideas.

We have described some of the elements of learning environments in Reggio Emelia preschools as we believe that many of the characteristics educators value for children's development are essential to adult learning as well.

Adults in early care and education centers need to be lifelong learners. They need the freedom to imagine, to explore, and to develop their ideas, and to think of things otherwise, too.

> To learn, after all, is to become different, to see more, to gain a new perspective. It is to choose against things as they are, to anticipate what might be seen through a new perspective or through another's eye. (Greene, 1988, p. 49)

The women in the Belenky et al. (1997) study described earlier could not have broken their silence if they were not able to think of themselves differently, in new situations. It is not unusual for those of us in supervisory and administrative positions to become frustrated because of the problems associated with daily routines or to feel bogged down because of increasing paperwork and bureaucratic requirements. Yet we need to persist in invoking our imaginations, to think of ourselves, staff members, and programs in new and different ways. Without imagination, we cannot move forward; we succumb to the press for conformity and accountability. Our vision becomes narrower, we lose our motivation, and we become numbed by the ordinary.

The multiple perspective–taking that Reggio teachers foster in children is central to adult caring, knowing, and imagining. As staff work with children, with parents, and with each other, the ability to see things as others see them, to explore a problem from many different angles, and to generate alternative solutions is a critical one for them to possess. Through encounter with supervisors and each other, this ability can be nurtured.

> We have begun to understand that for children's experiences to be as wonderful as possible, teachers need to reacquaint themselves with the wonder of the world and begin to see and understand it through children's eyes. (Cadwell, 1997, p. 103)

Just as Reggio teachers encourage the development of multiple literacies in children, supervisors, too, can assist staff in finding or expanding their voices by thinking of alternative ways for them to express what they know or are learning. Through different projects and particular responsibilities, staff can bring their special knowledge and competence to their everyday work and share them with others.

As Maxine Greene (1995) points out, "All we can do . . . is cultivate multiple ways of seeing and multiple dialogues in a world where nothing stays the same"(p. 16). Preschools, child care centers, kindergartens, and the primary grades as centers of imagining create openings for children and staff to see in many different ways, to think of things otherwise. Greene adds, "imagining things otherwise may be a first step toward acting on the belief that they can be changed" (p. 22).

CONCLUSION

In our exploration of child care programs as centers of caring, knowing, and imagining, we see several commonalities. An ethos of trust, respect, and openness is necessary in nourishing these characteristics. Dialogue is critical in the caring relationship, in bringing people out of silence and into freedom, and in developing different ways of seeing as well as learning about the perspectives of others. And lastly, it takes courage to care, to know, and to imagine.

EXERCISES

1. Set some time aside during a staff meeting to explore ways that you and your staff members can nurture and care for yourselves.
2. Make a list of your staff members. Think about their particular strengths or intelligences—the different ways that they express what they know. When working with them, try to recognize what they do well.
3. What are some additional ways that your program can encourage imagination in children and staff?

5

The Developmental Dynamic

Supervisor, *supervisee*, and the *context* in which they work are three components of a complex, dynamic process in which development occurs. Supervisor and supervisee grow and change in an environment that also changes. The interaction between these two individuals and the context in which it takes place can create energy, force, and power for continued professional and personal growth.

A major assumption of developmental supervision is that there is no single best method of improving the performance and facilitating the professional growth of supervisees. By assessing the developmental characteristics of staff members, supervisors can select and use an approach that best matches the individual with whom they are working and the specific problem or concern at hand. This diagnosis takes into account staff members' cognitive abilities, their level of professional development, and their stage in life. Basic to this view of supervision is the ability to "read" staff members to determine which strategies to use with them and to shift from one supervisory approach to another.

Knowledge of self is also fundamental to developmental supervision. By understanding ourselves and the impact of our early life experiences and cultural backgrounds, we increase the control we have over our own behavior and can more easily modify and redirect it when necessary. The literature on developmental supervision has focused primarily on changes in teachers. Yet supervisors' perceptions of self, life situations, and levels of competence change too, and these changes affect the supervisor and teacher development that takes place.

Supervisors and staff members interact within a context. They work with people; they confront problems; they feel pressures that affect the dynamics of the supervisory process. The situation and setting in which they work make up the third significant variable in the developmental dynamic. Figure 5.1 illustrates these three components, which will be discussed further in this chapter. Contextual issues are also addressed in Chapter 13.

Figure 5.1 Supervisor, Supervisee, and Context: Three Components of the Developmental Dynamic

CONTEXT: Workplace characteristics; Relationship between supervisor and supervisee; Issue, problem, concern at hand

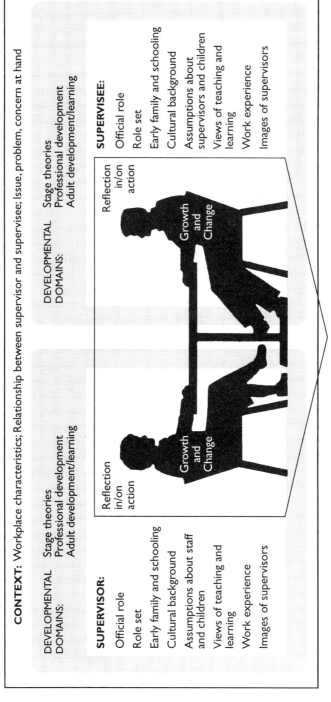

DEVELOPMENTAL
DOMAINS:

Stage theories
Professional development
Adult development/learning

DEVELOPMENTAL
DOMAINS:

Stage theories
Professional development
Adult development/learning

SUPERVISOR:

Official role

Role set

Early family and schooling

Cultural background

Assumptions about staff
and children

Views of teaching and
learning

Work experience

Images of supervisors

SUPERVISEE:

Official role

Role set

Early family and schooling

Cultural background

Assumptions about
supervisors and children

Views of teaching and
learning

Work experience

Images of supervisors

Reflection
in/on
action

Growth
and
Change

Reflection
in/on
action

Growth
and
Change

Supervisor and Supervisee Strategies
|
OUTCOMES

SUPERVISORS AND SUPERVISEES

As supervisor and teacher work together, each brings to the encounter an accumulated set of experiences, perceptions, beliefs, and values that make them who they are, shape their behavior, and influence supervisory outcomes. These include early childhood experiences, cultural perspectives, images of supervisors, previous work experiences, assumptions about people, and views about how individuals learn.

Early Childhood, Cultural Background, and Work Experiences

Supervisors and staff members live with emotional remnants from their early experiences with authority figures. Family training, education, culture, and socialization play a part in how they see themselves and how they express their own authority with others. A supervisor/teacher illustrates this point in describing her background and style of supervision:

> My father expected immediate action following a command. My parents usually fought in front of us over authority issues. Teacher was boss and unfair at times, not listening to my reasons. As a teacher and supervisor, I try to right the wrongs which were done to me; however, I often fall back into the pattern of wanting things done immediately from kids and of being didactic to staff.

Cultural background also has a particular impact on how supervisors and staff members view and carry out their authority. Cultural factors that may affect the supervisory dynamic are verbal and nonverbal language patterns, concepts of dependence/independence, cooperation and individuality, and the value placed on time and punctuality, as well as issues of gender and age. These factors are discussed further in Chapter 10.

Through employment in various settings, staff members and supervisors have had experiences with supervisors who have served as role models and who have left impressions about what it is that supervisors do and how they behave. Both supervisors and staff bring these lasting images with them as they interact with each other.

Assumptions and Philosophy of Learning

Assumptions about human nature also affect how supervisors and teachers work with children and adults. Supervisors who see staff members as basically good, honest, and trustworthy are likely to display behavior patterns that are quite different from those of supervisors who regard teachers/caregivers with distrust and suspicion.

Another significant factor in determining how supervisors or teachers interact with others is their point of view about learning. Some individuals believe that behavior is mainly caused and shaped by outside forces. Supervisors and teachers with this orientation select goals and objectives for learners, organize the material to be learned, and develop ways to reinforce learners as they strive to attain established goals. This *direct mode* of teaching can help learners organize skills and knowledge essential to specific tasks, and it can shorten learning time since learners do not have to go through the process of discovering new concepts. But direct teaching can foster a cycle of dependency between instructor and student (Brundage & Mackeracher, 1980) and does not encourage problem-solving and reflective behavior.

However, some individuals learn best through a direct approach because of their personal learning style or because they come from cultural or class backgrounds that value and respect directness. They expect teachers and supervisors to be directive and may have little respect for them when they are not. Although some teachers and supervisors are uncomfortable with this style, it can be considered a starting point. A direct mode does not eliminate the need for listening to learners, and becoming familiar with who they are and how they think.

Other people believe that learners need the freedom to explore and discover knowledge through a natural self-directed process. Supervisors and teachers favoring this view work in a *facilitative mode*.

Facilitating helps learners to discover and create new meanings, skills, and structures from experience. It requires that the facilitator be a catalyst, resource, reflective mirror, and co-inquirer. The structure, objectives, and direction of the learning are negotiated, although the context, in the form of personal meanings, comes from the student (Brundage & Mackeracher, 1980).

Interaction between the individual and the environment is central to yet another view of learning, which emphasizes collaboration and mutual problem-solving between teacher and student. A *collaborative mode* requires that learners and teachers jointly engage in the processes of discovering and developing new understandings, skills, and strategies. As co-learners, they act interdependently, dividing tasks on a mutually acceptable basis, building a "community of learners" (Brundage & Mackeracher, 1980).

Views about how people learn and the connection between a supervisor's or a teacher's personal philosophy of learning and personal style of working with others are, of course, not quite as simple as described above or as distinct in practice. An underlying premise of developmental supervision, however, is the recognition that humans learn through self-exploration, collaboration, and conditioning. We believe approaches to teaching and supervision that build on these philosophies of learning are valid and can be used appropriately with adult learners depending on their needs, the context, and the setting.

Criteria for Determining Supervisory Approaches

Related to these modes of teaching and learning are three orientations to supervision— *nondirective, collaborative*, and *directive*—described by Glickman, Gordon, and Ross-Gordon (1998). They recommend that supervisors determine the strategy to use with teachers by assessing their levels of development and expertise, and their commitment to solving the problem at hand. This can be accomplished by observing teachers up close and by engaging in dialogue with them.

A nondirective supervisory orientation is most effective with expert teachers who accept full responsibility for solving the problem. Decisions are in teachers' hands as they have high levels of development, expertise, and commitment. They can examine a problem from multiple perspectives, generate solutions to it, and follow through on implementing a plan of action. The supervisor's role is to help teachers think through their actions by listening, paraphrasing, and asking clarifying questions. We discuss these and other communication skills in Chapter 10.

In a collaborative orientation, teachers are operating at moderate developmental levels. Supervisors and teachers share the responsibility for solving the problem they are facing. Both are equally committed to finding a solution and have similar levels of expertise. In comparison with the nondirective role, the supervisor takes a more active stance, engaging in a give-and-take, joint problem-solving discussion with the teacher. Both supervisors and teachers make decisions and may generate solutions. They operate on a level of parity.

In a directive orientation, the decision making shifts to the supervisor as the teacher is at a low level of development or is not very interested in solving the problem. Glickman et al. (1998) make a distinction between directive control and directive informational strategies.

Directive-control supervisory behaviors are used when supervisors are committed to resolving an issue and carrying out the resolution and teachers are not so inclined or may not understand its importance. The decision making rests with the supervisor, who determines solutions and sets expectations and time-lines.

Directive informational behaviors are used with teachers who want to do well, but who do not have the skills, experience, or knowledge of an issue. They may feel confused and may even be unable to identify the problem. Supervisors take responsibility by identifying alternative solutions to a problem, and laying out the necessary structure and support for the teachers to succeed. For example, teaching techniques are modeled, and ongoing feedback and follow-up are provided. Directive informational supervision is a first step toward building teacher confidence and a baseline of competence in order that more self-directed problem-solving can take place at a later point.

We have found that supervisors are often more comfortable using a collaborative approach; however, skill in directive and nondirective supervisory behaviors is needed as well, as staff members require different interventions at various stages in their development.

A major goal of staff supervision is to assist teachers in increasing the control, authority, and responsibility they have for their own teaching and professional development. As we described in Chapter 4, with caring and patient facilitating by supervisors, staff can gain confidence in themselves as constructors of knowledge.

Learning to "read" or assess supervisees to determine how to best work with them is a sophisticated skill. The professional literature on the developmental characteristics of adults offers supervisors useful information in determining appropriate strategies and in learning about themselves.

DEVELOPMENTAL DOMAINS

During the 1970s and 1980s, in particular, researchers turned to theories of adult development to gain insight into teacher development, to be more responsive to teachers' needs, and to effectively support their professional growth.

Cognitive-Developmental Stage Theories

Cognitive-developmental stage theories such as those of Piaget (1961), Kohlberg (1984), Loevinger (1976), Hunt (1971), and Perry (1969) were studied to predict an individual's level of functioning. These theories assume that humans process experience through cognitive structures called stages. The sequence of stages is hierarchical and becomes increasingly more complex. Movement from lower to higher stages is not automatic but is based on interaction with facilitating environments (Thies-Sprinthall, 1980). The assumption is that individuals who function at higher stages are more conceptual, reflective, and independent (Bents & Howey, 1981).

The research that examined the relationship between stage theories and teacher development and effectiveness led to the notion of matching the stage characteristics of the individual with intervention strategies to assist that individual. Some researchers also experimented with ways to help individuals move to higher stages of development and explored the implications of matches and mismatches of cognitive-developmental stages between supervisors and staff members.

Hunt (1971), for example, described the conceptual development of individuals in terms of a continuum from a low conceptual level characterized by concrete thinking to a high conceptual level where thinking is abstract. He proposed matching the degree of structure in the environment to the learner's need for it, based on the person's conceptual level.

Bents and Howey (1981) studied the implications of conceptual systems theory for staff development and suggested that staff developers should plan training in tune with the developmental characteristics of staff. They suggested that teachers who are lower conceptual learners benefit from staff development that is very organized and practical and specific to their teaching situations and classrooms, while teachers at high levels would be expected to organize more of their own staff development and work in teams with colleagues.

Oja (1981) and Glassberg (1980) found that teachers who are at higher levels of cognitive, moral, and ego development function more effectively in a number of ways. They appear to be better able to think more abstractly about a problem and to generate more solutions to it than teachers at lower levels. They are also better able to see differences in the children they teach. As a consequence, they utilize the learner's frame of reference and adjust their teaching styles and methods to meet the needs of individual children.

An important finding was that the developmental stages of student teachers were raised when they used teaching methods such as role-playing, dilemma discussions, active listening, videotaping, individual conferences, and empathic responding exercises, illustrating the point that developmental levels are not fixed. Thus, supervisors, staff developers, and teacher educators who provide opportunities for staff to be reflective about their practice can help them to become more autonomous in their decision making and problem-solving.

Researchers have also examined the implications of this cognitive-developmental perspective in terms of the pairing of supervisors with supervisees. Grimmett (1983) studied the conceptual functioning and communication behavior of four supervisors and their supervisees during conferences. He found that supervisors who functioned more abstractly showed "flex" in their communication behavior. They were able to "read" their supervisees' needs and the situational constraints. Supervisors who functioned more concretely seemed unable to do this. The term *flex* suggests the supervisor's ability to vary or adapt his or her approach from a range of alternative behaviors. During a conference, for example, a supervisor might change from being directive to being collaborative to meet the personal, cultural, professional, or situational needs of a supervisee.

Grimmett (1983) also noted an increase in the conceptual functioning of teachers who worked with supervisors who were more abstract and conceptual, and a reduction in the conceptual levels of those teachers who were working with supervisors who functioned at more concrete levels. A study of student teachers and their supervisors by Lois Thies-Sprinthall (1980) had similar findings.

In a qualitative study of graduate students learning to be supervisors and their partner teachers, Arredondo (1998) examined the effects of support and challenge dialogues between them, based on an assessment of the cognitive complexity of the participating teachers. During conference dialogues, less support and more challenge was provided to teachers who evidenced high levels of cognitive complexity, while more support and less challenge was given to teachers who evidenced low cognitive complexity. Although results are not generalizable, participant pairs showed evidence of developing complexity and reflectivity in their thinking.

Since the cognitive-developmental stage theories noted above were constructed, however, investigators have become more sensitive to those whose experiences have been excluded from the literature because of gender, race, culture, or social class. The pioneering work of Gilligan (1982), for example, has broadened our understanding of human development to include women's lives. She found that women placed priority on the understanding of responsibility and on connection and caring, traits that labeled them deficient in an earlier conception of moral development based on men's beliefs (Kohlberg, 1984).

Keeping in mind our goal of promoting development in individuals and expanding opportunities for learning, cognitive-developmental theories, taken into perspective, can provide helpful information for supervisory practice. A second important developmental domain is the professional career development of teachers and other staff members.

Stages of Professional Development

The phases and stages of teachers' professional development and their needs and concerns at various points in their career paths are another source of information for supervisors, staff developers, and mentors as they strive to provide supportive and stimulating professional environments for teacher growth.

Francis Fuller (1969), who examined teacher concerns across time during the pre-service experience, was a pioneer in this way of thinking about teacher growth and its implications for teacher preparation. Fuller and Oliver Bown (1975) described the stages of learning to teach in terms of the individual's concerns rather than the content that is being taught.

Although there are many conceptualizations of teachers' career phases, those of Katz (1977) and Vander Ven (1988) are particularly relevant to early childhood educators. Katz (1977) identified four stages of preschool teacher development and the training needs for each stage. Stage 1, *Survival,* usually lasts through the first year of teaching, when the individual experiences self-doubt and feelings of insecurity. Katz recommends that teachers in this stage receive direct on-site support and technical assistance. During Stage 2, *Consolidation*, a teacher consolidates the gains made during the first stage and begins to focus on specific tasks and skills. Supervisors can support training needs during the first several years of teaching by providing on-site assistance, access to specialists, and advice from colleagues and consultants.

By the third or fourth year, the preschool teacher begins to tire and to feel a need for *Renewal*, Stage 3. By attending conferences, joining professional associations, and analyzing their teaching, teachers can meet their needs at this stage. Finally, Stage 4, *Maturity*, which extends beyond the fifth year, is the time when the teacher benefits most from attending conferences, participating in institutes and degree programs, and writing for journals.

Vander Ven (1988) examined levels of professionalism of early childhood practitioners a little differently. She described a series of five stages, their accompanying role level functions, adult/career developmental stages, and the level of guidance needed at each one.

Practitioners at Stage 1, *Novice,* function as nonprofessionals; they have the lowest legally permissible levels of education, as well as the lowest salaries. Needing a high level of direct supervision, they often view issues based on their own personal experience. Individuals in Stage 2, *Initial* stage, also need direct supervision, but they have had some training and are seriously considering a career in early childhood education. They are usually receptive to supervision. Professionals at Stage 3, *Informed,* have a strong commitment to the field, hold a bachelor's degree, and are more likely to use developmentally appropriate practices. They have a broader perspective, identify with parents and families, and are becoming more self-reliant. Professionals at Stage 4, *Complex,* and Stage 5, *Influential,* take on leadership roles, supervise others, and have high levels of self-direction and autonomy. Guided by their wisdom, age, and expertise, professionals at Stage 5, in particular, are likely to have a significant impact on the early childhood field.

An assumption behind these theories of teacher growth is that pre-service and in-service teacher education and supervisory support should change as the needs, concerns, experience, and preparation levels of teachers vary throughout their careers.

A third developmental domain that can be helpful to supervisors as they work with staff members is that of adult development.

Adult Development: Life Stages and Transitions

Staff members working in early childhood programs represent all adult age groups. There may be high school and college students, women beginning or returning to work as their children grow up, and senior citizens working part-time to earn extra income or to have something interesting to do. These adults are at varying points in their life cycles. As they develop and change, so do their personal and professional needs and priorities.

As early childhood educators, much of our thinking has focused on child development, but development does not end with childhood. The important work of life-cycle theorists such as Erikson (1980, 1982), Gould (1978), Sheehy (1976, 1998), and Levinson (1978, 1996), which place adulthood within a context of a life course or journey, has implications for supervisors, mentors, and staff developers.

Erikson (1980) studied a life from infancy to old age in terms of a series of conflicts or main concerns representing the inner and external worlds. Of the eight phases in his theory, three apply to adulthood. *Intimacy vs. Isolation*, Stage 6, takes place in young adulthood and deals with the search for partnership in friendship and love, and social patterns of cooperation and competition. In Stage 7, *Adulthood* (ages 40–65 or so), the central concern is *Generativity vs. Stagnation*—that is, one's relationship to the next generation or absorption with self. And finally, during the last stage, old age, *Integrity vs. Despair and Disgust: Wisdom,* a major focus is coming to terms with one's life and life experiences as one strives to balance integrity and despair.

Gratz and Boultin (1996) propose that early childhood educators consider Erikson's (1980) scheme in looking at their own development and the early childhood profession itself. For example, establishing teams within a program so that teachers can share ideas and work together is a way of reducing isolation and building intimacy in Stage 6; planning professional development opportunities for others and participating in classroom research that furthers the field enables one to help the next generation in Stage 7; and viewing accomplishments with satisfaction and knowing that we have made a difference for many children and families are ways to consciously develop the ego integrity that Erikson describes in his final stage.

Gould (1978) became aware of a predictable series of preoccupations in life through his work in supervising resident psychiatrists. He identified a series of false assumptions and illusions that individuals hold at each life phase that are challenged as they gain more competence. This thoughtful confrontation, which requires changes in viewpoints, enables them to make a transition to the next phase. For example, during the period between the ages of 22 and 28, *I'm Nobody's Baby Now,* the age level of a majority of child care workers, one of the major assumptions is, "There is only one right way to do things" (p. 88).

This assumption might play itself out in early childhood classrooms in several ways. For example, beliefs about what a teacher does or how a teacher should relate to children that are imprinted on our minds in childhood may interfere with the reality of working with children on a daily basis as they may not represent good practice.

The view of a teacher as someone who must be perfectly loving toward all of the children all of the time is one that is often held by novice teachers and one that makes it difficult for them to set limits with children. The process of asserting their teacher authority can be painful as they often feel guilty when they are forced to do so. Yet they cannot move forward in the role until they reconceptualize this idea of teacher authority.

The assumption held by many that teaching is telling or directing may also present challenges for supervisors as they explore ways to positively support beginning teachers by helping them to experiment with other ways of teaching so that development in them and in children can occur. Helping practitioners to share, explore, and challenge their own assumptions about their work with their colleagues can lead to clearer communication, greater competence, a better understanding of colleagueship (Levine, 1989), and the creation of shared values.

Arin-Krupp (1981) synthesized much of the research about adults at certain ages and stages and identified implications for staff development. She advocates that supervisors match support strategies to an individual's key concerns at each stage in life (see Table 5.1).

In thinking about their staff members and strategies to use with them, supervisors may find that, in some cases, one of the developmental domains described above may offer more information and greater relevance than the others, depending on the individual teacher and the issue at hand. Supervisor and teacher, each at his or her own phase of development, are two components of the supervisory dynamic. The third is the context in which they work.

THE CONTEXT

Not only is information derived from the various developmental domains important in determining supervisory strategies, but equally significant is the relationship established between the supervisor and the teacher, the particular concern at hand, and the organization of which they are a part. These salient contextual elements that influence supervisor-supervisee behavior can have a bearing on the approach that a supervisor might take with a particular supervisee and how a staff member might respond to a supervisor.

Relationship

The existing relationship between supervisors and supervisees affects supervision. Staff members who trust supervisors and who believe that supervisors care about them and their professional growth are more likely to be open to a range of supervisory behaviors. If teachers feel secure with supervisors, for example, there is less likelihood that they will be offended or threatened by criticism or information offered by them. Of course, relationships that are too close can create division among staff and make it harder for supervisors to be objective. A professional/personal balance in the relationship between supervisors and supervisees is most desirable.

The Problem

The nature of the problem being addressed also influences the approach to take. In working with a provider who arrives late and leaves early every day, for example, or a caregiver who talks roughly to children, or a teacher who simply does not have the skills to organize a small-group experience with children, a supervisor may have to be direct. On the other hand, if a teacher is involved in an emotionally laden issue with a particular child and cannot gain a clear perspective of the problem, the supervisor may have to reassure and comfort the teacher yet make an executive decision that may be disliked by that teacher.

In dealing with interpersonal conflicts among staff members or with intercultural issues, in planning for children who have special needs, or in exploring ways to improve the effectiveness of a program, collaborative strategies may be most appropriate. A supervisor may use listening, clarifying, encouraging, and other indirect behaviors with a teacher who is disheartened when a lesson that was thought to be exciting falls flat or with a young, inexperienced staff member who is involved in a family crisis that interferes with performance. The specific problem, issue, or concern at hand is always a significant variable in planning for supervision.

Workplace Characteristics

In her analysis of the school as a workplace, Johnson (1990) has identified a constellation of workplace variables that influence workers in all settings. We believe that these variables affect the supervisory dynamic and that an analysis of them with staff can serve as an important development and planning tool. They are economic, political, physical, organizational, cultural, psychological, and sociological.

Economic factors include salary, benefits, job security, incentives, and rewards. We know that early childhood educators leave the profession because of low wages and minimal benefits (Whitebook et al., 1993), although they love their jobs. Staff turnover greatly affects the supervisor's role, particularly with respect to recruitment and training, and it interrupts the flow of the supervisory process.

Table 5.1 Stages of Development and Implications for Staff Development

STAGE	KEY CONCERNS	CHARACTERISTICS	IMPLICATIONS FOR STAFF DEVELOPMENT
Late teens and early 20s 17–(22–24)	*Independence-dependence:* Breaking away from parents and family *Identity:* Fitting into the adult world Searching for a mentor	Physically at peak Explore intimate relationships Time perceived as endless Males concerned with occupational choice Females concerned with family or occupation New teachers concerned about confidence Males ponder viability of teaching Male-female differences abound Active social life	1. Provide these adults with clear definition of what is expected of them 2. Provide an opportunity for independence whenever possible, but recognize a need for dependence as well 3. Try to make a young teacher see the need for change by facilitating growth rather than by directing 4. Facilitate growth by encouraging participation in areas where teacher has background 5. Be sensitive to the ups and downs of intimate relationships 6. Foster exploration of all the ramifications of teaching 7. Do not encourage poor teachers to stay in the program 8. Provide social activities for staff
The 20s 18–28	*Identity and Intimacy:* Family obligations create stress Marriage and parenting Want to demonstrate competence on the job Males busy working and achieving, no in-depth questioning of occupation	Unsure of being boy-man or girl-woman Physically in their prime Emotions are modulated Very active socially Time is extensive Idealistic and optimistic	1. Clearly define the parameters of the job 2. Create a climate that permits discussion of life stressors 3. Discuss means of effecting change in areas of defect; teachers will try new techniques if they feel it is the responsible or supportive thing to do

66

	Flexibility and stability: Maintaining a balance between the two		4. Help young teachers select realistic goals 5. Female teachers may be unsure about their relationships with male administrators; frank discussions of the relationship may help alleviate some initial fear 6. While males avoid self-searching, females want to explore own development
Age 30	*Individuation:* Who am I? What is my place in the world? Males are restless and begin to re-evaluate Women investigate identity and role options Marital conflict is common Men establish career goals Women become more independent and career oriented	Physical and mental abilities still in their prime Children replace parents as central concern Decreased interest in social activities Males continue to be assertive Females continue to be nurturing Family life is major stressor	1. Teachers who are self-centered are less able to consider needs of others; may be willing to try new things if those new ideas relate to aspects of self 2. Do everything in your power to make teaching a rewarding, self-fulfilling experience 3. Be prepared for the more assertive, independent, active woman by age 35 4. Provide support to those questioning teaching 5. Find out why teachers have recommitted to teaching and help those individuals explore ways of finding satisfaction 6. Know your staff. Use persons with similar mindsets as support people with one another 7. Be flexible with teachers who have family-career conflicts

Table 5.1 (Con'd)

STAGE	KEY CONCERNS	CHARACTERISTICS	IMPLICATIONS FOR STAFF DEVELOPMENT
The 30s **(28–35)–40**	*Stability-Advancement:* Wants to feel a sense of accomplishment Women become more independent Men move toward career advancement Accomodation and constancy sought in marriage and family *De-illusionment:* Remove unrealistic aspects of the dream and modify it Become one's own person *Authority-Mutuality:* Interdependence	Past physical prime Family a strong priority for males Time is limited Social life revolves around family Men full of doubts and anxiety, while women are content and have more self-direction	1. Discuss career-family duality 2. Consider long-term staff development 3. Women working for the first time need support 4. By the end of this period, male teachers need support; they tend to be more open to the field need mentors 5. Women returning to the field need mentors
Age 40 Transition 40–(45–47)	*De-illusionment:* Career—to change or not to change? Marriage—each partner respects autonomy of the other Changes are greater for males than for females Task—to integrate best of youth and best of old Mortality-immortality Generativity—using self-knowledge to help humanity	Time left to live Strength and endurance have peaked Mental activities still in prime Friends are more important Men emphasize interpersonal experience Women emphasize social-service-oriented values	1. Know teachers—individualize to meet teacher needs 2. Support those who feel they have failed 3. Help teachers set realistic goals to avoid depression 4. Teachers need to be facilitated rather than educated 5. Value the insights of middle-aged staff 6. Respect differences among teachers

68

Middle Adulthood (45–47)–50	*Stability-Satisfaction:* To live out life within established structure Mellowness	Signs of aging continue Marital satisfaction is high Males more concerned about sharing their adult careers Talk about retirement begins Socialize to meet self-defined needs Males more affectionate and expressive Women want to "get ahead"	1. Teachers less willing to change—know teacher, build trust and understanding 2. Teachers may be more willing to work after school 3. Teachers need advance warning of changes 4. Encourage teachers to be mentors 5. Encourage older teachers to share
The 50s 50–60	Mellowness Feel creative, productive, and self-satisfied Integrity—acceptance of life lived to best of ability Death is accepted	Serious health and physical changes Mental ability is acute Attempt to capture life now Spouse is valued as companion Emphasis is on sharing joy and sorrow Women have more roles than men	1. Provide for comfort in school 2. Include teachers in decision-making 3. Let complaints be aired 4. Discuss problems 5. Continue to listen to be supportive 6. Listen to what staff has to say and act on it
60 Plus 60–retirement	Integrity—they demonstrate wisdom Accept selves as part of the elder generation	Lessening in general well-being Mental ability is slow but effective Task—to create new roles in retirement Time is finite Enjoy leisure pursuits	1. Find and capitalize on the unique contribution that these teachers can make 2. Prepare teachers for retirement 3. Counsel those who are ineffective 4. Provide single or small group staff development

Source: Judy Arin-Krupp, *Adult Development: Implications for Staff Development* (Manchester, CT: Adult Development and Learning, 1981).

69

Equity and the opportunity to participate in governance issues are *political* considerations. In parent-run programs, for example, a supervisor's behavior may be governed by others who have influence over a program's policy and operation. Or a center-based director in a large system may receive pressure from an executive director with different values about people and programs. The agency might not allow adequate planning time for supervisor and staff to work together, forcing the supervisor to give up a process approach with staff in favor of issuing orders. Staff participation in decision making is an important factor in building a professional community within a program.

Physical issues are also important. Lack of adequate space for a program may create problems and pressures, as classrooms may be congested and there may not be facilities for private conferences or for staff to relax. The environment should be safe for adults as well as for children.

Staff workload and autonomy are aspects of a setting's *organizational* structure, along with such factors as opportunities for staff to collaborate, the manner in which they are supervised and evaluated, how authority is delegated and vested, and how professionals such as social workers and psychiatrists are integrated into a program.

Each organization also has its own *culture* (Schein, 1985), which may be strong or weak or supportive or nonsupportive of staff. Deal and Kennedy (1982) have described organizational culture in terms its values, heroes and heroines, rites and rituals, and cultural networks. What is a program's philosophy? Are the center's values public and shared? Heroes and heroines personify an organization's values. They may be figures from the past such as Dewey or Piaget or Froebel or present-day individuals such as a program's founder or director. Rites, rituals, and ceremonies celebrate a program's culture. Gossips, whisperers, and storytellers are characters within a cultural network who transmit and interpret information and can reinforce a program's values and norms. A critical role of supervisors is to understand the culture and to work with staff to build and maintain a positive school culture.

Psychological variables such as job stress, meaningfulness of work, and opportunities for learning and growth are other significant workplace features. And finally, *sociological* features, which include the characteristics of peers and of children and families served, job status, and clarity of roles, are factors that can have an impact on job satisfaction and the supervisory process.

REFLECTIVE PRACTICE

A final aspect of the supervisory dynamic essential for development is reflective practice. The issues and problems that supervisors encounter on a daily basis are often unpredictable and complicated. Problematic situations may arise that require immediate decisions, yet a supervisor may have little previous experience in solving the specific problem faced. In these cases, supervisors may spontaneously draw on their inner resources and improvise as they make intelligent and important decisions. Schön (1987) refers to the competence that practitioners display in these situations as professional artistry. Reflection-in-action and reflection-on-action are essential components of this artistry.

Reflection-in-action (Schön, 1987) is the process of thinking about something while doing it. Teachers often experience this phenomenon while in the midst of teaching when they make on-the-spot adjustments such as re-explaining concepts in different ways or shifting from one activity to another when children become restless.

Conferring with staff members is a form of supervisory artistry that requires such reflection in which supervisors analyze the conference while it is taking place and make decisions as they work their way through it, striving to resolve the issue at hand. In these cases, a supervisor becomes a researcher in the practice of supervision, often experimenting and inventing new solutions. Both teachers and supervisors may engage in this reflective process as they "read" each other and plan responses to each other while conferring together.

A second type of reflective practice is reflection-on-action, which is reflection on reflection-in-action, a process Schön (1987) describes as a dialogue between thinking and doing that results in more skillful practice. Certainly this is a very sophisticated skill that has the potential to increase a supervisor's self-awareness and effectiveness and to deepen an understanding of one's work in supervision.

CONCLUSION

We believe that supervision is a reciprocal process by which the supervisor and the teacher influence each other's behavior. Both individuals function within a context that offers constraints and advantages and has a bearing on each person, the interactions, and supervisory outcomes.

We have reviewed three developmental domains—cognitive development, professional development, and adult development—that offer cues for facilitating the growth of staff members and for understanding ourselves. Contextual characteristics of organizations have also been described as they have a bearing on supervision. Lastly, we have emphasized the importance of reflection as a means of improving supervisory practice.

You may wish to refer to Figure 5.1, which illustrates the major concepts presented in this chapter. In the chapters that follow, we will elaborate on some of the ideas presented here.

EXERCISES

1. Think about your family and schooling experiences and your assumptions about your supervisees. Describe how these factors may influence your supervision.
2. Do you have a preferred supervisory style? If so, describe it. When does it seem effective, and when has it not worked as well?
3. Analyze your setting in terms of some of the contextual elements mentioned in this chapter. In what ways do they help or hinder you with your supervision?

6

Supervisor Development

As supervisors gain experience in their roles, they undergo a series of changes in how they view themselves and their jobs. Their feelings and concerns about supervision change over time.

We have identified three general phases that supervisors experience as they grow in their roles: beginning, extending, and maturing. Characteristic patterns of thinking and behaving tend to emerge during each of these phases as supervisors acquire new realizations concerning the supervisory role and the people with whom they are working. The significant characteristics of each phase are summarized in Table 6.1.

Since our first edition, supervisors have indicated to us that there is a pre-phase characterized by imagining what it would be like to be in a supervisory position and preparing for the role by enrolling in graduate course work or by moving up the career ladder in intermediate steps. Thinking about a job change and its implications, garnering support from friends and family, and taking some small steps in a new direction are all part of the process of separating from one position and anticipating and accepting the challenge that a new one can provide. And, of course, there is a phase toward the end of one's career when individuals begin to think about "passing the torch" on to others and limiting one's work in the field.

PHASE 1: BEGINNING

Beginning supervisors, like most novices, tend to have personal concerns: Will I be able to carry out the responsibilities of my position? What is my role? What is going to happen to me? Will I be able to meet the expectations that others have of me? These are some of the questions they ask themselves.

Beginners develop a number of coping strategies to survive the early months on the job. One such strategy is to play the role of supervisor by imitating role models from past experience such as parents, teachers, managers, directors, grandmothers, nuns, or deans. These role models have left

Table 6.1. Supervisory Development

PHASE 1: BEGINNING	PHASE 2: EXTENDING	PHASE 3: MATURING
Concerned with self	"If only I . . ."	Knows self and can evaluate self openly
Anxious	Accepts leadership with ambivalence	Sense of being in charge
Critical of self	Can discuss problems and concerns more objectively	Greater sensitivity toward and understanding of supervisees
Seeks support from many sources		
Rewards are self-centered		
Copes in several ways	Concerns are centered on others	Recognizes expertise of supervisees
Plays the role of supervisor	Better understanding of others and of program	More realistic about job and what can be done
Avoids responsibility		Concerned with ideas/issues
Orients self to role	More comfortable with authority	Has well-defined philosophical frame of reference
Uses trial and error	High expectations for self	
In process of conceptualizing the role	More confident, more relaxed	Stimulated by outside contacts; gets rewards from solving problems
Uncomfortable with authority		
Develops new realizations about self		Continues to be critical, but sees self as learner

74

indelible imprints as to how individuals in authority positions should behave, and it is only natural to imitate these familiar behaviors. Yet there is risk to coping by imitation, since the learned authority behavior may be inappropriate for early childhood programs, although it does give supervisors the feeling that they have "taken charge" and are "in control." This increases a supervisor's confidence, but only until problems develop. Solving problems requires meaningful deliberation and interaction with staff or board members based on an in-depth exploration of issues. Playing supervisor does little to resolve problems.

A second survival strategy novices use is to avoid the responsibilities of the role by appearing not to have adequate time to devote to supervision because they are preoccupied with other urgent administrative issues. These supervisors continually find themselves preoccupied with other business and somehow never take on their supervisory responsibilities. Some may believe that supervision is not their forte, a rationale for devoting all their time and energy to administrative duties where they do have competence. Avoidance behaviors enable supervisors to pretend they are doing a good job and their programs are running smoothly. In the meantime, problems snowball.

A third way beginners cope is to reserve a period of time to assess and orient themselves to their new setting if circumstances allow. They do this by observing and gradually getting to know people, programs, and routines. A new director explains how she is going about this task:

> Right now I am sort of filling the role of somebody that had been with the center for, I guess, 6 years who is very well loved and, in some ways, a mother figure for a lot of the staff. I have been listening to a lot of the kinds of interactions that went on with this person in terms of staff meetings and that kind of thing. I have been sorting out for myself what I would like to do without rocking the boat too soon. So, I'm following a lot of the things that were set up by that person.

Information gathered during this initial period can be valuable in making important decisions later.

New supervisors also learn through trial and error, even more so when they do not have an experienced teacher or other support system to point them in the right direction. They often try different approaches to solving problems in search of one that works.

Learning to Handle Authority and Confrontation

It is not at all uncommon for new supervisors to feel uncomfortable about directly confronting a staff member about a particular problem. Beginners are often concerned about being too bossy or offensive. They are not sure they can deal with problems in a sensitive and constructive manner. These feelings are understandable, as early childhood supervisors have frequently moved into their new roles from teaching and are still learning to shift from nurturing children to working with adults.

Although supervisors may have worked out their authority relationships with children in their previous roles as teachers or parents, working with adults is quite different. The diversity of caregivers in terms of cultural background, experience, age, and maturity levels can present serious challenges to the authority of an unsure supervisor. Coming to terms with authority is part of the process of defining and formulating a conception of the supervisory role. It is often painful and worrisome, as this director describes:

> I think basically confronting and being able to say I am not happy with this or I don't like it is very hard, even though that is not exactly the way I would say it. I am trying to sort through in my own mind how to confront some situations and I haven't done particularly well.

The new supervisor is faced with authority dilemmas daily in dealing with staff, parents, and curricular issues.

Conceptualizing the Role of Supervisor

Sifting, sorting, assessing, and testing are typical behaviors beginners use as they learn what a supervisor is and what a supervisor does. A conceptualization of the supervisory role emerges slowly, first in a narrow and ambiguous sense, and later with greater clarity and scope. Inexperienced supervisors, for example, tend to view their supervisees in general terms rather than as complicated individuals with special needs. They describe staff in terms of numbers and categories—"I have one head teacher and three aides" —rather than in terms of personal characteristics, strengths, and weaknesses, as experienced supervisors do. They simply don't know their staff members well enough to differentiate among them or to make discrete assessments of them.

New supervisors must also develop a total picture of the programs in which they are working. During the first months on the job, they have to learn about personal relationships among staff members, the political implications of decisions they may make, the special needs and problems of the community being served, the expectations of outside funding agencies or institutions that supply temporary staff, and other factors that will affect their success on the job.

Seeking Professional and Emotional Support

Beginning supervisors function in their own world, concerned and pre-occupied with self. Most are aware of their own weaknesses and are interested in becoming more skilled. Self-critical beginners willingly identify deficiencies and are open to experimentation. They want to improve their supervisory behavior.

First-year supervisors need and seek professional and emotional support from many sources, including administrators, parents, board members, and staff members, as well as friends and relatives. As one supervisor put it:

> I guess I need support. I need support from the staff. I need feedback from people in terms of what's happening from my end of things and how it is coming across to other people. I need open communication. I guess that is why I keep trying to work at building relationships because I feel it is really important that teachers be fairly open with me. And I need to learn a lot. I feel a little overscheduled sometimes about the role that I do play and I guess I need to develop my own skills.

A number of supervisors we interviewed gained assistance from other directors who were part of a local group that met on a monthly basis. Such nourishment from others helps beginners acquire the confidence they need.

Rewards for novices tend to center around self, since they are less other-person oriented than more experienced supervisors. Compliments from parents or from people in superior positions, such as chief administrators or board members, are especially appreciated. Solving difficult problems and accomplishing important tasks bring feelings of satisfaction to beginners.

Supervisors in this phase, and in the ones to follow, are continually learning about themselves. They are forced to reflect on their personal style, philosophy, and goals as they confront such challenges as implementing change; supporting, training, and evaluating other people; coordinating many activities within one program; raising funds; and conveying a center's philosophy and activities to the outside world. After 4 months on the job, a new supervisor talks about what she has learned about herself:

> I guess what I think about is that there are a lot of things that I can handle simply by jumping in and doing them. I don't panic. I'm not afraid to do things although I still have my nervous moments. I know what I feel like when I am nervous, but I still follow through. I can try new things and accomplish them. In terms of myself, I guess that I have learned that I am somewhat approachable and that is nice. I have

relearned that I am a real workaholic in some ways. I have a hard time
cutting down my hours. I guess that my feelings about being able to
confront others is something I have wanted to develop.

PHASE 2: EXTENDING

Supervisors in this phase are no longer novices, yet they have not yet
reached professional maturity. They are consolidating gains made as beginners, extending their knowledge and competence, strengthening their leadership, raising their expectations, and reaching out to staff.

Wishing for a magic potion or a wand that could make every part of a
program perfect is the quintessential fantasy of supervisors in this second phase.
As one day care director put it:

> If only I had more time! If only we had more money! Wouldn't it be
> wonderful if I could send some of my staff to NAEYC? I wish we had
> greater racial and economic diversity represented in our enrollment. I
> wish I had somebody who was observing me and telling me what I'm
> doing wrong and what I'm doing right. . . . And I'm not at all satisfied
> with my performance or my role or anything. I think that I wish I had
> some magic . . . some magic potion.

Having survived the first year and gained greater confidence and assurance in
coping with daily crises, supervisors in this phase are concerned with perfection. Now able to look beyond personal wants, the supervisor thinks about
the needs of others, the prevailing conditions under which the staff operates,
and the positive and negative aspects of the learning environment created for
the children.

Reflecting an innocence and naiveté, supervisors in this phase tend to
believe that if they work hard and do their best, all of a program's problems
and weaknesses will be corrected. Transitional supervisors set lofty goals, determined to make their programs exemplary ones, with visions of walking off stage
with the "Early Childhood Emmy" flashing through their minds.

In contrast with beginners, who do not feel like supervisors and may even
reject the notion of being boss, transitional supervisors accept the leadership
role but are still ambivalent about it. As one day care director explained:

> I feel strongly that supervision is a big job, and there are a lot of people
> to supervise. I do feel like a supervisor in the sense that I know people
> are looking for supervision, and I try to do it. In the sense of feeling
> that I am really supervising every single person as it should be done,

absolutely not. I know that there is no time. I don't have enough time to spend in classrooms really looking at what everybody is doing.

Another Phase 2 supervisor was still unsure as to how to enact authority appropriately:

> My problem is how do you get somebody to see that she needs improvement in a particular area? Just because it is my problem doesn't mean it is going to be theirs. How do you get them to be motivated to change? How do you get them to ask, "How do you do that?" How do you tell them that you are not 100 % satisfied with their work without sounding like you're extremely unsatisfied?

Unable to meet their own expectations of perfection, supervisors in this phase are often faced with frustration. They constantly fall short of mastering the art of supervision, yet continue to try to do better. One director commented, "There is this story that no matter how much you do, it is always less than what you want to be doing." In some respects, these feelings are prerequisite to realizing that all of one's goals cannot be achieved. They are part of a process of acquiring a truer picture of what a supervisor can accomplish and what is beyond his or her control. Reassessment and reconceptualization of the role of supervisor occur over time as supervisors engage in trial and error and meet with success and failure.

Phase 2 supervisors who are extending their leadership can begin to discuss problems and conflicts more objectively. They are better able to separate themselves from their roles, to stand back and look at problems analytically, rather than ignoring them or feeling overwhelmed as beginning supervisors do.

Concerns, then, move away from self and are centered to a far greater extent around other individuals and specific issues. Supervisors in this extending phase are more conscious of the need to provide reinforcement and support to staff members. They begin to see themselves as mentors who can guide staff members toward new realizations and self-improvement. They strive to provide an atmosphere of trust and openness to enable staff to identify and engage in group problem-solving experiences. They recognize the need to develop good group-facilitation skills in order to foster positive interpersonal relationships among staff members.

With more experience, Phase 2 supervisors begin to make distinctions among staff members, to see them as unique individuals with special needs and concerns. They begin to realize that some supervisees need specific direction while others respond well to casual suggestions or praise. They provide different kinds of training for volunteers, part-time staff, and experienced full-time staff. This ability to vary one's approach to working with others, to individualize supervision, is more characteristic of supervisors toward the latter part of this second phase.

Gaining a greater understanding of a program, its people, and its parts is also characteristic of Phase 2 supervisors. This new awareness of a program's complexity is linked to the development of a less idealistic and more realistic sense of what a supervisor can and cannot do or change.

Supervisors in this phase often feel isolated. They discover that there really isn't anyone on the job at their level in whom to confide. They look for sources of support among associates in similar fields and other supervisors in similar positions. Reliance on new professional contacts for support lessens the burden on family and friends on whom beginning supervisors usually depend for nurturance.

Although there continues to be some self-centeredness in what Phase 2 supervisors find rewarding, they derive greater satisfaction when they receive praise from individuals they supervise rather than from those who supervise them, and when they see others making progress. As one supervisor stated: "I love it when people get excited about teaching children, when people can learn to relax and enjoy teaching." Seeing the center run smoothly, observing supervisees improve their ability to work with children, or motivating a caregiver can be especially rewarding.

Supervisors who are extending their leadership also feel more relaxed, less panicky, less overwhelmed, and in greater control. It is at this time that they make enormous gains in professional development. They move from being anxious, self-centered beginners to individuals who grapple with issues, strive to support others, and feel a sense of accomplishment. Although still occasionally subject to feelings of ambivalence, guilt, or frustration, supervisors in this phase develop greater confidence and the security that comes from success and familiarity with the job, the program, and its people.

The experiences supervisors have during this middle phase affect whether they remain in a particular setting or even in the profession. It is during this transitional period that many supervisors make a commitment to the field or decide to look elsewhere to fulfill their career aspirations.

PHASE 3: MATURING

Phase 3 supervisors possess the characteristics of mature professionals: self-knowledge, self-confidence, in-depth understanding of the problems and issues associated with their work, and the skills necessary to do an effective job. Maturing supervisors bring rich and disparate life experiences to their roles and can look back and understand how those experiences have made them who they are and how they contribute to present-day success.

Seasoned supervisors know and evaluate themselves. A college laboratory school director discusses her strengths and weaknesses openly:

> I keep reminding myself that I need to listen to people very carefully. I think that this is essential. It has been an improvement in my supervisory style to be a better listener; it is a positive development in my personality.

> I have become conscious of the way I must come across to people, and I am cautious because these are young people. I think a supervisee is in a very vulnerable position very often, so I have to be sensitive to that and cautious about being too overwhelming or too opinionated or coming on too strong. . . . I think that I see my work all the time as a process of growth for me.

The supervisor who made the above statement shares some of her anxieties about being too overwhelming or too directive with caregivers, a common concern of her colleagues who are in earlier stages. A difference, however, between individuals in this mature stage and those who are less experienced is the ability to make accurate assessments of behavior: to acknowledge their weaknesses and to be conscious of them as they strive to change, to compensate, or to live with them. Maturing supervisors have a sense of being in charge of their lives, of making conscious decisions, and of being accountable for their actions.

One of the most striking characteristics of experienced supervisors is their sensitivity to supervisees as unique individuals and their ability to individualize supervisory strategies. Mature supervisors view being able to assess each supervisee and plan appropriate interventions as a special challenge, as exemplified by this supervisor who talks about the teachers in her program:

> In terms of personality they are all different and I enjoy the differences. I think that because of their differences, they bring various agendas to supervision sessions. I do feel that supervisors can fall into all kinds of traps with supervisees—among them being overnurturing or undernurturing, being too critical, being too demanding. A supervisor has to be careful not to fall into that kind of trap. I think that we need to look at people's personalities. I think that our supervisees have different needs which evoke different kinds of responses.

In the following comments an experienced supervisor shows great insight and understanding of her staff members, and values and appreciates the special qualities each of them has:

The three head teachers in this school are three different kinds of personalities and lead very different kinds of classrooms. For example, the head teacher upstairs works with the younger crew. I think that she is one of the most successful nondirective teachers I have ever come across. She is a rather young woman. This was her first job. She was trained here; she did a year's internship here and she became a head teacher after that. She has a unique way of communicating with children. One never hears her voice in the classroom. And yet, she is always talking with them or is at their side listening and communicating in other ways. Her presence is very much felt. The children are very busy doing their own thing. It is wonderful to see. That is a very special kind of personality and a very special set of characteristics.

Downstairs we have a teacher who has had a lot of experience in a lot of settings with special-needs children and so on. She is mature, experienced, and a very directive person. She understands children and her values are right, and I trust her explicitly. There is a vast difference in her approach. She does the right things for children. She is very good.

In the afternoon, we have another teacher who has . . . who is a very chatty, very warm, very connected with everybody. She is very interested in doing special projects with children. She has a special kind of energy that is just perfect for children who are tired in the afternoon. She works from 11:00 A.M. to 5:00, yet she doesn't get tired.

Supervisors who are professionally mature recognize and respect the strengths of their staff members. They are willing to share their authority, demonstrating a trust in their supervisees. They encourage their staff members to share their knowledge and skill with each other, recognizing that their diverse strengths provide mutual support for all and bring a richness to the program. Sharing authority is not intimidating to the mature supervisor.

Unlike beginning supervisors, who may not be aware of the problems around them, or moderately experienced supervisors, who acknowledge problems but are unsure of how to deal with them, experienced supervisors recognize and comprehend the depth and range of existing problems. They understand how much needs to be done and see problem-solving as an ongoing task. Supervisors in this phase are less frustrated because they understand that, even if certain goals cannot be achieved, at least they can be addressed.

Seasoned supervisors tend to be less emotionally burdened by the problems they encounter. They have gained greater perspective and have acquired skill in managing time, coordinating and keeping track of tasks, motivating staff members to change, and building morale within a program. They are still concerned with resolving interpersonal issues among staff members, and they still need the emotional support of others, but they are no longer as overwhelmed by the demands placed on them. They don't feel as helpless or as powerless as colleagues who are in the earlier phases.

Maturing supervisors tend to be concerned with ideas, with groups, with relationships, and with broad issues. They possess a well-defined philosophical frame of reference and a commitment to standards of education for children. They are perceptive, sensitive, discreet, and tuned in to staff members. They seize opportunities for leadership:

> What I do is observe a lot, see a lot, and then confront a lot. From time to time, I remember calling a meeting of last year's staff to redefine our ideas for curriculum before we started again this year.
>
> I thought that was the best way of saying, "Look, gang! This is the way I would like it to be here," without telling any one person that . . . and they had a lot of opportunity to discuss this. I don't really have to have it my way. There is room enough for other people's ideas. Every once in a while, I feel as though I have to pull things in and pull things together. I think this school has style. I like us all to be sure we know what it is that we are doing and why we are doing it. These are very important times when we talk about children and our ideas about curriculum.

Like their less-experienced colleagues, seasoned supervisors enjoy a "pat on the back for a job well done." The rewards they receive from the job now tend to be other-person, program, and professionally oriented rather than centered around self. They receive stimulation from work in their own centers and in the educational community at large, interacting with other professionals through local and national professional organizations, boards, and committees. They achieve satisfaction from the gradual resolution of difficult problems, from developing and improving their programs, and from new responsibilities. Supporting staff members as they strive to accomplish their goals provides maturing supervisors with additional satisfaction.

Supervisors at this stage are wise and skilled. They view themselves as individuals who are still growing, still learning, recognizing the need for renewal, reeducation, and challenge. They believe they can play a vital role in making this a better world for children and families.

CONCLUSION

Supervisors undergo a process of growth and development over time. They face similar problems and frustrations in each phase, but their ability to handle problems changes as they move toward maturity (refer to Table 6.1). The context in which they work, the nature of problems they encounter, personal characteristics, previous experience, and job training and preparation are factors that can influence the path of development from early to later phases.

The presence of support for supervisors is also critical to their development; yet it is often lacking. This means that individuals may have to take the initiative to seek out and build a support system for themselves. Support may take the form of a local network of directors or educational coordinators. Finding a mentor, shadowing others to observe how they carry out their roles, visiting nearby programs, taking courses and workshops, and joining and becoming active in professional organizations are all ways to build knowledge and competence and to meet people in similar positions who can be called on for help and suggestions when needed.

Supervisor growth during the beginning, extending, and maturing phases is ongoing but frequently uneven. Supervisors move back and forth from one phase to another during their careers, and even mature, educated, and talented supervisors may demonstrate some characteristics of beginners when they work in new roles, in unfamiliar settings, or with people they don't know. Some supervisors may never move beyond the first or second phase.

EXERCISES

1. Which phase would you place yourself in and why?
2. Describe the ways in which your present phase of supervisory development affects your job effectiveness.
3. What kinds of support do supervisors in each phase need?
4. Keep a journal; record your thoughts about your supervision.

7

Supervisee Development

In interviews about their work, caregivers of different ages, in contrasting roles, and at various stages of development described key areas for professional growth, which resemble in some ways those that supervisors go through as they become more familiar and expert in their jobs. The competencies we describe below do not represent the full range of skills and abilities needed to work effectively in early childhood programs, but they can serve as guides for informal mutual assessment of staff members and as a basis for planning for continued improvement.

LEARNING TO COMMUNICATE EFFECTIVELY

In order to teach and care for young children, staff members learn to communicate with a variety of people for different purposes as part of their daily experience. As team members responsible for a group of children, teachers learn to plan together, to share duties, and to cooperate with each other to support the children they serve. They participate in the supervisory process with head teachers and/or directors. They interact with outside consultants such as doctors, social workers, psychologists, and community workers who provide support to children and their families. Being an effective communicator is critically important to forming relationships with colleagues. Working productively with other staff members requires mutual exchange, which can take place only in an atmosphere of openness and respect, where people are honest with each other.

Sometimes, caregivers become board members and teacher educators, roles that require good listening and effective speaking skills. And one of their most important and difficult jobs is working with parents, helping them to increase their understanding of young children. The caregivers we interviewed who appeared to be the happiest and most successful in their roles were those who had become effective communicators.

BECOMING A SELF-CONFIDENT TEACHER

Some teachers enter the profession with little experience or knowledge of the field of early childhood education. In fact, quite a few of those we interviewed became involved in child care because their own children or younger siblings were enrolled in day care or Head Start. They often began their careers as volunteers, some eventually returning to school to complete requirements for a high school diploma. For those who dropped out of high school to marry and have children, the position of aide or assistant teacher may have been their first job as a professional, although they gradually moved up the ranks to become a teacher or head teacher.

Teaching young children, which requires an understanding of child development and an ability to communicate with other professionals, can be threatening to persons with previously unsuccessful experience in school settings or to those who are holding a regular job for the first time. Beginners require time to become comfortable in the work setting. It is common for them to feel timid when leading children or when talking to strangers, as this caregiver describes:

> When I first came here, I was very shy as far as talking to parents. I was very shy at starting out like leading songs in front of a big group, sitting on floors, and really getting to play with the kids. Now, I don't think anything about going up to a parent and saying, "You know, your kid had a great day!" or "You know, he didn't have such a good day." I don't feel funny about leading songs in a great big group; I don't feel funny about getting down on the floor and pretending to be an animal with the kids where, at first, I was a little shy about it.

As they become more confident, caregivers tend to be less dependent on supervisors. They no longer have to be told what to do and how to do it. In supervisory roles themselves, they make their own judgments about whether to step in if a teacher is having a difficult time with a child. They act without needing a director's assessment and opinion. A teacher shares her thoughts about responsibility:

> When you're a trainee, you have someone who is, more or less, directing you and telling you what to do. You don't have as much responsibility as you do as a teacher. As a trainee, all you have to say is, "Well, I have a problem with this. Will you help me? I'm not sure how to do this!" and someone will say, "Well, do it this way." You have a teacher to kind of fall back on. But when you're the teacher, you are the one who's doing the supervising and who has the responsibility for the

children in the classroom. The health and safety of the children is all your responsibility. Everything falls back on you.

Training and staff development can have an exciting effect on the self-confidence of caregivers who began at different developmental levels. One teacher describes the profound changes that participation in an associate's degree program had in her confidence:

> I think, too, that my education had a lot to do with making me feel more confident and being able to relate to people on different levels of a profession. This past year, I had a meeting at Children's Hospital about a child I had in my room who had a special problem. I had to meet with the social service director, the educational director, two doctors, a psychologist, and a dietician. They wanted to hear my opinion. "What!" I thought. Six or seven years ago, I probably would have died, "Oh, my God!" But I knew what I was talking about. I felt comfortable because I knew what I was talking about.

UNDERSTANDING CHILDREN

Working with children on a daily basis over time advances a caregiver's knowledge and understanding of child development. Even though many supervisees are parents before they become early childhood professionals, they often lack such basic information about child growth and development as when most children should be speaking or walking or using alternate feet to climb stairs. As a result of their experience in early childhood programs, two workers help us to realize the metamorphosis that some caregivers undergo:

> I now look at children differently. I looked at them before as more of a parent than as a teacher because I am a parent. I would be saying, "Oh, you don't want to do that because you're going to get yourself all dirty." Whereas now, I let them go ahead and do it. We can always take their clothes off and wash them. I was looking at children from a parent's eye rather than with a teacher's eye.

> All I can think of is there was a time in my life when I know I didn't know that a baby doesn't go to sleep when they're tired. You know, my conception was that they just fell asleep. The fact that you have to put them to bed was pretty obvious, I guess, but I didn't have basic knowledge of how infants should be treated.

Caregivers report that their understanding of young children deepens as they learn to observe children and be more in tune with their needs. As beginners they might have overlooked the clumsy, withdrawn, or abused child, but as experienced teachers with new understanding, they are more sensitive and can note and address important problems. Caring for children who may be unloved, undernourished, or delayed in their language development increases a child care worker's ability to look at the whole child and to recognize the interconnectedness of a child's emotional, social, cognitive, and physical development.

UNDERSTANDING ONESELF

The very nature of work with young children—observing children, interacting with parents and other professionals, teaching adults and children, and participating in in-service education activities—challenges staff members to change their own attitudes and behaviors and to reflect about their own growth and development. As one infant caregiver puts it:

> I look at infants and I am constantly learning about myself; just how people become and how they are. It all starts when you're born and then, I think about how I was treated in a certain way . . . and how I turned out the way I did. You see how infants are so honest and uninhibited and unable to cover up anything about themselves. I mean, it's all written on their faces. You know, the older you get, the more and more you learn how to protect yourself, to cover up.

Some supervisees completely change their own attitudes toward learning. They come to view themselves as learners, embracing and valuing education. This new perception of self can represent a transformation from an earlier time characterized by school failure or dropout. A caregiver's motivation to enroll in workshops and courses, some leading to a General Educational Development (GED) certificate and even a college degree, is an indication of this new outlook. Involvement in such activities, at a stage in life when one has obligations as spouse and parent, can create family disruptions, stress, and conflict. But staff members often see these opportunities to achieve new meaning in life, to enhance their self-concept and self-respect, as outweighing the inconveniences and sacrifices they might endure.

Strength derived from supervisory support can help supervisees to understand themselves better as they cope with crises confronting the children with whom they work. An assistant teacher talks about contending with child abuse:

> When I first came here, I just did not want to talk about or even think about child abuse. I mean I could not accept it. I didn't want to deal with it. I felt that there was just no way that I could deal with it myself. . . . As time went on, we had a lot of workshops, a protective service course, and I really got to understand where child abuse might begin, things to look for, and ways of working with children and families. I had a lot of support.

As they gain more experience on the job, supervisees are better able to deal with the developmental tasks that are part of the life cycle. Supervising others, as well as having support from a supervisor, provides caregivers with experience and nurturance that, as one worker describes it, stimulates them to "think about how I would like to be, where I am, and what I need to do to improve. It also makes me think about what's going on with me that I'm not performing the way I'd like to."

RESPECTING OTHERS

Developing a deeper understanding of oneself also promotes greater understanding of and respect for others. Working with children, families, and professionals enables caregivers to meet people they might ordinarily not have had the opportunity to know.

For those who come from backgrounds where relations outside the immediate neighborhood or community are limited or who have associated mainly with white, middle-class individuals, exposure to people from other cultures and who speak other languages can be especially meaningful, as this co-teacher points out:

> I've learned to respect other people's ways. We have a lot of Hispanic people here. I was brought up in another part of town where there were not many Hispanics, so I did not understand the culture. By working here, I understand. I have really broadened my thinking about other people's cultures: they might be different, but they're not strange, they are okay. I've learned about all different types of holidays because we are a multicultural school. We celebrate many holidays, including Three Kings Day and a black holiday which I had never heard of. I've learned a lot of things about other people's cultures. You can respect them.

Supervisees learning to appreciate the cultural and ethnic differences of others will often need help and training. Staff development experiences that provide information and allow discussion of stereotypes and feelings can be of great value in helping staff gain this understanding.

Staff members show that they value other human beings in their daily work by the empathic and understanding ways that they communicate with parents, by the approaches they take to resolve differences with colleagues or supervisors, and by helping peers in times of need.

DERIVING SATISFACTION AND STIMULATION FROM PROFESSIONAL GROWTH

Like supervisors, staff members with less experience and limited expectations about their roles tend to be satisfied with rewards that are personal and immediate. Foster grandparents or high school volunteers, for example, are likely to receive adequate gratification from a child's spontaneous hug or kiss. They derive satisfaction from loving and taking care of children and from getting to know their families. Displays of affection brighten any caregiver's day of course, but as an individual grows and develops professionally, other rewards come into play.

More experienced caregivers, for example, gain satisfaction from observing children for diagnosis of problems or to obtain greater understanding of their lives. More abstract rewards for experienced caregivers are the challenges of the job; the planning, development, and implementation of new programs; teamwork with colleagues; and participating in professional groups and associations.

One of the most remarkable aspects of the growth process of teachers is the way in which their roles change over time when they are fortunate enough to work in nurturing environments. Centers that lack organization and flexibility, where supervisors ignore staff development in favor of administrative duties, are environments that foster burnout, rather than excitement, creativity, and growth. In programs where individuals are valued, it is not uncommon for supervisees to begin their careers as volunteer workers or floating substitutes and take on new roles with major obligations as they gain experience. They may broaden their roles by training and supervising other adults, by greater involvement with families and communities, and by assuming such administrative duties as recruiting aides, helping with supplies, formulating agendas for team meetings, planning menus and preparing food, organizing social functions, and doing general paperwork. In centers where caregiver interests are considered, staff members create new roles and responsibilities for themselves based on their personal interests, which may vary from playground or classroom design to child advocacy work.

Children, of course, always come first, but professional growth opportunities for staff increase their competence and enable and motivate them to explore new dimensions of their jobs. Supervisees who feel challenged, stimulated, and enriched by their daily work may be willing to remain in their jobs over longer periods of time, despite the low pay and occasional frustration.

FORMULATING A PHILOSOPHY OF LEARNING

With experience, teachers tend to develop strong points of view about how children learn best. Early years in the education profession are usually characterized by tentativeness and ambivalence regarding teaching the right or the best way. Over time, these feelings of uncertainty are usually replaced with well-developed views of what comprises good education and child care.

As beginners, staff members are concerned with survival: learning new routines, meeting supervisor's expectations, and coping with hard-to-manage children. Everyday challenges prevent the neophyte from thinking about deeper issues pertaining to educational philosophy. Lack of experience and education, combined in some cases with little knowledge or expectation of their roles, can also slow the pace of development of a set of values and beliefs about what is best for young children. With experience and training, however, supervisees begin to formulate their views of how things should be done. Disagreements with supervisors or conflicting opinions with colleagues about how certain children should be handled or how a play area should be designed can be viewed as a positive sign of professional maturation. This comment made by a day care provider reflects the type of growth we are describing:

> Three years ago, I had much less confidence in how I felt about my work. You know, I was the one who would watch everybody else and often I worked with teachers whom I disagreed with. I wasn't sure if I was right. I knew that I didn't agree with them, but I had no idea if my ideas were better. I just knew they were mine. Now, I can definitely walk into a situation and observe and see if the program is good or not.

VALUING GOOD SUPERVISION

Staff members also grow and change in their expectations about the type of supervision they want to receive. Expectations differ depending on supervisees' age and experience, the positions they hold, whether they are full or part-time, and whether they are volunteers or part of the regular staff. The standards that supervisors set for them also affect their views of the supervisory process.

Part-time volunteers, for example, who help out several mornings a week with routine tasks and who provide various children with individual attention, expect little from a supervisor. They do not expect to be trained, observed, or evaluated. They often view themselves as ancillary help who are not an important part of the program. They may not anticipate that their roles will expand or change in any way. Supervisors who do not perceive volunteers to be an integral part of a center's operation may provide them with some initial direction and then leave them alone unless they create problems. This is hardly a desirable state of affairs.

The picture is quite different for regular, full-time, paid staff, particularly those who are experienced and who have gained confidence as professionals in the field. They have high expectations for supervisors and can be critical when adequate supervision is not provided. Our interviews with caregivers reveal that they hold definite opinions about the qualities they want their supervisors to have.

Honesty is one quality that was mentioned repeatedly. A caregiver who works with infants and toddlers sums up her feelings about supervisors this way:

> First of all, a supervisor should be someone who can be honest. Someone who can tell you what they think. Someone who can criticize you and praise you productively in ways that you can learn and understand and get whatever reinforcement you're supposed to get from them. Somebody who is sensitive to your needs and to the job. Somebody who believes in what you're doing, not somebody who thinks that babies would be better left at home with their parents. Somebody who knows what they're doing and knows the field.

Many supervisees emphasized the value of a supervisor who is willing to spend time with them, to listen to their thoughts, feelings, and concerns. They also wanted to be supervised by someone knowledgeable in the field. As one teacher noted:

> Somebody who can really talk about things, you know, very personal things about families, kids, and yourself. Somebody who can really, really see before a problem hits and be able to talk about it. Someone who can say, "Is something wrong?" To be able to come out and ask you this. Somebody who really has a lot of training, who can really understand because we are dealing with a lot of people who have very little in common. Supervisors need to understand how to help out families and how to help us out.

Supervisees appreciate receiving criticism that is direct and constructive. As one caregiver put it, "To give constructive criticism that would help you, not make you kind of back down. Also, to let you be creative. To make you feel that your creative ideas flow a little, too! And to be there when you need help." She also commented on the importance of feedback: "Giving feedback and following through on actual goals and work responsibilities rather than being palsy walsy; being practical and to the point."

Staff members believe, too, that they should be able to give their supervisors constructive criticism. As one caregiver stated: "Just because their title is supervisor doesn't mean they're perfect. They shouldn't act defensive when they are criticized when it's good criticism."

Supervisees want supervisors who seek their input when making important decisions, who engage them in group problem-solving activities, and who are good role models. Such ideal supervisory qualities are not easily found in one person. A major point, however, is that staff members, especially those in advanced stages of their professional development, have high expectations for supervisors.

SEEING THE BIG PICTURE

Supervisees often begin their careers with a limited understanding of themselves, of the children and adults with whom they come in daily contact, and of the programs in which they are employed. Like supervisors, they progress through stages of concern from self, to task and others, to impact. Experience and maturity enable supervisees to see themselves and their work not only within the context of their programs and communities but within society at large.

With maturity, they gain understanding of the complexity of the problems facing children and families; of their social, political, and economic contexts; and of the relatedness of people and programs and the dynamic forces affecting them. This new awareness enables caregivers to be more realistic about their work and to set priorities for the future. By knowing who they are and what they want to do, they gain a sense of comfort and power.

CONCLUSION

We hope the growth shown by caregivers in our interviews offers encouragement to supervisors. Staff progress points to the value of education and supervisory support. Professional maturation does not come about automatically, quickly, or in a natural progression, but all staff members have the capacity to improve. In Parts III and IV, we will describe the specific strategies supervisors can use to help staff reach their potential.

EXERCISE

Use the instrument in Figure 7.1 for an informal assessment of staff members in your program who are at different points in their development.

Figure 7.1 Growth Areas of Staff

Directions: For each area of development, consider the criteria listed, and circle the number on the continuum that best describes the staff member at this time. Have your staff member complete this inventory as well. Get together and share perceptions.

Name of Staff Member _____ Age ____

Number of years in program/school _____ Sex ____

Number of years in the profession _____

Education/Training _____

A. Learning to Communicate Effectively

1	2	3	4	5
Ineffective				*Effective*

1. Communicates effectively with colleagues
2. Communicates effectively with professionals outside the program who interface with it (doctors, social workers, consultants, and so forth)
3. Communicates effectively with parents
4. Communicates effectively with children
5. Communicates effectively with supervisors

B. Becoming a Self-Confident Teacher

1	2	3	4	5
Insecure				*Secure*

1. Feels comfortable when working with children
2. Talks to parents readily
3. Believes in own ability to care for children
4. Participates in staff-meeting discussions
5. Is willing to deal with conflict
6. Easily interacts with other professionals
7. Displays independence/takes initiative
8. Uses own judgement
9. Can cope with change

C. Understanding Children

1	2	3	4	5
Limited				*Extensive*

1. Has realistic expectations for children
2. Recognizes children's various stages of development
3. Is sensitive to children's individual needs
4. Has good observation skills
5. Recognizes the interconnectedness of social, cognitive, emotional, and physical development
6. Understands that many factors affect a child's growth and development

D. Understanding Oneself

1	2	3	4	5
Limited				*Extensive*

1. Is reflective and analytical of self
2. Views oneself as a learner
3. Can confront self and grapple with personal issues
4. Can cope with children's crises
5. Has self-respect and sees self as important part of program

E. Respecting Others

1	2	3	4	5
Low level				*High level*

1. Respects individuals (children, parents, colleagues) who are culturally and linguistically different
2. Supports colleagues when needed
3. Respects opinions and feelings of others

F. Deriving Satisfaction and Stimulation from Professional Growth

1	2	3	4	5
Low level				*High level*

1. Finds challenge of job rewarding
2. Participates in professional groups and associations
3. Enjoys team work with colleagues
4. Likes to plan and implement new programs
5. Likes to take on new and different roles and responsibilities
6. Is extensively involved with families and community

G. Formulating a Philosophy of Learning

1	2	3	4	5
Undefined				*Well-developed*

1. Can disagree with supervisor and colleagues
2. has strongly held and well-developed educational views

H. Valuing Good Supervision

1	2	3	4	5
Low				*High*

1. Can be critical of supervision if adequate supervision is not provided
2. Has firm opinion about qualities a supervisor should have
3. Has high expectations about supervision and program

I. Seeing the Big Picture

1	2	3	4	5
Limited				*Broad*

1. Sees self and work in context of program and community
2. Is realistic about work, sets priorities
3. Sees children, families, community, and programs as interdependent and interrelated

8

The Developmental Dynamic at Work: A Case Study in Supervision

In Chapter 5, we discussed three components of the developmental dynamic: supervisor, supervisee, and context. We also pointed to the necessity of assessing a staff member's developmental level and the problem being addressed to determine the most appropriate supervisory strategy. In Chapters 6 and 7, we elaborated on some of the developmental characteristics of supervisors and staff members. The purpose of this chapter is to illustrate the elements of the developmental dynamic at work.

BACKGROUND

The Supervisor

Rebecca is a graduate of a liberal arts college where she majored in politics and government. After graduation, she spent a year as a trainee in a large department store chain but left since she did not like the work. She is single, 29 years old, and lives on the outskirts of a major city on the East Coast.

Rebecca received her master's degree in early childhood education after teaching in a Head Start program for 3 years. For the past 3 years, she has been the director of a medium-sized day care center. As a third-year supervisor, Rebecca feels pretty comfortable in her role. She has a strong theoretical base in child development. The experience she had working in Head Start has been enormously helpful to her. Rebecca is reasonably confident in her ability as director of this program but occasionally gets thrown off guard when conflicts arise.

The Supervisee

Mrs. Warren is a 66-year-old widow who lives with her daughter and two grandchildren. She belongs to a senior citizen's organization that has provided her with part-time employment in this children's center. The job enables Mrs. Warren to earn spending money and to feel that she is doing constructive activity in retirement. She has been on the job for 3 months. She is in excellent health, dependable, and always at work early. Mrs. Warren enjoys her work, especially the unqualified love and affection she receives from most of the children.

The Context

Located in a small city, the East Side Child Development Center is a nonprofit center funded through the state department of social services. Most of the children are from low-income families, and about 15% are "protective" children, placed in the center because of abuse or neglect. The center has two groups of 3–year-olds, two of 4s, and a kindergarten. Each classroom has a teacher and an aide, and at least one senior citizen aide from a state-funded program. There are also several practicum students from the local community college. Rebecca has the help of a head teacher who is released half-time to work on curriculum and staff development.

Rebecca has strived to establish a collaborative atmosphere in her program where people work together. She places great trust and confidence in her staff members, but she does find it difficult to confront them about problems, as she does not want to be disrespectful to them or tarnish the humanistic climate she has worked so hard to establish.

The Problem

Mrs. Warren is great with kids, except in areas of discipline. When she does take disciplinary action, she often shouts and sometimes overdoes the punishment. For example, when a little boy was flipping a plant around on a wire hanger, she went across the room and shouted loudly at him to stop and made him sit in a corner. After 5 minutes, the head teacher told the child to return to his play. Mrs. Warren felt that her authority had been undermined. The one time that Rebecca raised the issue of disciplining children with Mrs. Warren, Rebecca was flabbergasted when Mrs. Warren admonished her for letting the children get away with certain things.

ASSESSING THE SUPERVISEE

At this point in her life, Mrs. Warren has developed strongly held views of child rearing. Whether she is open to learning and to modifying her ideas and values is a question Rebecca plans to explore. Mrs. Warren has been in this position for only 3 months, however, and there is much that she could learn about group care for young children.

Mrs. Warren does not see herself as an important part of the center. She keeps pretty much to herself. She carries out assigned duties, as a beginner, but she does not have a total picture of the operation and mission of the program.

Rebecca has noted Mrs. Warren's enjoyment of her work and that she is effective most of the time; on the other hand, her apparent lack of flexibility is an area of concern to Rebecca.

Based on observations over time, Rebecca views Mrs. Warren as being at the lower end of the continuum in terms of level of abstract thinking and in the middle to upper range in terms of commitment to her job. Taking this information into account with what she knows about Mrs. Warren's status as a beginner in the program, and what she has summarized about her strengths and her needs and goals during retirement, Rebecca has determined that her initial supervisory approach will primarily be directive, with the intention of moving into a collaborative mode when possible.

ASSESSING THE SUPERVISOR

Two years ago, Rebecca probably would have ignored this problem. Although she is anxious about her upcoming conference with Mrs. Warren, she is determined to go through with it, since she knows she cannot permit staff members to use such punitive measures with children.

Although she is certain she will feel uncomfortable in being directive with a proud woman who is old enough to be her mother, Rebecca has been gaining confidence in herself as a supervisor. She knows which behaviors are developmentally appropriate for children, and she is very clear about the nature of the environment she wants to create for them. Because of her graduate work and previous teaching experience, Rebecca is aware of resources she can use to train her staff, and she has definite ideas as to what the content of the training sessions should be and how to conduct them. Rebecca is determined to make her program a model one, and she devotes a great deal of time and energy to her work.

THE SUPERVISORY PLAN

Rebecca has formulated a plan for working with Mrs. Warren. She may use all of the possible strategies she has identified or may choose from among them. These include:

1. Going out of her way to make Mrs. Warren feel like a special person and recognizing the good work she has been doing.
2. Working out a structured daily schedule for Mrs. Warren that emphasizes routines and clarifies her role in working with 5–year-olds.
3. Holding an immediate conference with Mrs. Warren to deal with the issue of shouting at children. She expects to be very directive in dealing with this issue.
4. Taking time to observe Mrs. Warren in the classroom.
5. Holding individual conferences with Mrs. Warren on a regular basis. Recognizing that Mrs. Warren is a mature adult who has a high degree of self-respect and self-esteem, Rebecca believes that through these conferences, Mrs. Warren will feel respected, even though she and Rebecca may disagree on when and how children should be reprimanded.

    During these conferences, Rebecca hopes to learn more about Mrs. Warren's previous work and family experiences. She also plans to discuss the issue of disciplining children by eliciting from Mrs. Warren descriptions of her past experiences in raising children and connecting those to the conditions, needs, and behaviors of children in the program.

    By providing feedback to her from observations and by raising questions to clarify situations, Rebecca expects Mrs. Warren to begin to reflect on her behavior in disciplining children.

6. Providing monthly training sessions for Mrs. Warren and the other two senior assistants to deal with child care techniques and to provide them with opportunities to share their thoughts with each other and with Rebecca. These sessions will include demonstrating and role-playing behaviors, which will illustrate how to respond to children when they misbehave. Child growth and development issues will be discussed. In this way, Mrs. Warren will be able to test new behavior in safe situations and test her thinking with peers.
7. Inviting Mrs. Warren to staff meetings with the full-time staff so that she will feel part of the program and learn from other staff.

CONCLUSION

In formulating her supervisory plan, Rebecca has considered Mrs. Warren's stage of professional and personal development and the specific issue at hand—how and when to discipline children in light of their own growth and development. Rebecca has also made some judgments about Mrs. Warren's commitment to the job and her ability to analyze problems and generate solutions to them.

Rebecca and Mrs. Warren are at different points in their lives and careers. The knowledge, experience, competencies, and goals that each has will, of course, affect the outcome of this case. By taking into consideration personal, professional, and contextual factors relating to Mrs. Warren and to this particular problem, Rebecca has been able to develop a plan that is both realistic and growth-oriented. She has mapped out a variety of avenues for supervision, so that she can confront the problem while also providing support. She will then be able to move toward a collaborative style, and perhaps eventually to a nondirective mode, while maintaining the humanistic climate that she values.

EXERCISES

1. What aspects of the "developmental dynamic" described in Chapter 5 are illustrated in this situation?
2. Develop your own case study based on a problem that you have encountered with a staff member. Use the information from the chapters in this part to make a plan for supporting your supervisee.

Part III

A FRAMEWORK FOR SUPERVISION

9

Clinical Supervision

Developed in the 1960s at Harvard University by Morris Cogan (1973) and Robert Goldhammer (1969), clinical supervision focuses on the improvement of teachers' performance through direct interaction of supervisors and teachers in natural settings.

Originally, clinical supervision was designed as a collaborative process among teachers, interns, curriculum specialists, and professors. Today, it has primarily become a one-to-one encounter between administrator and teacher whose main goal is the evaluation of a teacher's performance. Supervision that concentrates mainly on evaluation is, however, limited in its ability to assist staff members in improving the ways in which they carry out their jobs. In contrast, we believe that the focus of clinical supervision is the ongoing professional development of staff members.

Both individual and group clinical supervision can take place within a program that has a multifaceted approach to supporting staff. Some teachers benefit from one-on-one supervision with a director, coordinator, or head teacher some of the time; however, pairs of teachers on their own or groups of teachers with or without their supervisor can learn to work together and take responsibility for their own growth and development.

THE FIVE STAGES OF CLINICAL SUPERVISION

Clinical supervision is carried out through a series of stages that are repeated to form an ongoing cycle. The five stages are the pre-observation conference, the observation, the analysis and strategy, the supervision conference, and the postconference analysis (Cogan, 1973). The behavioral content of these stages varies depending on the purpose that supervisors and/or staff members establish.

Stage 1: Pre-observation Conference

During pre-observation conferences, participants have an opportunity to begin to establish positive working relationships with each other, laying the groundwork for the development of mutual trust and respect throughout each stage of the supervisory cycle.

Initial conferences are occasions to diffuse anxiety and to explain the cycle of clinical supervision and the roles of each participant in this new relationship. Pre-observation conferences, in general, offer opportunities to discuss serious concerns, to review the purposes and procedures of an upcoming lesson with children, to make plans for an observation, to agree on its focus, and to establish a time for the postobservation conference.

Stage 2: Observation

Supervisors or peers may observe teachers and/or children at work during formal lessons or informal periods. The specific purpose of an observation is usually agreed on during the pre-observation conference, during which the type of observation to be made and the tools for observing are determined. The observation is the link between the plans made during Stage 1 and actual practice. It affords supervisors or peers an opportunity to see the situation in which the teacher's questions and concerns originated and to determine whether answers can be found (Cogan, 1973).

Stage 3: Analysis and Strategy

As teachers often prefer to talk with their supervisors right away, it is tempting to provide immediate feedback at the conclusion of an observation; however, taking the time to analyze observational data and to think about the conference that is to follow increases the success and power of the clinical supervisory cycle. During the analysis and planning stage, supervisors or peer teachers "reconstruct" observed events, note the context in which they occurred, identify patterns of behavior and critical incidents that developed. Observed events are analyzed in terms of the concerns raised during the pre-observation conference and strategies are formulated for use in the postobservation conference. The teachers who were observed also need time to reflect about their teaching and to plan for the follow-up conference.

Stage 4: Supervision Conference

Cogan (1973) states that "the conference is a shared exploration: a search for the meaning of instruction, for choices among alternative diagnoses, and alternative strategies for improvement" (p. 197).

The conference is a time for teachers to reflect on the lesson and to share their analyses and for the observer(s) to provide feedback to the teacher about the observation. Both parties can jointly formulate strategies for dealing with problems and can raise issues of concern. During the conference, observers can also offer specific help if appropriate, explore the rewarding and satisfying aspects of a staff member's performance, and plan for the next observation. Each conference varies in purpose, in content, and in the nature of supervisor-supervisee or peer interaction, depending on the individuals and circumstances involved and the balance of power and control between them.

Stage 5: Postconference Analysis

The postconference analysis is a means of self-improvement for supervisors and staff members. It is a time when participants assess the nature of their communication during the conference, the effectiveness of strategies used, the role that each individual played, and the extent to which progress was made on the issues discussed.

GROUP CLINICAL SUPERVISION

While a director, coordinator, or head teacher may carry out this five-stage cycle with individuals, opportunities for staff to engage in group or collaborative clinical supervision maximize a supervisor's use of time and place supervisors in the role of facilitator, which can be very rewarding.

In her classic study of workplace conditions for school success, Little (1982) found that continuous professional development—that is, "learning on the job"—is most likely and thoroughly achieved in those schools that provide opportunities for teachers to discuss their classroom practice, to observe and critique each other's teaching, and to work together in preparing curriculum and in improving instruction. Group clinical supervision can foster these conditions.

Group clinical supervision also has the potential to create a culture of community and collegueship among staff members. Cogan (1973) viewed clinical supervision as professional company for the teacher. This notion of "keeping the teacher company" conveys a positive image of supervision. Groups of staff members working together with a supervisor can have the effect of reducing isolation and bolstering self-confidence and morale because of the company and support provided.

We view group clinical supervision as a process whereby teachers, other professional support staff, and supervisors engage each other in planning, observing, and assessing instruction. Each program will have to develop its own format for group clinical supervision; however, we do make some suggestions for a structure in Chapters 10 and 11.

CONCLUSION

Clinical supervision offers early childhood supervisors a framework for working with staff members. It is a planned and systematic procedure for fostering the development of caregivers. It is one approach that early childhood supervisors can use to support individuals who are undertaking different personal and professional tasks and who have varied preparation and experience levels. For a more detailed description of clinical supervision, we suggest that you read the texts cited in this chapter.

In the two chapters that follow we will discuss aspects of clinical supervision in more detail. In Chapter 10 we describe the purposes of the supervisory conference, communication skills that supervisors need in order to conduct successful conferences, and the key ingredients in any supervisory conference. The material in Chapter 10 is directly connected to Stages 1 and 3–5 of clinical supervision. And in Chapter 11, we describe some approaches to observing staff, Stage 2, and give specific suggestions for constructing observation instruments.

10

The Supervisory Conference

The conference is the heart of clinical supervision. It enables supervisors and supervisees to come together to jointly solve the significant problems of caregiving and teaching. In addition to ensuring ongoing and systematic communication between supervisor and supervisee, supervisory conferences are held to

- Discuss, interpret, and evaluate issues pertaining to teaching/caregiving
- Develop long- and short-range plans with staff members
- Discuss issues regarding specific children and/or families
- Enable supervisors and supervisees to raise concerns and to resolve problems
- Transmit and discuss basic information about program policies and procedures
- Plan for an observation or to discuss staff performance after an observation
- Show interest in teachers' work
- Convey a planned disciplinary action
- Present and discuss a formal evaluation
- Enable the supervisor to obtain advice and information

Regardless of the reason for meeting with teachers, a goal of the conference is to help staff members think about, think through, analyze, and make decisions about their work with young children. Through the conference dialogue, which includes asking questions and offering information, supervisors can assist teachers in the decision-making processes involved in planning for teaching, reflecting on their practice, and applying what they learned.

Although a supervisor may have informal conversations with a supervisee during the course of a day, these meetings are not good substitutes for scheduled conferences where issues can be explored in depth and in thoughtful ways. When supervisors make a commitment to confer with staff members on a regular basis, and not just for evaluation purposes, caregivers believe that supervisors value them and their work.

THE CONTEXT

The success of the supervisory conference is largely determined by the nature of the existing relationship between supervisor and staff member and the professional culture in which they are working. The climate, context, and mood of a conference are affected by previous contacts that the two individuals have had and by the assumptions, beliefs, expectations, and perceptions that they have about themselves, each other, and each other's roles.

Power and Control

As supervisors are in official positions of authority and power, they set the tone for the supervisory conference. Pickhardt (1981) suggests that supervisors think about helping as a power. What kind of powers do early childhood supervisors have, and how can they use them judiciously?

Individuals in supervisory positions possess knowledge and expertise about young children and strategies for facilitating their cognitive, social, and emotional development. These can be shared to strengthen a caregiver's capacity to interact with young children and to cope with problems. Supervisors have access to material resources and to a network of human resources that can make the caregiver's role easier to carry out. They have control of the ways in which caregivers spend time within a program, which permits them to limit the demands placed on a staff member. They can directly influence how peers and those in higher positions think about particular staff members. Most important, they can use their power to encourage supervisees to become more independent.

Supervisees also have power. They have expertise, in some cases more than their supervisors. They have contractual agreements, especially in public school settings, that guarantee them certain rights and privileges and that protect them from abuse. They can influence the opinions and attitudes of their peers. And they have the power to refuse help.

Either party can control a conference. The person doing most of the talking may be dominating and controlling the conference if he or she allows the listener few opportunities to ask questions or to make a point. On the other hand, supervisors who *consciously* refrain from talk to permit supervisees to express their thoughts and feelings are in control and are helping without dominating.

Establishing the conference agenda is another form of power. If all or most of the issues discussed are supervisor-initiated, then the supervisee may not have had an opportunity to set priorities and may not have thought about those issues prior to the meeting. Such "ceremonial" conferences lead to feelings in staff members of being cut off from expressing immediate concerns so they often choose instead to end the ritual as soon as possible.

The pace and timing of conference dialogue are other indicators of who is controlling the conference. One party or the other may rush through or abort discussion of a certain issue. Refusal by the supervisee, or the supervisor for that matter, to elaborate on a problem and to express true thoughts about it is a way of exercising power.

Developmental Levels

The stage of development of a staff member is a factor for the supervisor to consider in determining the nature of help to provide during a conference. Staff members who have difficulty analyzing problems and thinking of solutions may be assisted by supervisors who probe and ask clarifying questions that focus and gradually lead supervisees toward solutions. In other cases, supervisors can be enablers by holding back, listening to teachers think through problems without offering information. By informally assessing the developmental characteristics of staff members described in Chapter 5, supervisors can make better decisions about which strategies to use with which individuals.

Communication Skills

We believe that much of the success of a conference depends on the clarity of communication that takes place between supervisors and staff members. The characteristics of people who facilitate the growth of others as, Carl Rogers (1962) has described, have special relevance within the context of helping:

> The helping person is more likely to make the relationship a growth promoting one when he communicates a desire to understand the other person's meanings and feelings. This attitude of wanting to understand is expressed in a variety of ways. When he talks, the helping person is less inclined to give instruction and advice, thus creating a climate which fosters independence. He avoids criticism and withholds evaluative judgments of the other person's ideas, thoughts, feelings, and behavior. He listens more often than he talks and when he speaks he strives to understand what the other person is communicating in thoughts and feeling. The comments of the helping person are aimed at assisting the other individual to clarify his own meanings and attitudes. Such behavior on the part of the helping person communicates the all important desire to understand, which in turn breeds the trust and confidence which are so essential to growth and development. (p. 417)

By conscious use of specific communication skills, supervisors can increase the possibility that they will attain shared meanings and understandings with supervisees. Listening, questioning, and offering information are three of these communication behaviors. Paying attention to nonverbal messages is also a consideration when conferring with staff.

Nonverbal Communication

Galloway (1974) developed a set of well-known categories of nonverbal communication for use in analyzing teacher-pupil interaction. Nonverbal expressions of enthusiastic support, helping, and receptivity encourage communication, while nonverbal expressions of inattentiveness, unresponsiveness, and disapproval discourage communication. These categories can be useful for analyzing supervisor/teacher conferences.

Facial expressions that imply understanding and approval and those that exhibit patience, interest, and attention to a partner's talk encourage communication. So do actions that portray acceptance, attentiveness, greeting, and praise. Voice intonation or inflections that indicate pleasure, acceptance, and approval also facilitate communication. Much of what Galloway (1974) describes as behavior that encourages good communication is also behavior that is an expression of active listening. It is important to keep in mind that different cultural groups give different meanings to various nonverbal expressions.

Active Listening

Active, attentive listening is one of the most critical supervisory conference skills in facilitating open and effective communication without dominating. Like teachers, supervisors often believe that they are not helping another unless they are telling, advising, and offering suggestions. The tendency by supervisors to talk a great deal during conferences can have the effect of making them feel good but can also cut off serious communication and, despite good intentions, can prevent helping.

Listening is a difficult skill and a complex act. It involves showing respect for the individual, being sensitive enough to discern various levels of meaning expressed by the individual, and being aware of assumptions that underlie the words being spoken (Morimoto, 1973). The good listener works on several levels to understand both the person and the message.

Silence

Supervisors striving to be good listeners need not fear moments of silence. In certain situations, silence is golden (Johnson, 1979):

> *Silence almost never offends.* While almost anything someone says can be seen as offensive under some circumstances, silence is gloriously neutral. It calls for no rebuttals, defenses, or new evidence.

Silence is a verbal cathartic. Most people are unable to tolerate silence for long. If two people are in a room together and one is silent, the other will feel a compulsion to say something, if only to fill the silence. If you want someone to speak, keep quiet, and before many seconds have elapsed he will.

Silence is nonjudgmental. Most people are careful of what they say because they expect to be judged. When a subordinate tells you he hates his job and would rather [not] . . . work another day, and you respond with silence, he will be greatly relieved at your failure to make a judgment. If you aren't more careful with your silence, he may even wind up thinking you're a nice guy. (pp. 75–76)

Asking Questions

Questioning is critical to accomplishing conference goals and in training supervisees to think through and analyze their behavior. Supervisors ask questions for different reasons, so the form of questions should change based on their purpose. For example, soliciting information from a supervisee usually requires *simple questions* to bring out facts or to clarify a problem so that both supervisor and supervisee have a common basis to build on for discussion:

- Can you tell me something about how you and your aide plan together?
- Why don't you describe your daily schedule so I have a clearer picture of how free play fits into the whole program?

Supervisors also ask questions to help teachers understand children's behavior, the causes of behavior, and the relationship of observed behaviors to previous behaviors. *Probing questions* invite the caregiver to think about the teaching act and to articulate reasons for behavior:

- Mario was throwing paper and hitting other children during cleanup. I've noticed that he has done this before. Do you have any thoughts as to why he tends to act out during these times?
- Tell me your strategy for working with Yolanda. She has improved so much. Why do you think she is responding?
- What would you like the children to gain from the lesson you plan to do on the calendar?

Questions that solicit consideration of *alternative decisions,* and *predictions* of what might happen with each alternative, help the caregiver make plans for future teaching:

- Can you think of some ways to change the arrangement of the dramatic play area that would encourage the children to put the clothes away when they are through?

- What do you think they're likely to do if there are cartons for the clothes versus having them on hangers?

Questions that *ask for opinions*, whereby supervisees evaluate something that has taken place; questions that encourage supervisees to *express their feelings* about a particular situation; and questions that ask supervisees to *clarify* by repeating a statement or by providing an example or illustration also contribute to clear communication:

- That was the first time that you used the "Wiggly Fingers" song with the children. In your opinion, was it effective? Why? Why not?
- The children really got into finger painting. You seemed a little overwhelmed. Did the mess bother you?
- When you say "It's always so wild," are you saying that they are too excited about going out or that they aren't sure what they're supposed to do?

Offering Praise

Regular conferences, whether to discuss particular problems or for other purposes, are a perfect opportunity for the supervisor to offer praise. Praise must be authentic, however, before its true value as a positive reinforcer and climate builder can be realized. Most teachers understand themselves well enough to know when praise is deserved. They can easily distinguish between superficial "stroking" and sincere encouragement, appreciation, and praise.

Praise is more effective when it is specific, as it enables supervisees to know which behaviors supervisors are pleased about. Reinforcing staff with praise when they demonstrate desired behaviors encourages them as they struggle to develop skills or to overcome problems. Pointing out these behaviors and avoiding the use of "good" is a more effective way of praising:

- When the children were pushing each other and you quietly walked over and gently placed them in line, they quieted right down.

Supervisors are often preoccupied with staff members who have problems and sometimes overlook and take for granted those caregivers who meet their expectations. These individuals need support as much as the others. Offering special encouragement or recognition when a staff member believes that he or she has just overcome a hurdle or made a significant accomplishment can also have lasting benefits.

Offering Information

Supervisors frequently offer information to supervisees during conferences. As leaders with knowledge and experience, supervisors are expected to share their expertise with staff members at appropriate times.

One of the most difficult supervisory habits to overcome, however, is offering too much information too often. This tendency probably arises out of a supervisory perception of "information giving" as helping, coupled with a need and desire to help.

A different conception of helping is to hold back information in favor of listening or questioning. This is a valid means of providing the supervisee with "thinking space" to arrive at his or her own solutions to problems. The trick, of course, is to make the right decision about when to offer information and when not to, keeping in mind the goal of enabling staff to be effective in their work and to assume responsibility for their own improvement.

There are many instances when giving supervisees specific information is appropriate. Staff members may need new ideas and suggestions. They may want to be connected to human and material resources to provide for an enriched program. They might benefit from particular illustrations of individual or group behaviors as a way of understanding themselves or the children with whom they are working. But this information is best brought forth after they have had time to try to discover it for themselves and when they are ready to hear it.

Another consideration in offering information is how to disclose data. Supervisors often confer with supervisees after a classroom observation, during which they collected data about teacher and child behavior and/or the learning environment. Showing this information to staff members in a nonevaluative manner can become a basis for mutual discussion. Supervisees then have an opportunity to select which issues to explore and to determine whether their behavior is congruent with their values and goals.

Listening, questioning, praising, and offering information are communication behaviors that need practice to become natural parts of the supervisory dialogue.

Intercultural Communication

Harris and Moran (1991) describe intercultural communication as a process of sharing perceptual fields. Our distinctive perceptual field, consisting of our family, education, religious, and social backgrounds, enables each of us to process information uniquely. Two individuals can thus receive the same message, but interpret and filter it differently. Each processes those segments that are consistent with his or her own cultural background and reality. When the originator of the message is from one cultural group and the receiver from another, the interaction is intercultural communication.

As a supervisor, when you confer with staff members who come from cultural backgrounds and have perceptual fields different from your own, you have opportunities to practice communication that is culturally sensitive. Realistically, it is not possible to be intimately knowledgeable of the language and the cultural patterns of every culture represented among families and staff members within a program, but it is possible to be aware of those cultural variables that have a bearing on communicating with understanding, and to learn about a culture that is represented by a majority of staff members and children in a program and even to study their language if it is different from your own. There are several specific cultural factors that can affect communication and supervision.

Time Sense

Mainstream American culture places importance on being prompt for appointments, meetings, classes, and work. Some groups, however, have a different sense of time. Supervisors sometimes strive to get things accomplished in a short amount of time because there is so much to do. This situation can create pressure to rush through supervisory conferences, causing internal conflicts in supervisors and dissatisfaction in supervisees, particularly if supervisees come from cultural backgrounds that place a great value on human relationships. Supervisors and staff members who come from cultures where individuals have a "long view" of time and/or prefer to allow more time for activities involving human interaction may be offended by hastened communication.

Space

Some Americans, depending on cultural background, like to have some distance, a comfort zone, between themselves and others when engaged in conversation (Hall, 1973). Others come from cultures that prefer closer speaking distances and may have considerable body contact when greeting each other and during conversations. Individuals who are comfortable with contact may view those who aren't as unfriendly; those who prefer closeness may be perceived as being forward, loud, or aggressive by persons accustomed to distance.

Verbal and Nonverbal Communication

Metaphors, stories, or examples used in conversations to explain an idea or a concept may be culture-bound and can impede understanding between individuals. When conferring with staff who speak a native language different from theirs, supervisors need to be aware of the complexity of language used. Bowers and Flinders (1991) suggest that it is best to employ a common vocabulary, avoiding words with multiple meanings. Further, how something is said is as important as what is said; loudness and softness and pitch and rhythm have various cultural connotations. Loudness in one culture, for example, may set an accusatory tone, while in another, it is simply a common way of speaking.

The pace of conversation is also culture-bound. Whereas some individuals may be comfortable with fast-paced dialogue, others may come from cultures where conversation is slower, where more time is taken for questions and reflection, where pauses are longer, and where our partners have greater opportunities to respond.

As supervisors and supervisees "read" each other during conferences, they often pay attention to nonverbal cues in order to make decisions about when to speak and what to say next or about the content direction that the conference should take. Facial expressions, body posture, gestures, and eye contact convey meaning; these messages can vary from culture to culture.

Values

Cultural attitudes, assumptions, beliefs, and values held by supervisors and staff members influence decision making and behavior in the workplace and are likely to be at the heart of many discussions between them, particularly when they do not have the same background. For example, a supervisor may believe that (1) change is needed in the program;(2) a staff member's primary obligation should be to his or her work; and (3) each staff member should express his or her opinion freely. A staff member, on the other hand, may (1) value tradition, continuity, and stability and thus resist change; (2) place family responsibilities and the pursuit of relationships first, and (3) defer to the supervisor as the person in authority and, therefore, say very little, raise few questions, and be reluctant to express opinions in supervisory conferences. It's not hard to see how these assumptions on both sides could cause confusion or miscommunication.

Concepts of Authority

Concepts of authority are formed in one's early family and schooling experiences. In some cultures, children are raised in very protected family environments where dependence is encouraged as well as strict obedience to the authority figure, who is often the male head of family. Women are not expected to take on authority roles and girls, in particular, are taught not to question authority. In schools, giving a teacher a correct answer may be valued over independence of thought. Also, individuals from cultures where the political climate is autocratic expect those in school supervisory positions to be authoritarian and may view nondirective supervisory behavior as a form of weakness.

Values; concepts of time, space, and authority; and aspects of verbal and nonverbal language are factors that have a bearing on intercultural communication. By observing, asking questions, and careful listening in pre- and post-teaching conferences, supervisors and teachers can come to know each other's assumptions and presuppositions about teaching and value systems that affect their decisions in the workplace and relationships with children, colleagues, and supervisors (Bowers & Flinders, 1991). Sensitive intercultural communication among adults in the early childhood settings can contribute to positive experiences for children.

STRUCTURING THE CONFERENCE

Each type of conference has a different focus and purpose, which can alter its structure. Different approaches might be required, for example, to resolve a particular problem, to plan an upcoming observation, to discuss a completed observation, or simply to maintain good communication. A conference requested by a staff member to discuss serious concerns might be open-ended in nature, while a postobservation meeting might be formal and highly structured. There are, however, common elements to all conferences, regardless of the topic being discussed: preparing, climate building, purpose setting, guiding, closing, and analyzing.

Preparing for the Conference

Careful thought about an upcoming conference offers greater assurance that it will be productive and successful. The extent of preparation necessary varies depending on the purpose of the conference and the sensitivity and seriousness of topics being discussed.

Location is an important consideration. Finding a suitable and private place to talk is most desirable, although it can be a problem for supervisors who work in more than one site or in a small or crowded center.

Arranging for a block of uninterrupted time, free from telephone calls and other disruptions that disturb the flow of communication, can also help both parties relax and think more clearly. Having adequate time yet setting a time limit is also helpful.

As a supervisor, in preparing for a conference, you might want to ask the following questions:

- What do I want to accomplish in this meeting?
- Are there specific understandings to develop with the caregiver?
- If the conference is one of a series that has focused on a staff member's behavior in certain situations, what do I want that individual to know or to learn in this meeting about his or her behavior?

You may also wish to plan conference questions or statements ahead of time to use as needed, especially when anticipating difficult conferences concerning interpersonal or evaluative issues. If it is a postobservation conference, it is helpful to study the data collected at the time of the observation to refresh your memory. If it is an evaluation conference, it may be useful to review notes kept over time and to examine the materials in the staff member's portfolio. Re-reading the program's evaluation policy statement, having at hand pertinent materials such as evaluation forms or the center's handbook, and thinking about how they might be used during the conference are also steps that can be taken to increase supervisory confidence, and to facilitate and add depth to the meeting.

You may find it helpful to identify a conference agenda beforehand and to prioritize issues that should be discussed. Flexibility is important, however, since an agenda may have to be abandoned to deal with a supervisee's immediate concerns. A conference should be focused so as to address one or two main issues in depth, instead of superficially covering a range of issues, which can serve to raise the anxiety level of a supervisee.

Teachers should also be encouraged to prepare for the conference by thinking about their goals and by laying out a tentative agenda ahead of time. The purpose of the conference and developmental levels of the teacher and supervisor will determine the extent of each party's participation and the agenda that unfolds.

Creating a Climate

The supervisor who is competent, helpful, and in control of the situation creates a positive conference climate. Actions that convey honesty and professionalism and that focus on performance contribute to the image of supervisor as a qualified and supportive individual.

Conferences can be threatening to staff members, since topics that are discussed often have to do with their performance. If a delicate issue is to be raised, the supervisor might also be anxious about the meeting. Anxieties are lessened when the supervisor, as leader, takes the initiative to set a working tone for the meeting.

The physical arrangement of the conference space—the placement of furniture, noise level, ventilation, and so forth—adds to or takes away from the tone the supervisor wishes to achieve. A supervisor who sits behind a desk establishes a formal atmosphere, one in which the supervisee is clearly in a subordinate role to an authority figure. There may be times when a supervisor will need to reinforce and execute his or her authority through a formal setting, but in most cases conference environments that help staff members feel at ease, raise concerns, and ask for suggestions and advice are preferable. An informal arrangement, which puts supervisor and supervisee face to face on the same level without artificial physical barriers, is much more conducive to these goals.

Friendly comments, a cup of coffee, or a humorous story can break the ice, diffuse anxiety in either individual, and lay the foundation for a productive meeting. On the other hand, if both parties are braced for a tense encounter, it may be best to get to the issue directly. The decision of when to address the key concern often has to be made on the spot.

Setting the Purpose

When the purpose of a conference is clear and agreed on, there is no need for you and your supervisee to guess the reason for meeting. You can focus on the agenda much more quickly. You might wish to set aside a few minutes at the beginning of the session to clarify its purpose and to enable the caregiver to suggest issues to be explored. Once an agenda is mutually agreed on, items can be prioritized.

For example, the following issues might be discussed in a postobservation conference after a single classroom visit:

Making cleanup go smoothly
Settling the children into nap-time
Handling a disruptive child
Extending children's thinking during free play

Although the overall conference purpose would be to analyze the activities observed, each specific issue could become the central theme of one or several conferences so it is important to narrow the agenda. The staff member may raise issues independently and decide that getting help in working with the disruptive child is most critical at this time. Concurring, the supervisor will encourage the staff member to share that concern. If the teacher failed to raise this important matter, the supervisor would have to do so.

Unexpected issues, which cannot be planned for, also arise during conferences. Artful supervisors learn when to pick up on a thought, when to screen it out, and when to pull back from one issue or push ahead to another.

As mentioned earlier, the developmental characteristics of the staff member and the nature of the issue(s) to be discussed will, in large part, determine the extent to which the supervisor or the supervisee takes the lead in setting the agenda and the structure for the conference.

Guiding the Conference

The body of the conference is the part during which the issues selected are elaborated on, explored, and discussed. During this phase, the conferees describe the behavior of teacher and children, share and analyze data from an observation, raise problems, note progress, and exchange basic information. The supervisor has an opportunity to reinforce a staff member and to put into practice the skills of asking good questions, listening attentively, and offering appropriate information. By describing and asking questions, supervisors can assist teachers in the reflective process.

Describing means to provide the supervisee with an account, a portrait of what was observed, without making judgments about it; for example, having chosen *working with a disruptive child* as a focus, here is a nonjudgmental description by a supervisor:

> I noticed that Mark was poking Sharon and Gail during circle time. When it was over, he went into the block area and knocked over Josh's tower and kicked the blocks with his feet. He then took the cards that Josh was using to label his buildings and ran to the far corner of the room with them. You were getting ready for the cooking lesson when Mark was disturbing Josh in the block building area.

Once the behavior has been described, the supervisor can begin to assist the supervisee in interpreting and evaluating it by questioning and listening:

> Why do you think Mark was so disruptive today? He started to misbehave during circle time. How did you respond to him then? How else might you have handled the situation? What could you do to be more aware of what is taking place in various parts of the room?

When the conversation goes off on a tangent, a supervisor will find it necessary to bring it back into focus. If a staff member has difficulty thinking through an issue or arriving at possible solutions, then the supervisor may have to offer more information and ask fewer questions.

A way to signal the end of one discussion and the start of another is to summarize what has been said and change the subject by moving to another that needs to be talked about.

Planning Next Steps

In planning the next steps, supervisor and/or supervisee identify and develop problem-solving strategies, which usually involve changes in teaching behavior. Once new behaviors or possible strategies have been explored, supervisor and supervisee agree on which of these should be implemented, when, and how. The supervisee may say:

> Before I start circle time activities tomorrow, I plan to describe to the children how I expect them to behave. If Mark continues to misbehave, I will tell him in a very firm voice to stop, instead of ignoring him as I did today. I also will make certain that I am sitting next to him before we begin. I'm also going to set up the cooking area before school so I can move about the room during the transition from circle time to activity period.

The supervisor may respond:

> Those are excellent ideas. As you suggested, I'll come in tomorrow at the beginning of circle time. I'll especially watch Mark, and I'll pay special attention to the transition from circle time to activity period. Let's get together tomorrow afternoon to talk about the effects of these changes and share more ideas.

Or if a caregiver is unable to offer a solution, the supervisor might say:

> Tomorrow, I will serve as a role model for you during circle time. I would like you to observe my teaching and management techniques and pay particular attention to the ways in which I work with Mark. Write your observations down. We can discuss these when we meet tomorrow afternoon.

An agreed-on and limited set of steps that both the supervisee and supervisor will take before the next conference gives both individuals a sense of accomplishment and direction.

Closing the Conference

During the closing phase, the supervisor summarizes what has taken place during the conference period, reviews initial goals in terms of conference outcomes, and restates agreed-on future plans and time-lines. If progress has been made, both parties sense achievement. The closing is also a good time to ask caregivers to offer feedback about the conference itself. This is not a time to be defensive, but rather to be a good listener. Asking the supervisee to share thoughts and feelings about the conference builds trust and open communication.

After an evaluation conference, you may find it beneficial to write a brief summary of what has taken place. A signed copy of the summary can be forwarded to the supervisee for his or her signature. If the supervisee disagrees with the summary and both of you cannot agree on revisions, then the supervisee can have the option of submitting a written summary of his or her own. This procedure is especially important when a serious problem is being addressed.

Preparing, building the climate, setting the purpose, guiding, planning next steps, and closing are six phases that give a conference structure and flexibility, regardless of its purpose and the number of individuals participating. It is important to note that throughout the conference, a supervisor closely observes and listens to the supervisee, engaging in *on-the-spot* decision making about which communication skills to use and at which point; when to be direct, collaborative, or indirect; how to keep the conference in focus; and when to bring it to a close. A final, postconference stage is analyzing the conference.

Analyzing the Conference

One way for you to improve your performance is by consciously and systematically thinking about and questioning your own supervisory behaviors. This is an aspect of the conference that is often overlooked. Such self-analysis takes time, but the result makes the process worthwhile.

We recommend making audiotapes of at least a few conferences for the purpose of analysis. When told of the purpose, caregivers are usually receptive, since they recognize that their supervisor is striving to become a more effective leader. Supervisors usually find this experience quite revealing. Videotaping a conference allows one to later analyze both verbal and nonverbal behavior, but individuals sometimes become overly conscious of the camera, and making arrangements for videotaping can be overwhelming.

When reviewing the audiotape of a conference, it is best to listen to the entire recording first to refresh your memory and to get a holistic view of the meeting. Then, when playing the tape again, listen for specific purposes:

- In what ways and to what extent did you achieve your goals for the conference?
- In what ways were you successful in practicing the specific communication skills that you had set as a priority?

- In what ways did the supervisee respond to the conference climate and to your communication behavior?
- What are your goals for yourself for your next supervisory conference with this individual?

Scrutinizing your supervisory behavior during conferences fosters your own growth and development and advances the notion in staff members that all adults, including supervisors, are learners.

THREE-WAY CONFERENCES

Although most conferences include just a supervisor and a staff member, there is need on occasion to have a third party participate. Student teachers, job trainees, or Child Development Associate (CDA) candidates are often supervised by a representative of an outside program, who works in cooperation with the coordinator or head teacher. Although the caregiver may spend more time in the field setting and receive most supervision there, he or she must meet the requirements of both organizations and the expectations of both supervisors.

As the two programs and their representatives interface, it is critical that the staff member being supervised and both supervisors meet on a regular basis. Without ongoing communication among the three individuals, splits can develop whereby two develop mutual trust and common goals to the exclusion of the third. There is, therefore, the potential for misunderstanding and conflicting expectations.

Three-way conferences are also useful with individuals within a program. They can be especially effective in handling conflicts among staff members, in resolving contractual issues, and in dealing with parental concerns.

Conferences about grievances usually have clear and well-defined step by-step procedures that directors must follow. Conferences about serious interstaff conflicts are particularly troublesome and should be carefully planned as well. Kostelnik (1982) recommends a multistep problem-solving approach for these encounters.

She suggests that when directors initiate the mediation process, they should take the preliminary step of meeting with the individuals privately, before bringing them together in a face-to-face meeting. During the private sessions, the supervisor's skill of active listening is critical, for the supervisee needs that opportunity to present his or her view of the situation and to express feelings openly and fully.

Once this step is taken, both parties should be brought together for mutual clarification of conflicts. The role of the supervisor in this step is to be neutral and to manage the conference so that each party has an opportunity to present views and to state his or her ultimate solution with respect to the problem being discussed. By paraphrasing or reflecting what each supervisee has said, without evaluating, the supervisor can assist each caregiver in clarifying his or her own thinking, as well as ensuring that each person has an accurate perception of the other's notion of the problem.

Kostelnik (1982) elaborates on the supervisory role during mutual clarification:

> The supervisor should solicit from each person in turn a statement of the situation from that individual's point of view. The ground rule here is that the situation must be described in terms of personal aims rather than phrased as an accusation about another person. An acceptable statement might be, "I wish I spent less time on classroom maintenance." An inappropriate remark would be, "She makes me do all the cleanup and saves the fun things for herself." (p. 2)

Once each person has had an opportunity to state and clarify her or his position and the supervisor understands each worker's view of a desirable outcome, the supervisor should move both parties toward a resolution by defining the problem and making sure that each staff member accepts responsibility for the problem and its solution.

The parties then begin to generate possible alternative solutions to the problem, until a mutually beneficial solution is agreed on. The supervisor then praises each individual for his or her hard work in the problem-solving process and reminds them what the terms of the agreement are, including how the plan will be carried out and evaluated.

Kostelnik (1982) views this problem-solving process as one in which the supervisory role is that of a model and teacher, rather than a judge or disciplinarian. Although time-consuming, the problem-solving process does serve to reduce tension and create positive working relationships among staff.

While it is often difficult to find and arrange a time when all three individuals can meet, the three-way conference has several advantages. It builds relationships among individuals through a collaborative process where each individual has input. The presence of a third person can take pressure off the other two and that person can bring new insights into the conversation. Each person involved has an opportunity to hear and to understand each other's point of view about a child, the teaching role, or a problem. Usually, during a three-way face-to-face conference, individuals use more careful descriptive language, which promotes greater respect and understanding. Three-way conferences that deal with conflict have the overall effect of reducing stress and anxiety among those participating.

GROUP CONFERENCES

A supervisor may wish to bring small groups of staff members together using the five-stage cycle of clinical supervision described in Chapter 9. Groups may include teachers and assistant teachers of varying or of similar levels of experience and expertise who may or may not be on the same teaching team and/or any other relevant staff members such as curriculum specialists. Groups can be formed to explore a new curriculum theme or simply to become familiar with or to refine particular teaching strategies. Two of the stages in clinical supervision, the pre- and postobservation conferences, provide an opportunity for group planning and reflection and for building mutual support among staff members.

The supervisor's role in group conferences is that of facilitator. As teachers often have little experience in mutual planning, analyzing teaching, and giving feedback to others, the supervisor as leader creates an appropriate structure and format for group supervision, laying the groundwork by establishing a time and space for meetings and guiding the group until staff members are prepared, comfortable, and able to carry out group supervision on their own, with teachers eventually becoming group facilitators, perhaps on a rotating basis. Facilitating group conferences includes preparation, climate building, purpose setting, guiding, planning, and closing, the steps described earlier in this chapter.

If, as a supervisor, you decide to initiate group conferencing, we suggest you begin with a pilot group of volunteers who are enthusiastic teachers and who are likely to work well together. In this way, you have an opportunity to explore the role of group facilitator and to observe and listen to teachers engaged in the process before attempting group supervision with your entire staff.

Describing the purpose of clinical supervision and the five-stage cycle is an essential first step. Setting a positive tone, placing an emphasis on collegiality and staff development, while making clear that the purpose of group clinical supervision is not staff evaluation, are important points to emphasize early in the process. In addition, you should help staff to become aware of effective communication skills and to be conscious of using them during group sessions.

Pre-observation Conference

One way you could begin group clinical supervision is to ask a teacher to present an idea for a lesson to the group and ask the group to plan the lesson together. Giving group members an opportunity to ask the teacher questions about the children who will participate and the teacher's goals is an effective way to start.

You can provide group structure by offering participants some questions for discussion that can help to focus the dialogue. Below are some sample questions developed for use in a pre-service teacher preparation program (Caruso & Graham, 1994):

- What do the children need to know and/or to be able to do prior to this learning experience in order for them to succeed?
- What are your main objectives?
- What are the skills and concepts (cognitive, social, emotional, physical) that you wish children to acquire?
- What are some strategies and materials that you could use to accomplish your goal?
- What kinds of problems might occur during this experience?
- How might you achieve curricular integration through this experience?
- What are some different ways to assess children's growth as a result of this experience? (p. 1)

Pre-observation group conferences enable the teacher to think through the learning experience he or she is focusing on whether it is dramatic play, block building, or morning meeting. Dialogue with colleagues can help to clarify its purpose, to anticipate problems, and to obtain ideas and suggestions for teaching strategies. Other group members, particularly those with less experience, are also likely to benefit from the discussion. At its conclusion, the teacher reflects on the conference and creates his or her own lesson plan using the input provided.

During the conference, as supervisor, you should not dominate the discussion but should manage the communication flow, encouraging the participation of all group members. Being sensitive to the developmental levels of staff members and "reflecting-in-action" (Schön, 1987) can help you make decisions about the nature and extent of your participation.

You may conclude the pre-observation conference by asking the group to analyze the conference. You can contribute by helping to summarize the discussion, pointing out effective communication that took place, and outlining next steps.

The Observation

The teachers who helped to develop the plan during the pre-conference should have the opportunity to observe their colleague teach the lesson or facilitate the experience. The observation might take place by watching a videotape if teachers in the group cannot be released from their duties to observe it firsthand. The staff member who is teaching/facilitating may also be more comfortable with videotaping. One teacher from the group could assume the taping responsibility.

Analysis and Strategy

The teacher needs time to review the videotape, to reflect on his or her experience, and to prepare for the postobservation conference. Teachers may find it helpful to bring the tape home where they have ample time to watch it and can be joined by friends and family for an additional critique. The teacher may note critical incidents, patterns in behavior, particular children, and so forth. The teacher decides which highlights of the tape to show to the group and prepares an analysis.

Postobservation Conference

Once the teacher and observers have had time to reflect, a postobservation conference with the planning group can serve to build the teacher's self-esteem and to help others learn some effective teaching strategies.

As facilitator, you might open the conference by restating the importance of listening, questioning, and other communication skills as the observers respond to the video, and by emphasizing the supportive nature of the process and of being sensitive to the teacher whose lesson is being discussed. Reviewing the content of the pre-observation conference is also a helpful way to refresh the memories of group members and sharpen the group's focus.

The teacher who was taped takes a leadership role in the meeting by quickly sharing the final lesson plan he or she developed and by showing segments of the videotape to the group. Because one goal of the postobservation conference is to help the teacher become more skilled at self-assessment and reflection, the teacher should open the discussion by sharing his or her analysis first, followed by questions and comments by group members.

We suggest that group members be given the responsibility of offering feedback about specific aspects of the lesson. This helps to keep the discussion focused. An observation guide can provide members with a structure for conference discussion. Sample observation instruments appear in Chapter 11.

In our experience, these postconferences are lively and positive as group members have excellent insights and observations to share. Again, your role, as supervisor, is to facilitate communication by sharing thoughts, asking questions, and intervening to maintain the flow and the focus when necessary. The extent of your involvement will depend on the development levels of members of the group.

Postconference Analysis

At the conclusion of the conference, you may assist the group in reflecting about the conference by analyzing the effectiveness of their communication and the feedback given, and in summarizing the conference. Plans are also made for the next pre-observation conference, the beginning of another cycle in group clinical supervision.

CONCLUSION

A conference, whether two-way, three-way, or group, provides a director the opportunity to practice the art of supervision. Planning, problem-solving, and evaluating can take place in conferences, and teachers can express themselves and get recognition and praise. Conferences are central to maintaining continued communication between supervisors and staff and to ensuring that caregiving and teaching are of high quality.

PROGRAM ACCREDITATION

The National Academy of Early Childhood Programs (*Guide to Accreditation*, 1998) includes the following criteria for program accreditation related to conferring with and among staff members:

E-9 a. Staff interactions reflect mutual trust, respect, and support for each other.
E-9 b. Staff members seek out and acknowledge each other's ideas and opinions. Staff give positive recognition to each other's skills and accomplishments.
E-9 c. Staff provide appropriate supports for each other when dealing with stress.
E-9 d. Staff respect each other's rights to confidentiality.
E-9 e. Staff communicate with each other to ensure smooth operations. (pp. 68, 69)

Reprinted with permission from the National Association for the Education of Young Children

EXERCISES

As part of a staff training session in supervision, participate in small role-playing groups to consider the problem situations described below. Individuals take the roles of supervisor and caregiver. An observer whose primary function is to offer feedback to the supervisor should also be included. At the conclusion of an agreed-on time segment of role-playing, individuals switch roles so that everyone has an opportunity to practice supervisory behavior. The observer might create a category system for analyzing conference behavior to examine a particular type of communication skill such as questioning technique. Each role-playing sequence need not be long, and at the end the observer should report the results of the analysis to the supervisor. Practicing supervisors might write and discuss a hypothetical plan for resolving each dilemma.

Two-Way Conferences

1. George is concerned that his kids aren't playing well together, particularly with Keith. Keith is an aggressive and active 4-year-old. His parents have been separated for several months and are planning to finalize their divorce very soon. Keith does not see his father and has lots of babysitters. He is at school from 9:00 A.M. to 5:30 P.M. Role-play this conference with George.

2. Yolanda has come to you with a concern. She is very frustrated as the children are sloppy with their food during snack time. She complains, "The kids don't stay seated like they're supposed to and milk gets spilled all over the place!" She explains that some of the children finish their snacks early and get bored and others never have a chance to finish. The kids who finish early get up to throw their containers away and bump into others, and the children who don't finish get up and go to their activities leaving their partly filled milk cartons on the floor to get kicked over. Role-play this conference.

3. Diedre is an assistant teacher in your Head Start classroom. She is from a middle-class family and has a college degree. She has a hard time accepting and appreciating the lower-income children and families who are at the center. When her activities do not go well, she becomes angry and usually blames it on the children, "who don't know anything," "never learned manners," or "don't even speak the language." While she appears to be sweet with the children, you sense that there are a lot of feelings of anger and frustration underneath. Diedre is quite argumentative, and your suggestions have often been met with strong opposition. She feels that she is doing an excellent job, and your criticisms are usually dismissed because "you didn't really see what was happening." The tension is mounting. You have decided that it is time to talk with her about the situation.

Three-way Conferences

1. You are a head teacher in a day care center in a large corporation. All the parents are employed by the corporation and tend to be quite conservative. Your assistant teacher, Cassandra, is very imaginative and has a unique

and rather flamboyant style. She often wears sequined purple sneakers, brightly colored tights, and short skirts; at other times, it is flowing Indian skirts and a headband (a la 1960s). Her activities with the children are age-appropriate and creative but represent a different lifestyle from those of the parents (e.g., body painting, Yoga, Tai Chi, vegetarian cooking). She is wonderful with the children, and you feel that she offers a good balance to the daily businesslike atmosphere of the site. One day Diane, a parent, calls to say that she is distressed about the "crazy things" her child is learning and feels that Cassandra should dress and behave in a "more appropriate manner." You think that both people would benefit from hearing the other's point of view. Role-play that meeting.

2. You are a director of a day care center with a culturally diverse group of families and staff. You have recently hired an assistant teacher, Elena, who came from Russia last year. She is in her 40s and has the equivalent of a master's degree in education. Her head teacher is an American woman in her late 20s who has a bachelor's degree in education. Elena has had more years of teaching experience than Diane, her head teacher, but most of it was with older children. Elena is finding it difficult to take direction from a person with less education and experience, but at the same time she is not finding it easy working with 3-year-olds. Diane, on the other hand, finds Elena to be somewhat intimidating and is having a hard time establishing a good working relationship with her. Both have come to speak with you about their frustrations in trying to work together. You have decided that it is time to have a three-way meeting. Role-play that meeting.

11

Observation and Analysis

Observation provides the context for conferring with supervisees in the clinical supervision cycle. When supervisors and supervisees talk about what is happening in the classroom, their discussion is based not on speculation, but on what each has experienced directly, through either participation or observation. Through supervisory observations and follow-up conferences, staff members can receive accurate information and feedback on what they are doing, enabling them to compare it to what they think they are doing and what they would like to be doing. As Asa Hilliard (1974) has stated, "Two basic things help teachers to grow. One is relevant professional information, and the other is continuing feedback on what the teacher does" (pp. 18–19).

When observation is used within the cycle of clinical supervision, it can become part of a joint inquiry into what is happening in the classroom, an important process for adult learners. Within this context observation can:

- provide a mirror for staff members' actions so they can have objective feedback on what they are doing
- serve as a vehicle for working together with teachers to help them develop, improve, and maintain their skills in working with children
- provide information that supervisors and supervisees can use together to diagnose and solve teaching problems
- help teachers understand how the classroom/learning environment affects children's growth and development, and enable them to act on this information
- aid teachers in assessing the effectiveness of their program for children and of changes they have made in it
- provide data for evaluation based on shared criteria and standards (Acheson & Gall, 1980)

At its most basic level, observation is a way of gathering and recording data, yet it clearly involves more than entering a classroom, watching what is happening, and recording what is seen. The very complexity of the teaching/

learning process makes effective observation difficult. The many interacting forces—teaching staff, children, the physical environment, the time of day, the activity—must be sorted out in some way. Observers have opinions and feelings about what is going on, and their prejudgments must be accounted for in planning accurate and reliable recording of information. The many layers and subtleties of social meanings, contexts, and feelings present in the classroom must be revealed but not confused with the "facts." Finally, the information collected must be conveyed to the persons observed in ways they can understand, accept, and use. Thus, supervisors who are helping teachers become active participants in their own learning might describe observation more as a *way of inquiring* than as a way of gathering data.

OBSERVATION WITHIN THE CLINICAL SUPERVISION CYCLE

Most supervisors find it advantageous to use a variety of ways of observing. In a study of the methods used by 300 supervisors during observation and analysis, Noreen Garman (1982) found that they actually used five "modes" at various stages in the cycle of supervision. At each stage there were different assumptions and, therefore, different methods of observation and analysis. "Each has a different, yet vital, purpose in a comprehensive plan for supervision" (p. 50).

The first mode, *discovery,* is an open-ended search to discover the reality of the classroom and to begin thinking about what questions should be explored further. Various systems of observation could be used at this stage. At this point the data from these observations are usually analyzed by identifying the teacher's stated intent and comparing it with what has been observed.

In the second mode, *verification,* more objective and structured systems of observation are used. This is an important step, as it is used to verify the degree to which features or problems identified in the discovery stage do indeed exist.

In the *explanation* phase, both open-ended and structured methods (see discussion below) are often used. At this time the supervisor and supervisee begin the analysis process, together trying to come to terms with their individual and—most important—perhaps differing perceptions of reality.

Interpretation is the search for meaning, the attempt "to get at what really matters" (Garman, 1982, p. 51). The supervisor's knowledge, experience, and insights are used to help the supervisee find the deeper significance beneath the surface of literal descriptions and explanations.

It is in the *evaluation* stage that the supervisor and supervisee examine values and make judgments about specific aspects of the teacher's behavior.

The criteria for these judgments are the specific information gathered and the goals of the supervisor and supervisee. These become the basis for setting priorities.

The descriptions of approaches and methods that follow are presented in the context of an individual supervisor/supervisee relationship. However, most are appropriate for use by teachers and assistants as well, either individually or with a group of peers, with or without a supervisor. (See introduction to group usage in Chapters 9 and 10, and further discussion in Chapter 15.)

APPROACHES TO OBSERVATION

Observation can be approached in several ways: (1) informally, as a casual visitor to a classroom; (2) as a participant observer, having both involvement in the classroom and a systematic way of recording observations; and (3) formally, completely detaching oneself from the activities in the classroom, recording them in a systematic way.

Informal Observation

Because of the informality and open structure of most early childhood classrooms, adults who are not regular members of the classroom staff can usually move in and out without disrupting the children or the program. Children tend to ignore visitors or to welcome them as new sources of help, amusement, or interesting information. When a supervisor sits down with children during free play or pitches in with cleanup, teachers' apprehensions are often lessened. In fact, many teachers welcome informal visits from supervisors because they think that the supervisor will have a clearer picture of what their classrooms are really like and will be better able to empathize with their problems.

Many directors and educational coordinators make casual visits to classrooms because they like to be with children, to break the routine of their office work, or, more deliberately, to get the flavor of day-to-day center activity. From such visits, they can obtain a general sense of the tone of the room, a teacher's style, the ways staff work together, and the organization of the learning environment. This kind of information can add depth and dimension to a supervisor's knowledge and understanding of classroom life. It must not, however, be counted on as the major source of information for evaluation purposes.

Because informal observations are usually unfocused and are recorded, if at all, after the fact, what is likely to emerge is only a general impression of the room and the teachers, or a record of events or factors that stand out or are unusual in some way. If such visits are made to all rooms on a relatively regular basis, however, they decrease (but do not eliminate) the need for formal observation, and round out the supervisor's picture of life in the center.

Participant Observation

Participant observation is a method in which the inquirer has considerable involvement in the setting being studied. Anthropologists use this form of observation to "get inside" a culture so that they will be able to see the world as the members of the culture see it.

True participant observation goes beyond informal observation. Supervisors in this role must be very conscious of their perceptions, because they really play two roles: an observer who is responsible to the program as a whole, and a genuine participant in the classroom, who thus "has a stake in the group's activity and the outcome of that activity" (Guba & Lincoln, 1981, pp. 189–190).

Supervisors with teaching responsibilities who use observation as a supervisory tool are by definition participant observers of staff in their own rooms. When nonteaching supervisors use this method, however, they must take part in classroom activities and spend enough time in a classroom to immerse themselves in what is going on. Only then can they see the classroom through the eyes of the teachers and children and determine strategies for assistance from these viewpoints. This can be an especially valuable method for supervisors who work with staff or children whose cultural backgrounds differ from their own, or with teachers or programs whose early childhood goals or methods are very different from theirs. Teachers, too, can become participant observers. Some may be interested in learning to do "action research" (Cochran-Smith & Lytle, 1993) to study their own classrooms (see Chapter 12). Their journals and child observations can also be used as a basis for supervisory conferences or seminars.

Formal Observation

Formal observation differs from participant observation in that the supervisor remains aloof from the situation, observing as objectively as possible. Formal observations are recorded on the spot, and the observer does not take part in the classroom activity. A variety of recording systems can be used to observe in a formal way. These include open-ended systems, such as narrative descriptions of what is occurring, and systems that limit what is recorded to a set number of behaviors or events that the observer checks off or tallies. Because the observer is not taking part in the classroom activity and presumably has no stake in it, these records should be the most accurate of any of the three approaches.

METHODS OF OBSERVATION

The methods used in observing are usually divided into two categories: closed (also called quantitative) and open (also called qualitative or naturalistic). To some extent, each is based on a different assumption and point of view about the role of the observer. For supervisors, however, using both types contributes breadth and depth to their assistance to teachers.

Closed Systems

These systems grow out of the "scientific" view of supervision, stressing the use of methodology that limits the inferences that observers are required to make (thus "closed"). Methods of this type can be very useful when there is a need to focus on only certain elements out of all that is going on in a classroom. The observer tallies or codes behaviors as they occur, or checks off characteristics of the setting. When analyzing this data afterward the supervisor can see, for example, how many times a teacher responded verbally to children and how often she or he was unresponsive, or other similar information. The context, the exact words, and nonverbal nuances are not revealed, but the frequency of certain behaviors and, with some systems, the duration and sequence of events do emerge.

The limitations of these methods are that they can obscure individuality. The use of predetermined categories into which all teachers are expected to fit may, for example, make it difficult to take stylistic or cultural differences into account. Further, they do not lend themselves well to interpreting the meaning of behavior.

Procedures

The following procedures and instruments are those most commonly used for observing in classrooms. Each has its own advantages and limitations.

The simplest method is a *checklist*, a list of characteristics or behaviors that are simply checked off if they are present. See Figure 11.1 for an example.

Similar to checklists, is a method called a *sign system*. It differs only in that the observer tallies *every time* an activity or behavior occurs, either continuously or at time intervals.

A method that can be used when a supervisor and supervisee are interested in obtaining more information about a limited area of classroom life (for example, verbal interaction) is referred to as a *category system*. Within this limited area categories of behavior or events are listed ("praises," "responds using child's words," "asks direct questions"). Again, the observer tallies events as they occur or at specified intervals, sometimes using a coding system. The goal

Figure 11.1 Checklist

Teacher or aide available to talk to parent	
Teacher or aide greets each child	✓
Teachers encourage independence in taking off/hanging up coats	✓

is to see which of these actions take place and what their balance is within a segment of the day. An "other" category may be used to make sure that everything that happens is accounted for. (Examples of the use of sign and category systems are given in the case study later in this chapter.)

Rating scales have sometimes been used as observation instruments. However, they have limitations because the observer must decide on the spot the degree to which a teacher shows a particular characteristic (e.g., creative vs. rigid). These procedures are much better used to summarize information obtained from several observations and from other sources. Rating scales are discussed in Chapter 12, in the context of evaluation.

It sometimes makes sense to use or select from published teacher observation systems. The Child Development Associate (CDA) assessment system (Council for Early Childhood Professional Recognition, 1996) is very comprehensive. These systems, however, may not focus on the specific behaviors of concern at a particular time, so they may not be practical in day-to-day supervision. It often makes the greatest sense for observers to construct their own instruments.

Guidelines for Using Closed Systems

Consider the following points when creating or selecting observational instruments:

1. Decide on a focus. Think in terms of people, behaviors, context, and setting, and narrow the observation to the interaction of two of these.
2. Determine whether there is a need to record everything that takes place (category system) or only certain behaviors or events (checklist or sign system).
3. Decide whether merely noting that something is present is sufficient (checklist) or whether you would gain from having information on the frequency or sequence of events (sign or category).
4. Make sure that behaviors do not overlap. For example, "asks question" and "makes statement" are clearly different behaviors. "Asks question" and "talks to child" are not, since asking a question is a kind of talking.

5. Define each category precisely. Two people should be expected to agree that the behavior in question fits the category (one of the problems when using rating scales). Very broad categories ("warm behavior") make agreement more difficult. Very narrow ones ("points," "motions with open hand") usually do not provide much meaningful information unless they represent specific behaviors a caregiver is trying to develop or eliminate.
6. Keep the instrument simple. Since behavior is complex and occurs rapidly, it is better to make two or three different instruments than to cram too much into one.

Open Systems

In recent years, there has been a growing interest in open or naturalistic inquiry among both practitioners and researchers. At its most basic, this means writing down in continuous fashion everything that happens while observing in a classroom. Early childhood educators have used similar methods for observing children (Cohen, Stern, & Balaban, 1997), although perhaps not in systematic ways.

Narrative

Open systems, which make use of the ethnographic techniques developed for use in field studies, are based on the assumption that different people see events from different perspectives. The narrative helps them focus on "multiple realities that, like layers of an onion, nest within or complement one another" (Guba & Lincoln, 1981, p. 57). The observer tries to see the world from these differing points of view and to understand their relationships. Whereas observers using closed systems try to screen out human judgment from the process, naturalistic observers seek to sharpen and refine their judgment skills in order to become "more personally and environmentally sensitive" to what is unique in the situation and its meaning to the participants (p. 129).

The use of narratives can help teachers to become reflective, to construct their own knowledge about children and teaching, as discussed in Chapter 4. Elizabeth Jones (1993) and her colleagues have found this method especially helpful with adults with limited educational backgrounds, who have not had experience with constructive criticism. Narratives help teachers to "come to see themselves as *people who know*—thereby, people capable of making appropriate choices for themselves and for children" (p. xiii, emphasis in original). We have found this especially useful in CDA training.

Elliot Eisner (1982), in an approach he calls "connoisseurship," stresses the importance of recognizing each person's characteristic style, which should be developed and strengthened rather than molded into a particular "good teacher" model. This is especially important with supervisees whose interactions with children are influenced by a culture different from that of the supervisor. Eisner encourages supervisors to develop the ability to use rich language to convey their observations to supervisees.

Advocates of naturalistic methods point to their flexibility and to the detail that is made available to help observers discover what is happening below the surface. Teachers and supervisors are thus free to examine, interpret, and reexamine the descriptions in various ways as they make plans to improve performance. This process can enhance joint inquiry, reflection, and dialogue, helping teachers to construct their own knowledge.

There are limitations, however. Because observers are free to record anything that occurs but cannot get everything, there is a possibility of bias in what they focus on and in how they convey and interpret events to staff members. In addition, care must be taken so that descriptions do not become confused with judgments and interpretations.

A way to ensure that these two types of information are kept separate is to use a two-column format:

Description	*Comments*
Four children in house corner.	
Justin enters. Others continue	
with dialogue.	
J. gets down on floor.	
Marie (teacher) walks over, sits down.	M. is casual; doesn't intrude.
M: I like the way you're playing. . . .	
Who's the daddy?	
Beth: I'm the dog.	Has M. misinterpreted their
J: I'm the big dog.	theme?

We strongly advocate a system like this; it helps observers stay alert to the difference between description and interpretation, while making it possible to include feelings, thoughts, inferences from nonverbal cues, and questions to be followed up in the postobservation conference.

Guidelines for Using Open Systems

1. Develop an understandable (to you) shorthand system so you can get on paper as much as possible of what is taking place.
2. As soon as possible after the observation, while your memory is fresh, fill in whole words and details that you were not able to write down during the

observation itself. Edit the narrative where the language is imprecise or ambiguous.

3. As you become experienced in recording observations, try to use more descriptive language so that nuances can be conveyed more accurately. For example, instead of "T. goes over to Fred," use "strolls" or "strides with long deliberate steps" to convey the feeling tone of the child's actions. (Cohen et al., 1997, include wonderful examples of such language.)

4. When possible, get the exact words used by teachers or children. This helps teachers become sensitized to the impact of their words on others and become aware of their own verbal style. Describing or paraphrasing can change or make ambiguous the meaning of what was said. "Tells children to stop throwing sand" could have been "Stop that!" or "It's not nice to throw sand" or "Sand stays in the sandbox," each of which conveys a different message to the children.

5. Separate inferences and conclusions from the descriptive data. Avoid judgmental labeling such as "She was inflexible about that rule." Describe the behavior ("Immediately put child in chair") and perhaps add an interpretive comment ("Seemed to feel the rule must be upheld at all cost"). Recheck at the editing stage to ensure the objectivity of the narrative.

6. Note the time periodically in the margin to assist interpretation. If you become distracted or tired and lose some data, time checks alert the reader. Time checks also help portray the stream of events more accurately.

7. Finally, analyze the narratives for patterns of behavior or specific areas to be discussed in the postobservation conference or to be verified during subsequent observations. If the observation is made at the *discovery* stage of the clinical supervision cycle and with an open-ended agenda, you may have noted areas of concern or special interest during the observation itself for follow-up. If a specific focus was agreed on during the pre-observation conference, analysis should be made on the basis of that concern. A copy of the narrative can be shared with the supervisee to foster cooperative analysis.

Combined Systems

Supervisors have wide latitude in developing observation forms for specific purposes or situations, using any combination of closed and open systems. The specific needs or interests of the caregiver, the characteristics of the situation, and the supervisor's and caregiver's creativity are the only limitations beyond following the guidelines for construction of reliable observation instruments.

A system that combines tallying and description can be a very useful teaching tool. For example, a listing of behaviors that support a child's self-concept could include space for the exact language used by the teacher or a description of the specific incident (see Figure 11.2). Because both the specific behavior and the outcome are described, caregivers are able to see exactly what they do and how this behavior affects children. In the case illustrated, only positive behaviors are listed, allowing the supervisor to reinforce what is desirable, not emphasizing that which is not. This technique is especially useful with staff members who have had little experience with field supervision or training, and for whom positive feedback and confidence building are especially important.

Another method is to use a narrative but limit the focus to a few categories of behavior. In the example in Figure 11.3, used by a CDA trainer, some of the descriptors for the CDA Functional Area "Communication" have been listed (Council, 1996). This system provides a way for supervisors to observe and record only behaviors relevant to that area. Additional detail provides backup and feedback to the candidate.

Observations do not always have to be recorded in written form. Videotaping and audiotaping also have valuable places in supervisory observation, making available a permanent, credible record of what actually took place. The record is not limited by the observer's attentiveness, ability to write fast enough, or unconscious biases. Nonverbal as well as verbal nuances are captured, revealing the "feel" of classroom interaction. The material can be reviewed and analyzed in a variety of ways.

A major benefit of using such equipment is that caregivers are able to assess their own behavior, becoming less dependent on the supervisor, thus increasing the mutuality of the supervisory process. Since both supervisor and supervisee have the same information to work from—whether the teacher reviews the tapes alone, as is often desirable, or with a colleague, a group of colleagues, or a supervisor—real problem-solving can result. At the same time, hearing or seeing oneself directly is so powerful and even anxiety producing that caregivers should not be required to use these media. If you do use taping with your

Figure 11.2 Checklist with Comments

| Gets down to child's level | ✓ | Ch. tugs on T's shirt. T. squats down, asks Ch. to tell her what she wants. Ch. does. |
| Uses extended praise | ✓ | "You did a good job wiping up the spilled paint!" Ch. grins. Carefully puts sponge where it belongs. |

Figure 11.3 Focused Narrative

FUNCTIONAL AREA 6: COMMUNICATION

Name: __Chris G._____ Date: __3/5_____

Listens attentively to children, tries to understand what they want to communicate, and helps them express themselves.

Tran pulls at Chris's jeans. C: Yes, Tran, what is it? T. points. C: You'll have to tell me, Tran. T: Mark.... C: Yes — Mark...? T: Mark playing with my truck.

Talks with children about special experiences and relationships in their families and home lives.

Sees Teresa looking at Guinea pig. Picks it up and gives it to T. to hold. T: It's soft — like my kitty. C: Oh, you have a kitty? T: Yes. His name is Tigre. He gets lost sometimes. (Continues story.)

---

teachers, you should be especially sensitive in follow-up discussions as you try to assist the supervisee in identifying and analyzing what is significant and as you comment on or ask questions about the events that both of you have seen.

Group Observation

Most of these methods of observation can be used by teachers as well as supervisors as part of the group clinical supervision cycle described in Chapters 9 and 10. Very interesting insights can emerge when the information from individual observations is compared and analyzed. The data become "thicker" because each observer may record different aspects of what has been happening. The discussions that follow often bring broader or deeper meaning to the events than might be evident with a single observer.

Members of the group could be asked to observe different features of the learning experience they have planned to look at, based on the goals that have been set in the pre-observation conference. Some, for example, might focus only on children, others on the teacher. Different kinds of instruments could also be used, some using checklists or category systems, and others narratives. Again, in the postobservation conference this information must be integrated, along with the views of the teacher who was observed, in order to make it meaningful.

SPECIAL CONCERNS FOR SUPERVISORS
AS OBSERVERS

Observer Bias

At several points in our discussion of observation, we have emphasized the importance of discovering the meanings underlying the situations that you are observing. Any attempt to interpret meaning, of course, brings with it the possibility of misinterpretation, based on the limits of what you can perceive and on biases stemming from values and preconceptions. While these biases are natural and even legitimate at times, they must be brought to a conscious level or they will limit your ability to make accurate and meaningful observations.

Clearly, two people can see the same thing and interpret it differently: the parent who sees "just playing" and the caregiver who sees what the children are learning when they play; the teacher who sees May baskets for the children to take home and the supervisor who sees children who are bored or close to tears because the project is not developmentally appropriate; and the supervisor who is concerned because a Vietnamese caregiver does not use children's names while the caregiver is actually functioning in a culturally appropriate way (Binh, 1975).

One source of bias, as we noted earlier, is the complexity of the observational field, which can cause observers consciously or unconsciously to attend to some features and ignore others. One way to overcome this is for you to take time before recording to look around a room and take into account all that is going on and all the kinds of things that could be observed. Another is to practice recording with a colleague, noting differences in what you record. Reviewing your own observations periodically can also reveal patterns you may not have been aware of.

Another source of bias is preconceived expectations about a person or situation. Previous experience with a teacher as a fractious participant in staff meetings, a report on an aide indicating that she is lazy, or the observer's strong feelings about the use of nonstandard English grammar can influence what a supervisor looks for and the interpretation of what is seen. Conversely, when observing a person known to have especially good qualities, a supervisor may take more time to try to understand a problem situation or overlook issues that may be significant. Using a variety of observation tools, both open and closed, makes it more likely that you will view and interpret situations accurately, since they can be seen from different perspectives.

Cultural Differences

Teaching styles often differ based on the cultural values of individuals or a community. A study of Amish classrooms (Cazden, 1979) indicated that teachers used a very directive, even controlling, style of teaching. Because the teachers were from the same background as the children in this closed community, children understood this style quite differently than would children (or adults) who were not attuned to the expectations built up through a similar home and community environment. This directive style made sense for them within the context of everyday routines and was supported by an underlying trust, accountability, and warmth that outside observers may not have perceived or understood. Cazden also describes two bilingual first-grade classrooms, where children and teachers were all of Mexican-American background. Although their teaching styles (one open, one structured) differed, the teachers' styles of classroom control were quite similar. Both teachers used endearments and other behaviors characteristic of parents, such as kissing and holding children in their laps when working with them individually.

Supervisors unfamiliar with adult-child interactional patterns in either of these cultures might have judged the behavior of these teachers inappropriate. Conversely, the absence of such behaviors might seem problematic to an Amish or Mexican-American supervisor.

Observers in classrooms in which there are cultural or social-class differences must be especially concerned with looking for clues to the meaning of events to children and to adults. In such situations, data from both structured and naturalistic observations of children and adults aid in interpretation. Discussions with supervisees about the meaning of events during the *verification* and *explanation* phases of supervision are especially important when differences in cultural values are present. The discussions of cultural and linguistic issues in Chapters 10 and 13 provide additional information that can assist you as a supervisor and your teachers when observing in classrooms.

Personal Considerations

When one member of a classroom team is being observed, particularly if that person is an aide, staff relations may become strained. If you visit a teacher often for written observations, other staff members may feel inhibited, perhaps suspecting that they are being judged. Furthermore, when schedules are disrupted for supervisory conferences, even in a minor way, the change in normal routine can be unsettling and lead to hard feelings, especially when another caregiver has to take over in the staff member's absence.

You can avoid or alleviate much stress if you take time to make frequent contact with the teacher or other classroom staff members with an explanation of the purpose of the observations. Giving positive feedback from time to time to all classroom staff members and unobtrusively pitching in at busy times can temper many uneasy feelings. Staff members will often say that they do not mind these intrusions, but over a period of time, resentment can build if there are too frequent changes in patterns of responsibility or if communication is not maintained.

GENERAL GUIDELINES FOR OBSERVING

The following points relate to observing in classrooms in general. They can be helpful in establishing trust, making the act of observing a positive experience for you and your supervisees, and making records both reliable and useful.

1. When beginning an observation, especially if it is in an unfamiliar room, try to immerse yourself in what is happening. Try to become part of the world of the teachers and children so that the interrelatedness of its various aspects can be understood. It can be helpful to "map" the setting, noting the number of children and adults, including those who are non-English-speaking or bilingual, or have special needs; physical features, equipment, or materials that might affect what takes place, with perhaps a simple sketch of the room arrangements; and any other information that might assist in interpreting events.
2. Try to find an inconspicuous place to sit while observing. This decreases the pressure on the caregiver and lessens the disruption of the class as a whole. Curious children feel honored when told that someone is writing about what they are doing.
3. Plan with an individual caregiver or with the classroom team when formal written observations are to be made. This is basic to making them part of a cooperative learning experience, rather than subjects of an examination. Dropping in for a written (as opposed to informal) observation without notice or planning is seldom effective or necessary, except when there are serious concerns that cannot be documented in any other way.
4. Make several short observations so that you can discover and verify patterns of behavior. This avoids the problem of drawing conclusions based on a single observation.

5. Build time for observing and conferencing into your weekly schedule. This makes it more likely that it will actually happen. Even 10% of a 35-hour week is 3½ hours—a substantial amount if regularly planned.

PUTTING OBSERVATION TO WORK: A CASE STUDY

For the purpose of the following illustration, put yourself in the role of supervisor working with a teacher, Maria, who has been with your program for about 2 years. You will note that, in addition to a variety of observation methods, all the steps described in Garman's (1982) study are present. As supervisor you use a *discovery* mode in the early stages of observing the teacher. You then *verify* your hypothesis, *explain* by sharing points of view, *interpret* the meaning of events and behaviors, and *evaluate* in relation to what you and the supervisee think ought to be occurring.

Not all supervisors will be able to take the amount of time or use all of the methods described in this example—at least not very often. As you read this section, we suggest that you focus particularly on two things: the process of working with a supervisee using observation, and the use of various observational methods in context.

Sequence of Observations

As a result of her evaluation at the end of last year, you and Maria have agreed that she needs to work on improving how she organizes and manages free play. You have made informal visits to Maria's room in the last few weeks, sitting in with children during the free-play period. Your general impression was that she is warm with children and has a wonderful sense of humor. You observed that she has some interesting group activities that children are free to take part in during this time. The period is not chaotic, but a number of the children do a good deal of aimless wandering and occasional roughhousing. Not all areas of the room are used.

In your initial meeting with Maria to plan how you will work together, she seems unsure about the purpose of the free-play period. She knows that children "learn through play," but has never been quite sure what this means or what her role as teacher is. Her main concern about free play is that certain children "don't make use of their time effectively." You suggest that by observing what is actually happening, you may be able to find ways to help her restructure the program so that these children become more involved.

You begin with a naturalistic observation. Your mapping of the room indicates that there are a limited number of learning centers. The block area seems small, the furniture in the house and block areas is mostly lined up on one wall, there is a large open area in the middle of the room, and there are no places for privacy. Four to six children at a time were finger painting at one table. The others were in and out of water play, in the house corner, or at the easel. There was again a good deal of wandering and tussling, especially in the open area in the middle of the room.

In analyzing your narrative description, you note that Maria and her assistant seemed to function in two ways. Either they were in a kind of "rescuing" role, constantly responding to what wasn't going right, finding things for wandering children to do, cleaning up a spill, or stopping roughhousing; or they were "waiting on" children, responding to a child's request by getting materials, putting names on papers, hanging up wet paintings, telling children to let others have a turn, and even drawing a cat for a child who said he didn't know how.

During your next conference, you shared this observation with Maria, who said she was pleased with the finger-painting activity and that the children liked water play. In response to the description of aimless activity, she said that she had noticed that Roberto, Jared, and Vanessa often seemed to run out of things to do, acknowledging that she knew the block area of the room was not used much. She had recently seen a film on blocks and was interested in working on this area. When you discussed what she thought about the teacher's role in free play, she stated, "To make sure children have what they need, and to prevent and solve problems."

Although you are concerned about the overall picture of free play and Maria's limited perception of her role, you agree to work with her on the block area, using observation as a tool. It is something she is interested in, and by working in this limited area, you may be able to help her develop techniques that will help her with free play as a whole. It is also a logical place to involve the restless children.

Focus on the Children

You and Maria decide that your first focused observations will be used to verify what children do in the block corner and in the room as a whole during free play. There are several advantages to beginning with observations of children. First, it is often easier for teachers to look at children's behavior than at their own, especially if they have not been observed before. Second, observing children can serve as a means of verification and explanation of what actually is happening. Third, it puts the teaching role into perspective by looking at children first, focusing on learning rather than teaching.

The major disadvantage to an initial focus on children's behavior is that it may divert attention from the caregiver's behavior at a time when changes need to be made. Nevertheless, focusing on the children first can create a base from which to work with the caregiver because of the information that is revealed.

In order to develop a set of categories, you and Maria brainstorm about what could or should take place in the block corner. You discuss what kinds of behaviors she would like to see there, what might go on that is inappropriate, and how categories can be defined with as little ambiguity as possible.

A list of many possible behaviors is eventually whittled down to a few. They are described and defined as you construct a manageable observation tool. The discussion that leads to this point helps Maria—and you as supervisor—think more specifically about goals for children in the block area and in free play in general.

You choose the following categories:

- *Building*—Interacting with blocks in any constructive way, or with accessories related to blocks; knocking buildings over if clearly acceptable to those involved
- *Other constructive play*—Using materials from another area; playing exclusively with accessories (trucks, people) without involving blocks
- *Watching*—Observing; passive behavior; not actively part of block play but present in the area
- *Nonconstructive play*—Interfering with others, nonconstructive block play, unrelated rough play in area
- *Other*—All other behavior (where possible, note specific behavior)

Using this form you can periodically record the number of children in each type of activity. The "other" listing ensures that you can capture all of what goes on. The form can be refined if in actual use you find that you must use the "other" category too often, or that a category is too limited or too broad.

Recording at approximately 3–minute intervals during a 15-minute observation should provide enough data to reveal patterns of activity within one free play period (see Figure 11.4). By doing several of these over a period of days, you will get more meaningful information.

You also decide to construct an instrument to use in observing the free-play period as a whole, listing all the areas of the room. Here you record the number of children in each area. (When you use time intervals, it is sometimes possible to use two forms during the same observation period, alternating between the two.) Figure 11.5 shows the patterns of play on a different day from the block area observation above.

On examining the free-play observations, Maria discovers that they confirm the low use not only of blocks but also of manipulatives and books. At the same time, she is uncomfortable about the number of children who are "uninvolved." For Maria the use of this form has seemed more objective than your initial narrative.

Figure 11.4 First Instrument

Block Area Room **Maria** Date **10/20**

Time begun **9:15** Time ended **9:30**

Behavior	9:15	18	21	24	27	30
Building					2	2
Other Constructive Play		1	1 *			
Watching						
Non-constructive Play						
Other						

Comments: * Lenny takes out a truck, wheels it around for a while, then "drives" it out to central area.

Figure 11.5 Second Instrument

Free Play Room **Maria** Date **10/21**

No. of Children **14** No. of Adults **2**

Time begun **9:20** Time ended **9:35**

Activity	Time 9:20	:23	:26	:29	:32	:35
Directed	5	5	4	2	3	3
Manipulatives	2			1		
Blocks		1	2			
Easel	2	2		2	1	1
House			3	3	3	2
Books					1	1
Water Play	5	4	3	2	3	4
Uninvolved		2	2	4	3	3

Comments: Children in finger paint area changed. Water + house had same core of children — same ones as yesterday.

Maria goes to the center library and looks through *The Block Book* (Hirsh, 1984) and the section on blocks in *The Creative Curriculum for Early Childhood* (Dodge & Colker, 1992) to discover new ideas about what children can learn from block play, to formulate clear goals for that area, and to identify ways to arrange the area for greater involvement. After discussing these ideas with her assistant, together they make plans to rearrange the entire room to make the block area larger. Since this affects the other areas as well, Maria and her assistant rethink the goals of all the underused areas in the room. Over the next several weeks, things begin to change and Maria is excited! She is now concerned, however, that although children use the block area more, they are not building as elaborately as she would like.

Focus on the Teacher

As you and Maria discuss ways to enhance the children's play, you bring up your original concern that she and her assistant seem to spend much of their time rescuing things and waiting on children. She agrees that although the children are functioning more independently and she has more time, she still does not spend much time sitting with children while they play. It had not previously occurred to her that she could actually plan for free play. You suggest that she read "Interacting with Children in the Block Corner" (Dodge & Colker, 1992).

Based on the examples in Dodge's chapter, you and Maria develop categories for another observation (see Figure 11.6). This instrument uses a system that focuses only on specific behaviors (*sign system*), not all those that could occur.

As a result of this observation, you discover that Maria has relied heavily on direct questions and suggestions rather than on the indirect behaviors illustrated in the article. The change from asking convergent questions like "What color is it?" to "How could"–type questions or descriptive statements is not easy. Your postobservation discussion with Maria reveals that she isn't convinced that the children will learn as much if she uses indirect language. She needs a chance to come to terms with this idea, to practice new skills, and to find a balance that makes sense to her. You feel comfortable that she is now looking at free play in a different way and will continue to find ways to make it a positive experience for the children. You leave her with the suggestion that she do some participant observation and journal writing about children's responses to her statements and questions, evaluating which kinds encourage more elaborate building, problem-solving, and experimentation. She can call on you to observe her or the children again when she feels ready to do so.

This hypothetical sequence of observations illustrates some of the ways supervisors and supervisees can work together to improve teaching and learn-

Figure 11.6 Third Instrument

Teacher's Verbal Encouragement: Block Play

Labels what child does	|	*1*
Asks "What if" questions	| |	*2*
Asks child to label	┼┼┼ |	*6*
Makes direct suggestions	|||	*3*

Definitions:

Labels: "You've used a *square* block." "The truck went right *through* the building instead of going *around*."

"What if" questions: "What would happen if you used a bigger one?" "Would it fall if you used a different block?"

Asks child to label: "What shape is this?" "Is this taller or shorter than your block?"

Direct suggestions: "It won't fall if you put bigger ones on the bottom." "This one would work better."

ing. Many of these observations could have been made using a naturalistic mode, providing a more holistic, but less focused, view. Another alternative would be to have the caregiver do the observations of the children, which would allow him or her more direct knowledge of what is happening. This has the disadvantage, however, of removing his or her own influence from the dynamics of the situation.

Since there are a number of problems or situations that tend to recur with different teachers over the years, instruments that you have developed for one situation can be used with little alteration in a number of others. The free-play form (refer to Figure 11.5), for example, could also be used to examine teachers' activities during free play. By writing in staff members' initials at periodic intervals, a classroom team could have their own behavior mapped to help them plan strategies for cooperating more effectively.

CONCLUSION

Observation is a fundamental tool for staff growth and change, serving as the major source of the content of supervisory conferences. It enables supervisors to provide feedback on what actually goes on in classrooms, providing a credible basis for planning improvements in classroom practices. When supervisors are able to spend time in classrooms informally while regularly scheduling time for more formal observations, trust is developed, making it less likely that they will need to observe only in crisis situations.

As both supervisors and supervisees become skilled inquirers about classroom life they will find many advantages to planning together what is to be observed and discussed, analyzing the data and discussing how they will follow up.

EXERCISES

These excercises are most effective when done "live" in a classroom, but videotapes can also be used. Be sure to have a postobservation conference with the person observed.

1. Develop a list of categories that could be observed during circle time or small-group time. These could include teacher and/or child behaviors or environmental factors. Develop a form from a few of these, try it out, and refine it.
2. Develop a checklist or "sign" system, based on similar information, using either only behaviors you want to encourage or examples of both positive and negative behaviors. Try your system out and refine it.
3. Do a naturalistic observation using the two-column system—one for description, the other for comments. Role-play or carry out a conference with the supervisee to identify a specific focus for another observation.
4. If you are teaching, become a participant observer of your own classroom by setting aside a few minutes each day to focus on one dimension of classroom life. Use this technique to analyze your own program or as a way to assess strengths and needs of assistants or volunteers who work with you. (See Chapter 12 for more detail on action research.)
5. Participate in one of two groups who are to observe the same situation, focusing on the same concern, for example, a teacher's use of encouraging behaviors. One group should use a naturalistic system, and the other, a closed system. Compare the information, and discuss it in terms of the usefulness of each for ongoing staff development or evaluation.
6. Try out one of the published observation systems; for example, the NAEYC *Guide to Accreditation* (1998); CDA (Council, 1996); or Harms, Clifford, and Cryer (1998).
7. Discuss how supervisors in different kinds of settings can find time to observe.

12

Evaluating Staff

Evaluating, judging, examining, appraising, and rating connote behaviors that seem contrary to the humanistic ideals dear to early childhood educators; yet probably no other supervisory process has the *potential* to affect the quality of learning experiences for children as much as what staff members learn about themselves.

The great variability in experience and education levels among professionals and paraprofessionals within early childhood programs suggests a strong need for staff evaluation. It also places great demands on directors who struggle with the dual roles of fostering the growth of staff members at different points in their professional development and making personnel decisions about them, while confronting the serious problems associated with staff turnover.

Through evaluation, directors and other supervisors acquire information about their programs and staff members that can be used to make informed decisions as they plan for the future. Also, staff members receive formal feedback about their performance, which can be useful to them in making career plans. An informal survey of early childhood program directors yielded the following purposes of evaluation:

- To make judgments about staff performance
- To recommend that staff be rehired, fired, promoted, or reassigned
- To note the progress of staff members
- To reward staff
- To motivate staff
- To assist staff in improving their teaching/caregiving
- To improve the quality of overall services provided to children
- To meet requirements of outside funding agencies
- To ensure that program goals are being met
- To set goals for the future

Although there is overlap among the stated reasons for evaluating staff and among the implied tasks, the major purposes of evaluation remain: (1) to obtain information for making personnel decisions and (2) to foster the professional development of staff members in order to improve instruction and care.

EVALUATION TERMINOLOGY

There are several terms that are frequently used in connection with staff evaluation. These include *supervision, assessment, authentic assessment,* and *evaluation,* both *formative* and *summative.*

Throughout this text, we have equated the term *supervision* with the concept of ongoing support and professional development of staff members. Leaders in the field of supervision, however, continue to disagree over whether staff evaluation should be thought of as separate from or a part of supervision. As evaluation can be growth-promoting and as those holding administrative and supervisory responsibility are normally expected to evaluate staff as part of their job descriptions, we believe that a legitimate aspect of supervision is the process of evaluating staff—that is, the act of judging the effectiveness of a staff member's performance.

Formative evaluation is an ongoing process that provides teachers and others with regular feedback about their programs and their performance to effect transformation and growth. Staff members do not have to wait until the end of the year to receive constructive suggestions or to know what supervisors think about their work.

Supervisors and others collect data in a variety of ways, including conferences with staff members, videotapes, observation instruments, and checklists to *assess* the presence of and the degree to which staff members possess certain qualities and teaching/caregiver competencies. Formative evaluation is comparable to ongoing *assessment.*

Recently, the term *authentic assessment* has been used in connection with the evaluation of both children's learning and teachers' effectiveness. By having teachers document and collect data based on the work that they actually do with children each day in their classrooms, evaluation is more authentic and is broad in its scope.

In contrast to formative evaluation, which takes place regularly and over time, *summative* evaluation takes place at the end of a specified time period, when an administrator or supervisor "sums up" the effectiveness of a staff member's performance, letting that person know where he or she stands against certain predetermined standards. In summative evaluation, the "big picture" or overall performance is considered. The time established for summative evaluation may be set by a board, the director or a funding source. Summative evaluation is a formal, legal process; it must be described in a program's personnel policy or teacher contract and is usually approved by a board of directors.

SOME GUIDELINES FOR STAFF EVALUATION

Effective evaluation programs are characterized by a culture of professionalism. Directors are sometimes reluctant to evaluate staff members for fear of creating more staff turnover, but in reality, evaluation can have the opposite effect. It is a process that has the potential to assist staff members in internalizing the concept that they are professionals (Duff, Brown, & Van Scoy, 1995). Working in an environment in which there are high standards for staff can actually raise the professional self-images of staff members and promote greater retention of staff within a program. Trust, respect, openness, communication, and a commitment to strong evaluation are enabling conditions that foster a culture of professionalism within a program (McLaughlin & Pfeifer, 1988).

Evaluation processes and plans should recognize the various developmental levels of staff members. The purpose, frequency, depth, procedures, information collected, and personnel involved should be different for beginners, for example, than for experienced staff (Peterson, 1995). Evaluation should emphasize the strengths of staff members, building on the skills they have and assisting them in acquiring new knowledge and competencies so that it is viewed as a helping process rather than a punitive one (Bloom et al., 1991). A program's career ladder or lattice, with defined roles and rewards, can offer a structure for designing an evaluation plan and a basis for tying it to a program's professional development plan.

Teacher involvement is essential in the design and implementation of any evaluation plan if it is to be successful. A sense of ownership of the evaluation process enables staff to perceive it as meaningful, one that can have a positive effect on practice. This means that teachers should help to develop the evaluation plan and feel a sense of authority over the process. Whenever possible, staff members should have opportunities to work in pairs, teams, and groups as they design and implement the evaluation plan.

Opportunities for reflection and analysis should be woven into a program's evaluation plan whenever possible. Reflective journal entries in portfolios, conferences with peers and supervisors, and completion of self-evaluation instruments are examples of activities that can assist staff members in thinking about and refining their practice.

Evaluators who are culturally responsive take into account the cultural values they bring to the evaluation process, and the cultural lenses through which they view and interpret the teaching/learning process. They strive to assist staff in developing a cultural awareness of the impact of their teaching and caregiving.

Time is a valuable commodity in the daily lives of supervisors and teachers. Yet if evaluation is to be taken seriously by staff and if it is to be a thoughtful process, then adequate time must be set aside for evaluation activities.

WHO EVALUATES?

Should supervisors have the sole responsibility for evaluating, or should supervisees, other staff members, parents, and children be involved? We suggest that a broad range of individuals participate in the process of evaluating staff members. In this way, data are obtained from multiple sources.

Supervisors

Whether director, educational coordinator, or head teacher, the supervisor by virtue of position has the authority and responsibility for evaluating staff. The supervisor is accountable for the program and therefore is concerned about its quality.

Supervisors have the experience and expertise to make judgments. Most likely, they have observed and conferred with staff members over time and have conducted training sessions with them as well. This ongoing process enables them to assess the professional development of individuals and to have a sound data base for evaluation. They are also familiar with the children, parents, and community so they understand the context in which staff members work. Supervisors may also have developed the procedures for evaluating staff in cooperation with the staff as well as with board members.

For all these reasons, supervisors are central to the evaluation process, but, as indicated earlier, they need not be the only individuals who evaluate.

Supervisees

Self-evaluation requires that individuals take time to reflect about their progress. This can be an insightful and rewarding experience, enabling them to note gains and setbacks, and to set personal goals for the future.

Although all staff members benefit by evaluating themselves, our experience suggests that self-evaluation is easier for supervisees who are already analytical and reflective. Some staff members may need ideas and structure to help them think about their progress. This might take the form of an instrument in which they are asked to state goals and strategies for reaching them. Such a self-evaluation tool could be jointly developed with staff, who could be introduced to readings that stimulate reflection—for example, "Teachers Developmental Stages" (Katz, 1977) or "Pathways to Professional Effectiveness for Early Childhood Educators" (Vander Ven, 1988), referred to in Chapter 5.

Supervisory conferences lay the groundwork for self-evaluation, for it is through conference dialogue that staff members practice reflecting, predicting, judging, and suggesting alternatives to caregiving and teaching behaviors. Through practice, patience, and hard work on the part of supervisors and supervisees, most staff members can learn to become skilled self-evaluators.

A drawback to self-evaluation is that supervisees sometimes underrate or overrate themselves, but individuals usually know themselves and the quality of their work better than anyone else. Also, teachers may be reluctant to make statements about what they can't do well. If they feel free from external threat, self-evaluation can empower staff. They have an opportunity to judge themselves and to respect their own judgments. They also become better at it with the help of supportive supervisors.

Peers

In addition to assisting in the design of a program's evaluation plan, peers can be involved in the assessment and evaluation process itself. Directors may be able to establish a structure within programs to enable peers to assess each other's work. Colleagues can be particularly helpful to each other in working on areas that supervisor and supervisee have agreed need improvement, perhaps by serving in mentor roles, or by working in pairs or groups. When colleagues participate in peer supervision—that is, observing the teaching of peers and providing them with feedback—a program gains the advantage of their expertise, and staff members acquire further opportunities for growth. Peer or group supervision described in Chapter 9 can build colleagueship and allow the director more time to engage in other important tasks. Peers can also participate in the selection and evaluation of materials that a teacher places in a portfolio.

Parents

Parents informally evaluate early childhood programs. They judge staff members and programs by continuing to send their children to a center or by withdrawing them. Parents can be asked to evaluate staff more formally by completing anonymous questionnaires as is done in the Child Development Associate (CDA) credentialing process (see Chapter 14).

Soliciting the views of parents can increase their support and enthusiasm for a program and can enhance its climate. Critical to their successful participation, however, is the method used to involve them as well as the ways in which staff members are prepared for parental involvement. Parents need to be informed about why their help is requested, to understand the nature of the actual power they have, and to know appropriate protocol and behavior for participating in the evaluation process.

Children

Measures of children's growth and learning comprise another source of data to assess effective teaching. Vartuli and Fyfe (1993) believe that samples of children's work reflecting their language development and artistic, social-interaction, and problem-solving abilities could be collected to illustrate children's progress as well as teaching effectiveness.

SOURCES OF EVALUATION CRITERIA

In developing instruments for assessment and evaluation, program administrators, supervisors, and staff members will need to determine the criteria on which individuals in each role will be evaluated. There are several helpful sources for determining these criteria.

The concept behind the National Association for the Education of Young Children (NAEYC) career ladder and lattice of early childhood professional development (described in Chapter 3) is based on common elements that define what all early childhood professionals must know and be able to do (Willer, 1994). These are listed below. They represent a shared knowledge base for all early childhood professionals. The acquisition of these common elements will enable early childhood educators to assume higher levels of responsibility and to work in diverse settings (Bredekamp & Willer, 1992). The common elements are as follows:

- demonstrate an understanding of *child development* and apply this knowledge in practice;
- *observe and assess children's behavior* in planning and individualizing teaching practices and curriculum;
- establish and maintain a *safe and healthy environment* for children;
- *plan and implement developmentally appropriate curriculum* that advances all areas of children's learning and development, including social, emotional, intellectual, and physical competence;
- establish supportive relationships with children and implement developmentally appropriate techniques of *guidance and group management*;
- establish and maintain positive and productive *relationships with families*;
- support the development and learning of individual children, recognizing that children are best understood in the context of *family, culture, and society*; and
- demonstrate an understanding of the early childhood profession and make a commitment to *professionalism*. (Willer, 1994, p. 13)

Additional sources for identifying criteria for evaluation are administrators and staff members themselves. Asking staff members to keep track of their time, to describe their daily activities and their perceptions of their roles, and to identify the qualities, knowledge, and skills they believe to be important in carrying out their jobs is a worthwhile staff development endeavor as well as a practical source for evaluation criteria and job descriptions.

Other sources of criteria are the Child Development Associate (CDA) competency standards (see Appendix C), and those that appear in NAEYC's (1998) *Guide to Accreditation* by the National Academy of Early Childhood Programs.

APPROACHES TO EVALUATION
AND THE CAREER LADDER

In designing evaluation that is based on stages of career development, there are several questions to consider:

1. Which evaluation practices make sense for staff given their needs and experience levels?
2. Which evaluation practices should be required and which should be optional given staff stages of development?
3. How do the roles of the evaluator(s) and staff members change at different points of the career ladder?
4. As staff members acquire experience and expertise, should the criteria on which they are evaluated change?
5. As one moves up the career ladder from teacher aide to head or master teacher, should the frequency of evaluation vary?
6. At what point should evaluation focus less on determining the presence of competencies and more on professional development?

As you and your staff members design an evaluation plan within the career-ladder concept, you might wish to consider some of the approaches to evaluation described below. The first practice noted, using tools and reports, is a traditional one in which supervisors have major responsibility and control. The approaches that follow—portfolios, storytelling, learning communities, action research, and long-range goal setting—are more inquiry-oriented, place more responsibility in the hands of staff members, and are more closely linked to professional development. We consider them to be evaluation approaches, however, as they encourage staff to study, to analyze their practice, and to change it. You may want to use a combination of traditional methods with those promising practices that have been developed more recently, keeping in mind the career stages of staff members.

Tools and Reports

Tools and reports commonly used in evaluating staff have a quantitative emphasis, a qualitative orientation, or a combination of both; below we offer two examples.

Rating Scales

The quantitative approach is based on specific criteria that researchers, practitioners, and policymakers have deemed essential to professionals in a field. These criteria or competency statements, such as the CDA standards mentioned above, can be modified to create rating scales that ask evaluators to indicate the presence of specific competencies and to rate the extent to which a staff member manifests them. Figure 12.1 shows a sample page from a rating scale.

Rating scales can be administered with relative ease, depending on their length. The competencies to be evaluated are explicit and available to supervisor and supervisee at the beginning of the evaluation period. Those with numerous competency statements can seem overwhelming and perhaps a bit unrealistic to the supervisee, yet they can be useful as both formative and summative evaluation tools. Teacher rating scales do not provide the reader with personal or specific examples and illustrations of a staff member's behavior, and they should not be used as instruments for observing teaching in the clinical supervision cycle.

There are a number of published rating scales that are commonly used for assessing program, rather than staff, characteristics. These include the *Early Childhood Environment Rating Scale* (ECERS), (Harms et al., 1998), and those for family day care (FDCRS, 1989), infant and toddler care (ITERS, 1990), and school-age child care (SACERS, 1995).

Descriptive Reports

Descriptive evaluation reports, often called narratives, are qualitative in nature. A greater emphasis is placed on the meaning and quality of the experiences that children and staff members have in classrooms. Rather than rating a teacher on specific competencies, supervisors are more concerned with context and setting, with understanding and describing how teachers and children engage each other, and with discovering the assumptions that underlie classroom practices.

These narrative reports are statements that describe what a supervisor has observed over a period of time rather than during a single observation, as discussed in Chapter 11. As summative reports, they include a supervisor's judgments and recommendations with regard to a staff member's performance. The format of this report can be open-ended, but some narrative instruments provide evaluators with more structure by asking for comments on such general areas as knowledge of child development, planning, behavior management, establishing classroom learning environments, teacher-child interaction, interpersonal communication, professional development, personal qualities, relations with parents and community, and nonteaching responsibilities. Some

Figure 12.1 Evaluation Rating Scale

Understanding Behavior: Children

1. Is able to make natural, spontaneous conversation with children; appears to gain satisfaction and pleasure from interacting with them

0	1	2	3	4	5
serious problems	limited	adequate	good	superior	outstanding

2. Understands what is developmentally appropriate behavior for children of a given age (i.e., nature of play, interest spans, social relationships, and so forth)

0	1	2	3	4	5
serious problems	limited	adequate	good	superior	outstanding

3. Is aware of children's feelings and able to identify a range of affective behaviors such as fear, jealousy, anger, joy

0	1	2	3	4	5
serious problems	limited	adequate	good	superior	outstanding

4. Interacts with children with sensitivity to the possible causes of behavior; exercises an understanding of individuality

0	1	2	3	4	5
serious problems	limited	adequate	good	superior	outstanding

5. Actively seeks to understand and implement change in his or her own behavior as it affects working with children (i.e., issues of authority, anger, competition, insecurity, and so forth)

0	1	2	3	4	5
serious problems	limited	adequate	good	superior	outstanding

Source: Department of Child Study, Tafts University, Medford, Mass.

supervisors and supervisees like this type of instrument because it can help them sort out the important issues to be considered and what needs to be done.

The advantage of this type of evaluation approach is that it gives the evaluator(s) space to set a context and to describe and illustrate with examples; and it can be very thorough, offering the reader a substantial amount of specific information. Descriptive or narrative evaluation reports provide a lasting record, highlight patterns of behavior, and encourage evaluators to be thought-ful. On the other hand, writing a summative report is time-consuming. Its open-ended quality may not provide enough structure for the evaluator(s), who may overemphasize some areas and leave out others just as crucial. The narrative report is compatible with a naturalistic view of evaluation, but some believe it is simply too open-ended and relies on the evaluator's values to a greater extent than need be.

Following is an example of a summative evaluation written by the direc-tor of a program whose goals include a strong emphasis on play and child-initiated learning and on parent participation, including volunteering in class-rooms and active board membership. Kate is a kindergarten teacher in her second year in this program.

> Kate has been intrigued by open education and sees her most impor-tant goal as what she calls community building. As she is aware, at the beginning of this year, there were complaints from parents about Kate's methods of guidance of children's behavior, and that she was not doing enough to prepare children academically.
>
> As I observed Kate during the year, I found some real strengths in terms of her loving and nurturing interactions with children, her very special ways of developing positive communication among the chil-dren, and her work with individual children, especially those with problems. In the latter case, she worked all year with a child who had had a traumatic experience at home, developing relevant classroom experiences, and including his parents in her plans. In addition, her classroom has indeed become a community in terms of children's social exchanges, and their gaining respect for one another.
>
> It was evident, however, that the parents' concerns had some merit. I have been working with Kate to help her understand the need to set expectations for children, and to follow up on them. She is beginning to see that doing this helps children to become more self-disciplined, rather than pressuring them, as she feared. She no longer takes the phrase "open classroom" literally. For example, instead of sitting and waiting for long periods of time for children to pay atten-tion at the beginning of circle time, she has found ways within her own style to let them know what she expects them to do.
>
> Kate also needs to think about how to build in more specific ways to develop literacy and math skills. Her fear of overstructuring has made it hard for her to work in this area. She is beginning to see that children need to be challenged, and that this is different from pushing them. We have been discussing ways for her to arrange the room environment so that each area can contribute to the educational program.

Kate has moved a long way in her relations with parents. She has had a hard time understanding the legitimacy of the parents' concerns, especially in their wanting more academic preparation for children. She said that she didn't feel it was necessary to explain why she was doing what she was doing. She has developed a good system for sharing developmental information with parents, for example, but she is so indirect with them that they don't always understand what she means. Recently, Kate has begun to share her goals and methods with parents, and to respond to their questions, rather than telling them what she thinks they want to hear when she is criticized. This process has forced her to articulate her philosophy and given her confidence, and the parents love it!

Kate and I have agreed on four goals for her to pursue next year: to improve her skills in guidance of children's behavior; to find developmentally appropriate ways for children to acquire literacy and math skills; to design a more comprehensive means of documenting assessment, such as using portfolios; and to continue to improve her skills in parent communication.

Robert Fraser (1982) offers the following principles and suggestions for writing summative evaluation reports:

1. Focus on strengths; be specific in citing what it is you thought was good and why.
2. Try to be positive and supportive but be judicious about the use of superlatives.
3. Focus on specific behaviors; simply stating that someone is well-organized is insufficient. Be specific about the facts that have led you to make that inference.
4. Set forth any and all areas of concern. State exactly what you have observed which concerns you, why it concerns you, and what you expect to be done about it.
5. After you have written a statement, ask yourself how you would prove it to be true if you had to.
6. Use the written evaluation reports as a means of focusing on "growing edges."
7. Don't be afraid to set expectations relative to the next evaluation cycle or school year.
8. Avoid the use of "professional jargon"; write so that a third party who knows nothing about the situation will get a clearer picture of the teacher you are describing.
9. Don't use qualifying or equivocal terms. "Hedge words" have no place in

an evaluation. You are presumably an expert rendering an informed opinion about what you know.

10. Don't be apologetic if something is unsatisfactory; say it.
11. Have another qualified administrator read your evaluations in "draft form" before you present them to the teacher involved.

Portfolios

Portfolio development, long used in the Child Development Associate credential program, is a means of assisting staff members in learning more about themselves and helping advisors and evaluators to gain a more complete picture of teaching, caregiving, and learning in a particular setting. Portfolios are collections of materials designed to represent various aspects of a classroom's program, as well as teaching activities and teachers' reflections about their practice, often centered around particular competencies. These materials might include a combination of the following: a teacher's statement of personal philosophy and goals, sample journal entries, lesson plans, samples of children's work to document their development, photographs, videotapes, letters of recommendation, reports to parents, lists of professional activities, and a statement of self-evaluation.

An examination of portfolio materials should enable supervisor, staff member, and peers to raise questions and to draw inferences about the teacher's assumptions of how young children learn, what the teacher values, how children spend their time, and the ways in which teacher and children interact. These inferences can be validated by classroom observations and by engaging in dialogue with classroom teachers in portfolio conferences.

Supervisors can serve as facilitators in portfolio development by establishing a means for staff members to assist each other in the creation of portfolios and in the assessment of portfolio contents. Supervisors, for example, might lead group sessions with staff in which they discuss how they are going to illustrate a specific competency in their portfolios, form teams of staff members who assist each other in the selection of portfolio entries, or facilitate collaborative assessment conferences (Seidel, 1998) in which teachers come together to describe, discuss, and interpret a portfolio entry, such as a sample of children's art work or writing.

The use of portfolios as a form of assessment, however, raises several concerns (Wolf, 1991). Portfolios can be very bulky and unwieldy and evaluating their contents can be very time-consuming. Giving a portfolio a focus by asking staff to collect entries on a few competency areas each year, however, is a possible solution to this problem. How materials should be displayed in portfolios, how many entries are appropriate, and whether entries should demonstrate teacher growth or simply represent a teacher's best work are questions that must be resolved when formulating a portfolio assessment process.

Portfolios may undervalue the strengths of effective teachers who excel in areas such as personal interactions with children (Peterson, 1995), an area that is more difficult to represent in the form of materials. On the other hand, portfolios provide a rich data source for personal reflection and for dialogue on the quality of classroom events and experiences and shift the locus of control of the assessment process from supervisors to teachers.

Storytelling

Storytelling is a powerful communication tool that encourages reflection on practice and professional growth and development. Stories, whether oral or written, are a means of sharing our personal versions of the world around us, and by telling them or writing them down and engaging in dialogue with ourselves or others as we repeat our stories, we can clarify our thinking about particular issues, about people or contexts, and refine our behavior.

Storytelling is a way of learning (Egan, 1987). Bruner (1996) describes narrative as a mode of thinking and a structure for organizing our knowledge. In certain oral cultures, storytelling is an art form and important messages are embedded in stories. Stories also serve to strengthen relationships among community members and to transmit cultural values.

Personal narratives or stories, in the form of case studies, have been used as a means of teacher preparation to help develop professional ways of thinking. By reading and writing case studies, students learn to "think like a teacher," to frame problems, to design strategies, and to explore moral and technical issues that are a part of everyday teaching (Kleinfeld, 1988). Vignettes and case studies have also been used to successfully train mentor teachers (Shulman & Colbert, 1987).

It is exciting to think about how to incorporate personal narrative or stories into the assessment process. Certainly autobiography as a form of self-assessment and even short vignettes about daily teaching experiences, which can be shared and discussed with others, offer simple yet potentially effective possibilities for helping staff to gain confidence, discover their own knowledge, and reflect on their work.

Learning Communities

Another vision of an inquiry-oriented and collaborative approach to assessment and professional development is the concept of teacher learning communities. In addition to helping teachers to be more effective (Lieberman &

Miller, 1992; Little, 1990), learning communities offer teachers the possibility of being part of a caring and interconnected culture in which values are shared. Key ideas in the concept of learning communities are that the agenda of such groups arises from the needs and interests of teachers, that there is an emphasis on inquiring about and learning from practice, and that teachers have control over such groups.

Learning communities take a variety of forms and may include a range of people. Some groups might consist of staff members within the same program or from several programs. Others might include supervisors, advisers, and university professors. Communities might come together to conduct action research on a topic of mutual interest as described below or simply to engage in "story swapping" (Little, 1990), that is, sharing experiences and commiserating about their work with children. Communities might also take the form of study groups that explore a theme such as "Learning through play," in which group members select and discuss readings, view films or videotapes, and discuss personal observations. Between meetings, group members use new insights to improve their practice.

A promising new practice is the creation of learning communities called Critical Friends Groups. Meyer and Achinstein (1998) describe critical friendship as "a model of collective inquiry that champions the co-construction of knowledge through talk" (p. 6). It is one that builds on the notion of friendship. Our friends, after all, are our *advocates.* They *care* about us and we have a *shared history* with them. Because we *trust* them we can accept criticism and advice from them and offer the same in a relationship that is *reciprocal.* In groups of friends one is able to obtain multiple perspectives on an issue. Central to Critical Friends Groups is critique that takes the form of probing and questioning that fosters serious reflection and change regarding beliefs and practice.

In a study of Critical Friends Groups of novice teachers at Stanford University, Meyer and Achinstein (1998) describe a structure for group meetings, which last from 20 to 90 minutes. Groups begin with a "check-in" followed by a "charrette." Check-in is a time for group members to get to know each other and to eventually form a bond of friendship. This activity is one in which all members of the group give a brief update of their personal and professional lives. Charrettes, often used by architects or city planners when beginning new projects, are group-process brainstorming sessions, in which many new ideas are generated. During the charrette process in Critical Friends Groups, a teacher-presenter brings an artifact for discussion and sets the context for it. At the conclusion of often dynamic discussions around the issues, ideas, and experiences connected with the artifact, the meeting is summarized and sometimes members write in their journals.

Dunne and Honts (1998) found that Critical Friends Groups pass through several developmental stages. The first stage is one in which group members build trust with one another. In Stage 2, they begin to talk about what they do in classrooms and how to improve what they do. Fundamental questions, particularly as they relate to school and community, are addressed in stage three.

Critical Friends Groups, which meet outside of the school day and which consist of staff from a variety of settings, could be sponsored by a local professional association, a consortium of early childhood programs, or a college or university partnership.

Action Research

When Vivian Paley, whose insightful observations are contained in *Mollie Is Three* (1986) and other books, realized that being curious was a missing element of her teaching, she started using a tape recorder. She began to discover a lot about children's thinking and about her own responses to children, realizing that they were not necessarily the best ones.

Experienced teachers or providers often want to find their own answers to questions about the effectiveness of a classroom practice, about children's behavior or development, or family interactions. Perhaps they are concerned about something that isn't working, or something that did work, but they don't know why. These caregivers may be ready to learn to do action research in their own classrooms.

Action research is a process in which practitioners systematically reflect on their work, and as a result, change their practices. They use qualitative and sometimes even quantitative methods or combinations of both to observe and reflect, plan an intervention, collect data, and then make changes. They may use tape recorders to collect data as do Paley and the teachers in the preschools of Reggio Emilia, or an array of other ethnographic techniques, such as interviewing children, parents, or others; keeping journals; or using photographs or portfolios.

Supervisors can encourage and support teacher research by helping teachers and providers to find courses, workshops, or a university-based partner who could serve as a facilitator. They can also help them to identify an action research study group, perhaps through the public schools, training centers, or local professional organizations, or to start one themselves. It is helpful if supervisors have some experience in conducting action research so that they can lead staff in exploring issues that are of interest to them. A useful resource to learn more about action research is *The Art of Classroom Inquiry: A Handbook for Teacher Researchers* by Ruth Shagoury Hubbard and Brenda Miller Power (1993). *Sometimes I Can Be Anything* and other books by Karen Gallas (1998) offer examples of teacher action research.

Long-Range Goal Setting

Long-range goal setting can be used effectively with novices, with specific and frequent supervisory input, as well as with experienced staff. Individuals with experience, however, will have most likely attained a comfort level with core criteria and will have met a program's basic expectations. They may want to work on more specialized areas as they anticipate moving up the career ladder. As they are more competent and do not require frequent assessment, they are likely to benefit greatly from long-range goal setting. With this approach, teachers and administrators work on the goals together (Brandt, 1996). At the end of an agreed-on time period, the teacher and supervisor jointly write what has been accomplished, reflect about the experience, and plan the next steps. A unique aspect of this evaluation strategy is that there are no summative reports or ratings.

This idea can be advanced a step further by forming teams of staff members who develop a team professional development plan. In a conversation with Brandt (1996), Tom McGreal suggests that the advantage of teaming is that program administrators or supervisors become facilitators, coaches, and resource providers as they are responsible for getting the team together, assisting group members with their plans, and offering encouragement. The coaching of advanced teachers permits the supervisor to spend more time with those teachers who are at lower career-ladder levels and who need the most help.

We have described a range of evaluation practices that can be used to promote professional growth in teachers. Dialogue between supervisor and supervisee, and/or among staff, is a key component in each of them in helping staff to examine their practices and to plan for change.

SOME CULTURAL CONSIDERATIONS

Culturally sensitive assessment is dependent on supervisors' being aware of classroom cultural patterns as well as the cultural perspectives that they bring to the evaluation process.

In Chapter 10, we described cultural variables that have a bearing on communication. These and others are likely to come into play as supervisors observe teachers for evaluation purposes, communicate with them about their observations, and nurture teachers in learning about how cultural patterns affect children's learning. We offer several examples from the research literature to illustrate possible cultural misunderstandings and their effect on teacher assessment, as what constitutes good teaching varies across different cultural communities (Delpit, 1995).

Many cultural groups, particularly Native American communities, place great value on social, interdependent relationships verses individual achievement, prevalent in mainstream culture. A principal way of connecting with others in many Native American groups, for example, is through storytelling. In a case study of one Lakota master teacher, Kathleen Jeanette Marsh (1998) found that there was a pattern in the ways in which the teacher used personal narrative to help her students learn. In each of her lessons, she created a context for the discussion of the material she presented, shared some personal stories and perspectives related to the concepts being taught, and questioned and encouraged questions for clarification. While some evaluators might marvel at the way in which she connected with the students and their family and community values, a culturally insensitive evaluator or one with different values or a lack of knowledge of Lakota values might perceive the context building and personal sharing aspects of her lessons as not a good use of classroom time.

Among examples of cultural difference that might affect teacher assessment that Delpit (1995) points out is the level of emotion displayed by teachers. She refers to a study by Foster (1987) that revealed that black students view assertive, aggressive, and even angry behavior as acceptable teaching behavior for communicating intentions as long as the emotions are genuine. Students perceived subtle messages or messages lacking sufficient emotional quality as noncaring. Delpit (1995) notes, however, that in assessment situations, African-American teachers who display strong emotions are often viewed by evaluators as teachers who are too harsh, too authoritarian, too "pushy" with their students and thus receive poor ratings.

Jacqueline Jordan Irvine (1991) expresses concern that culturally responsive teachers often do not meet the expectations of traditionally trained supervisors. She describes some of the characteristics of these teachers:

> Responsive teachers . . . spend a great deal of classroom time developing a personal relationship with the minority children they teach. These relationship-building exchanges are recurrent and spontaneous daily events. These teachers understand that teaching is a social interaction involving affect as well as cognition. They listen non-judgmentally and patiently to their students and allow them to share personal stories and anecdotes during classroom time. Students often express themselves openly and with high affect and emotion violating mainstream rules about turntaking and raising one's hand to be recognized. These teachers also share their personal lives and experiences. These teachers report, however, that their behaviors are often misinterpreted by supervisors as time off task, unnecessary delays and digressions, or inappropriate relationships between students and teachers. I have noticed that these teachers wait longer for their minority students to respond, and they probe, prompt, praise and encourage lavishly. These teachers use an abundance of interactive techniques, and the pace is brisk and the activities varied. They move about

the classroom and use their bodies, voices, and facial gestures as teaching instruments. (p. 7)

As supervisors observe and interpret teaching and assist teachers in becoming culturally responsive, they should think about the cultural patterns of understanding they bring to an observation. Bowers and Flinders (1990) provide us with an example of how a supervisor, Karen in this case, uses her cultural knowledge to interpret an observation. She summarizes her observation of Glen's class by noting that he began his class by giving two Japanese pupils an individual writing assignment. While they worked diligently at this task, he carried on a discussion with the class as a whole.

Using her cultural understanding of language, Karen thinks about Glen's intentions and how the students may be interpreting his behavior. Glen, unsure of the students' ability to speak English, may have seen himself as supporting the two students by giving them individual attention, standing close to them, smiling, and having direct eye contact with them. The students, however, based on their cultural patterns, may view being separated from the large group as a form of rebuke and may interpret Glen's nonverbal signals as either rapport or reprimand.

Bowers and Flinders (1990) believe that Karen, as a culturally responsive supervisor, should make explicit her own cultural frameworks for interpreting the observation as she nurtures Glen to explore new ways of seeing and hearing by introducing a cross-cultural perspective.

Supervisors, then, must be willing to learn about other cultures and even to study other languages if they are going to assist teachers in thinking about their interactions from a cultural perspective and in creating learning environments that are responsive to the cultures of children and families in a program. Much can be learned from staff members and parents within a program, who can serve as "cultural brokers." Being a good listener and observer, being able to "put oneself into another's shoes," and spending time to get to know the workplace and its community are ways that supervisors can learn about cultural values and patterns and become more culturally sensitive as they carry out their work.

A SPECIAL CONCERN: THE MARGINAL PERFORMER

As a result of formative or summative evaluation, supervisors will occasionally have to deal with a staff member whose performance is marginal. According to Lawrence Steinmetz (1969), a marginal performer may be defined as "any employee who recurringly, although infrequently, fails to produce a reasonable quantity of acceptable work in line with his capabilities and management's expectations" (p. 88). Marginal performers may be tardy or absent from their work; they may be moody or aggressive; they may have many "blue Mondays" on the job; and they may offer many excuses for not performing up to par.

Reprimanding

When the need arises to reprimand an individual, Kenneth Blanchard and Spencer Johnson (1982) make a very strong case for criticizing the *behavior* and never attacking a person's worth or value. They believe that reprimands should not be based on hearsay, but that you should let the person know that the behavior is not OK as soon as you observe it. Significant improvement in people's behavior will occur if you tell them what they did wrong, tell them how you feel about it, and remind them that they are valuable and worthwhile.

In working with such individuals, determine the seriousness and the source of the individual's unsatisfactory performance. If the source is job-related, it may be possible to spend more time with the staff member and alter certain job conditions to improve the situation. Supervisors may have to correct or change their own behavior if they are the source of the problem—for example, if they do not give complete and clear directions for accomplishing a task. Sometimes a direct, take-charge approach is needed, whereby the supervisor sets up a very structured schedule for the individual or moves the staff member from one team to another. If the source of the problem is outside the program, the supervisor may have little control over its solution but may be of some help by listening to the supervisee and offering suggestions.

Firing

As every supervisor knows, it is sometimes necessary to terminate an employee. This is a very difficult and unpleasant supervisory responsibility. The decision to fire someone should come after careful thought, after the collection of solid data over time, and after a sincere effort has been made to examine the problem from different angles and to solve it. The collection of descriptive and relevant data is essential not only to make the reasons for the decision clear to the employee but as backup in case of a grievance or legal challenge to the firing.

There are many reasons why it may be necessary to terminate the employment of a staff member. These include lack of competence, attitudinal problems, and interpersonal conflict with others in the program. Steinmetz (1969) recommends these guidelines for supervisors to follow in discharging an employee:

1. Check and consult with trusted people in the organization who are knowledgeable about the circumstances, concerned, and likely to be objective in their advice.
2. Get into a relaxed frame of mind before making the decision. Do not make the decision while under stress.
3. Never make the decision to discharge an individual under conditions of crisis.
4. Don't try to anticipate all the eventualities that could occur as a result of the dismissal. Assume that the decision is the right one.
5. Don't expect that everyone else in the program will consider the decision to fire someone to be the right one.
6. Don't overdo in planning for the discharge.
7. Once the decision is made, carry it out in a simple, forthright, and clear fashion. Make it very clear to the staff member that he or she is being dismissed, why, and when the discharge is to become effective.
8. To avoid embarrassment and possible eavesdropping, carry out the discharge at the end of the day in a thoroughly private place.
9. Once the decision is made, carry it out. Don't wait several days or weeks.
10. Have all the facts relevant to the decision at hand.
11. Allow ample opportunity for the employee to offer explanations and to ask questions.
12. Have at your disposal information with respect to contract and program policy so that you can answer questions about procedures, final payment, transferring medical benefits, and so forth.
13. Make a record of what transpires during the final conference and note unfinished tasks or projects that will need to be completed by another staff member. (p. 88)

In many cases, although certainly not all, firing someone can be in that person's best interest. Sometimes, an employee who is unhappy, frustrated, or unfulfilled in the job simply cannot make the decision to "get out of a rut" and into a new job, routine, or lifestyle. In those cases, supervisors actually relieve pain by making the decision for the individual.

Staff members in programs with good systems for self-evaluation and frequent communication between supervisor and supervisee are usually not surprised by such actions, as they have been working with their supervisors to address problems over time. Suggesting ways that the person might find another job, redirecting the person to another career, and reminding the individual of the skills that he or she does have can be helpful. This is especially important for low-income persons who have few alternatives. Firing an employee can be almost as painful for the supervisor as for the staff member. You should assume, however, that you are in a supervisory position because you have expertise and sound judgment and that your decision, not taken lightly, is in the best interest of the program and the people in it.

CONCLUSION

Our emphasis in this chapter has been to address the changing landscape of staff evaluation by emphasizing its dual nature. We have described several approaches that link evaluation with professional development. These include making portfolios, telling stories, participating in learning communities, conducting action research, and setting long-range goals. And we have set evaluation within the context of a program's career ladder, encouraging supervisors and staff to jointly design evaluation programs and processes. We have also suggested that evaluation should be culturally sensitive. This is a topic that needs greater attention in the field of supervision. Finally, we offer directors some guidelines for reprimanding, and even firing, staff in those rare cases when such action may be necessary.

PROGRAM ACCREDITATION

The National Academy of Early Childhood Programs (*Guide to Accreditation*, 1998) includes the following criteria for program accreditation related to staff evaluation:

E-5a. Attendance records of staff and children are kept.

E-5b. Confidential personnel files are kept including resumes with record of experience, transcripts of education, documentation of ongoing professional development, and results of performance evaluation. (p. 67)

H-2c. New staff members serve a probationary employment period during which the director or other qualified staff person makes a professional judgment as to their physical and psychological competence for working with children. (p. 73)

J-1a. All staff, including the program administrator are evaluated at least annually by the director or other appropriate supervisor.

J-1b. Results of staff evaluation are written and confidential. They are discussed privately with the staff member.

J-1c. Staff evaluations include classroom observations. Evaluation is based on the employee's job description and previously established goals for improvement.

J-1d. Staff are informed of evaluation criteria in advance.

J-1e. Staff have an opportunity to evaluate their own performance.

J-1f. A plan for staff training is generated from the evaluation process. (p. 79)

(Reprinted with permission from the National Association for the Education of Young Children)

EXERCISES

1. Discuss the notion of the teacher portfolio with your staff members. Ask if one or two teachers would be interested in experimenting with the idea of developing a portfolio and discussing its artifacts with you. After reasonable time intervals, confer with the staff member(s) using the portfolio entries as a basis for discussion. You and the teacher(s) can practice analyzing the material in terms of your program's goals for young children.
2. Review your program's evaluation policy and procedures in light of the principles discussed in this chapter. If revisions are needed, begin by involving your staff members in a process of describing the competencies they believe are necessary to do their jobs effectively.
3. As you consider developing an evaluation plan with staff based on the concept of the career ladder, discuss which approaches described in this chapter are suitable for novice staff, staff with moderate experience, and staff with considerable experience and expertise.
4. Practice observing classrooms through a "cultural lens." Think about how you can assist staff in becoming more aware of the cultural implications of their teaching.

Part IV

STAFF DEVELOPMENT IN PRACTICE

13

Special Issues Affecting Early Childhood Supervision

Supervisors in early care and education often encounter issues and situations that those working with teachers in schools for older children do not. They work with teachers who may or may not have degrees or formal education in the field, and the need for further education, even at the kindergarten level, is often not recognized. Compensation remains low. In some programs staff work year round and spend long hours with children in work that is sometimes tedious, with few opportunities for adult stimulation. If not attended to, these conditions can lead to stress, low morale, and staff turnover, which in turn affect the quality of life for children.

Other issues that may need special attention from early childhood supervisors are not very different from those for teachers who work with older children. As in most schools today, staff members often need help in their relationships with children who are from a variety of cultural and linguistic backgrounds, or whose families have many problems.

In this chapter we examine issues affecting staff morale and turnover, and the need for addressing cultural, racial, and linguistic diversity. We look at how each can affect early care and education programs, clarify some factors that underlie them, and establish a basis for managing them.

STAFF MORALE

It is not easy for caregivers to focus on meeting children's needs when their own are not being met. If they are unhappy with working conditions, are not getting along with other staff members, and/or feel powerless to affect job decisions, their effectiveness is impaired (Willis & Ricciuti, 1975).

Employee morale is a major issue for any supervisor, whether in business and industry or in the human services. When morale is high, people are motivated to do exciting, innovative, and growth-oriented work. When it is low, they do their work in a routine fashion at best. They often withdraw, complain, become cynical, or leave.

Low Status

Almost everyone who works with young children has at some time, in one way or another, been given the feeling that their job requires few skills or that it is one that any woman can "naturally" do. Child care staff, especially those in home settings, are characterized as "just baby sitters," and many teachers are seen as "merely" supervisors of children's play. Helping staff members to view themselves as professionals can be difficult when the knowledge and skills needed for their work are not recognized by the public or sometimes even by state licensing standards. Low pay, which reflects a lack of recognition of the difficulty of providing a quality program for children and the staff training required, further erodes caregivers' self-image and their desire to stay in the field.

Public school kindergarten teachers generally have higher status than teachers in day care or nursery schools, causing many people with degrees in early childhood education to seek jobs at this level. Even they, however, along with public school preschool teachers, are often not seen as "real" teachers by their colleagues, especially if they use approaches that support children's play and thus their classrooms do not look like "real school" (Jones, 1994).

Exclusion from Decision Making

Control over day-to-day decisions, the flexibility connected with the job, and the opportunity to learn and grow are high on the list of satisfactions of teachers of young children. Bloom (1997) found, however, that more than three-quarters of teachers responding to a national survey felt that they had less decision-making influence than they thought they should have. The greatest concern was their lack of involvement in interviewing and hiring new staff, which had earlier been shown to be available to only 18% of teaching staff (Whitebook, Howes, Darrah, & Friedman, 1982). Although most teachers felt they had influence on planning and carrying out daily activities, many felt left out of determining program objectives and ordering supplies, areas that clearly have an impact on those day-to-day decisions.

The place of aides and assistants in this picture is of special concern. Early childhood educators often state with pride that all members of a classroom team are seen as "teachers." Job descriptions frequently reflect this view, since aides are able to fulfill many of the same roles as teachers. Although this is undoubtedly a source of real satisfaction to many assistants, it can also be a source of resentment. In spite of the fact that they carry equal responsibility for day-to-day classroom decisions and sometimes for curriculum planning, their pay and benefits are lower than those of teachers—sometimes considerably so. In addition, they are often arbitrarily excluded from certain tasks and are even less likely to be included in major decision making than are teachers (Whitebook et al., 1982). Since aides in multicultural settings are more likely to be people of color, while teachers in the same settings, especially where they are required to be certified, are predominantly white, these status differences gain added significance (Jones, 1994).

An important aspect of the findings of Bloom (1997) was that directors believe that they do give staff opportunities for involvement to a much greater degree than is perceived by teachers. These data suggest that supervisors need to work toward being open to hearing teachers' perceptions of lack of influence, and should review what opportunities are available to all staff, especially aides, for participation in decisions in areas that affect them. Through regular staff meetings and classroom team meetings, supervisors and staff can clarify what is actually happening and discuss how things could be improved. This can, however, open leaders up to uncomfortable criticism. Perceptions, of course, do not necessarily represent "the truth" on either side. But perceptions have their own reality, and it is this that must be dealt with.

Examining and updating job descriptions periodically with staff input helps ensure that expectations of both aides and teachers are clearly delineated. Pay scales can also be reviewed and brought closer together where job expectations are substantially similar. Perhaps most important, however, is to provide career ladders to help lower-level staff move into higher positions and pay levels, so that the skills and knowledge obtained through in-service training, experience, and college courses are recognized.

Tedium and Exhaustion

Watching children grow, creating successful learning experiences, and being warmly responded to by children are the kinds of rewards that attract people to the field of early childhood education. But the very humanness of children, which makes them loving and joyful, can be difficult to manage in group settings. Even with the warmest, most skilled caregiving efforts, children don't always respond positively, and handling one or more difficult children on a daily basis can be exhausting.

What Bloom (1995a) refers to as the "treadmill of activity" can consume teachers' time and energy. Infant caregivers spend much time in routines such as changing and feeding, and all teachers can become bogged down when they feel they know every puzzle by heart, have said, "Tell me about your painting" too many times, and have had their 40th cup of coffee in the house corner. This can easily lead to their losing sight of the importance and meaningfulness of what they are doing.

Isolation

A great deal of the caregiver's time is spent immersed in the world of children, and isolated from other adults. Their autonomy, which they value, may also lead to missed opportunities for collaboration and learning from one another. In family child care settings providers often have little contact with adults, and none with others doing the same job unless they are part of a support network or training program. In center- or school-based programs, although two or three adults usually work together, their focus is mainly on children and classroom concerns. Sometimes teachers solve this problem in their own way by engaging in personal talk when they should be interacting with children. It is easy to label this lazy or irresponsible behavior, but feelings of isolation may be involved.

Caregivers are really dealing with isolation on two fronts—personal and professional. Both are supervisory concerns. Times set aside for open discussion of daily problems in the context of professional sharing can help teachers deal with their feelings about themselves and the children. Supporting collaborative efforts in a variety of ways, such as through mentoring relationships, is also helpful. At the same time, purely social situations, from coffee breaks to staff parties, can provide opportunities for adult, non-work-centered interaction.

Stress and Burnout

At times factors such as those described above can come together leading to stress, sometimes resulting in what is often referred to as burnout.

Burnout occurs in many organizations where there is high person-to-person involvement. It can be either individual or organizational. It shows up in three ways: (1) emotional exhaustion, that is, being drained of energy and the ability to give to others; (2) depersonalization, characterized by negative attitudes toward oneself and work, cynicism, and a detached, callous attitude; and (3) a lack of a sense of achievement in the workplace (Boyd & Schneider, 1997).

Although a number of factors have been found to contribute to burnout in early childhood settings, Boyd and Schneider (1997) found that lack of involvement in decision making was the strongest predictor of both emotional exhaustion and depersonalization. They found, too, that lack of a feeling that the whole staff is working toward the same goals (goal consensus) was an important factor contributing to these aspects of burnout.

Administrators and supervisors, especially when they have little funding or other support for providing the kind of program they think is necessary, are also vulnerable to these feelings. One might speculate as to whether developing a process for staff input, especially identifying overall goals for a program, might strengthen supervisors' own emotional well-being, professional accomplishment, and sense of belonging.

Stress does not arise exclusively from factors within the workplace, however. The National Day Care Study (Ruopp et al., 1979) reported that fully 30% of caregivers were the sole income earners for their families and 69% provided more than half of their family's support. Low salaries are an especially important factor for these staff members. When a caregiver is confronted with major problems at home—a husband out of work, children in trouble at school, divorce—the daily task of caring for someone else's children can seem especially difficult. Wessen (1981) found that for low-income child care workers, life circumstances outside the job were much more anxiety-producing than were job-related problems. Even positive factors, such as an aide's growing confidence and competence on the job, can sometimes change his or her relationship with a spouse and family, creating tensions that can affect that person's work. Supervisors in programs where staff members are drawn from low-income communities should be especially alert to these concerns.

Raising Morale and Creating Community

Individual and group morale can and will be low from time to time without leading inexorably to burnout. Supervisors who recognize that morale is a legitimate supervisory concern and are alert to burnout symptoms at their early stages can work out both long- and short-term strategies for dealing with it.

Stanley Seiderman (1978) found that lower rates of burnout and greater job satisfaction tended to result where there were staff meetings during which people were able to socialize informally, provide each other with support, receive advice and clarify goals, and exert some influence on the policies of the center. More recent studies have reinforced these findings. Margie Carter (1995) suggests the idea of staff meetings as "circle time." When this setting is "physically comfortable, emotionally safe, and full of active listening" (p. 53), it can, as it does with children, build a sense of belonging and accomplish many of the above goals.

These and other authors (Neugebauer, 1980; Whitebook et al., 1982) also recommend:

- Creating an atmosphere of trust, inviting and giving honest feedback, especially in recognition of work well done
- Ensuring that the most basic personnel policies are adhered to, including sick, vacation, and holiday pay; making sure that a break policy is implemented; and hiring substitutes so staff members feel that they can take days off when they are ill

- Providing health and other benefits, with as much financial support as possible
- Providing stimulation through changes in routines and renewal experiences that give people a chance to grow—even having staff change age groups or the composition of classroom teams every few years, especially when opportunities for promotions are not available
- Setting short-term, reachable goals that provide opportunities for success
- Having flexible job responsibilities
- Allowing "responsible selfishness"—time off for a few minutes, hours, or even a day, when fatigue and stress become overwhelming

STAFF TURNOVER

It is a rare early childhood program that does not experience frequent changes in personnel from year to year. This turnover results both from changes in paid staff and from the movement of volunteers, students, and trainees in and out of programs. Supervisors are thus faced with the task of continually orienting and training new personnel and maintaining and building systems to support a cohesive staff while also trying to develop a quality program.

Regular Staff

As we indicated in Chapter 3, staff turnover rates are very high in this field: for teachers, as high as 25% or more per year compared with less than 10% for the U.S. work force as a whole (Kisker et al., 1991). For aides, rates are even higher. Many factors contribute to these high turnover rates. In their classic study in 1982, Whitebook and her colleagues found that centers with the greatest turnover tended to be those with the "highest adult-child ratios, the worst working conditions, the fewest benefits, and most stated tension" (pp. 224–225). The conditions discussed in the previous section, especially low pay, also contribute to lack of staff continuity.

The problem of inadequate pay, familiar to those who have worked in this field for any length of time, is confirmed by evidence from recent studies. The *National Child Care Staffing Study Revisited* (Whitebook, Phillips, & Howe, 1993) revealed in a study of 193 full-day year-round centers that as a group child care teaching staff earn less than half as much as comparably educated women and one-third that of similarly educated men. Bureau of Labor Statistics data from 1996 indicated that preschool teachers (defined as a person who instructs children, normally up to age 5, in a preschool, day care center, or other child development facility) earned less than data entry keyers, only two-thirds of the pay of bus drivers, and 40% of that of kindergarten teachers.

"Child care workers" (most of whom are classroom assistants or aides, but sometimes including before- and after-school caregivers) averaged less than 80% of the pay of preschool teachers, lower than that of parking lot attendants (Center for the Child Care Workforce, 1998).

While the pay of teachers rose about 8% in real terms between 1988, as reported in the original National Child Care Staffing Study (Whitebook, Howes, & Phillips, 1989), and 1992, that of the lowest paid assistants actually fell. The income of nursery school teachers and assistants, who work only half-days and no summers, can seldom be classified as more than supplemental, and family child care providers are paid less than half the salary of those in center-based programs (U.S. Department of Education, 1990).

The relationship of pay to turnover was clearly shown by the staffing study data: Of those with salaries of less than $5.00 per hour, 77% had left between 1988 and 1992, while 53% of those being paid $7.00 or more had left (Whitebook, Howes, & Phillips, 1989; Whitebook, Phillips, & Howes, 1993).

Further, fringe benefits such as paid vacations and sick leave, which are standard in almost every other workplace, are unavailable to some staff members, especially those in part-day or family child care programs. The *National Child Care Staffing Study Revisited* revealed that only 27% of early childhood staff had fully paid health care, and almost one-third of assistants in those programs were excluded (Whitebook, Phillips, & Howes, 1993). Breaks, though mandated by law, were found to be unavailable to as many as three-fifths of caregivers, either because they were not allowed, or because a shortage of time and staff made them difficult to take (Whitebook et al., 1982).

Administrators of sponsoring agencies and boards of directors may have little understanding of the skills needed by staff members in the preschool or school-age programs they sponsor. They may have as little knowledge of the effects of inadequate compensation on the lives of children as the public at large. Early childhood educators thus have the burden of finding ways to inform their own administrators, the public in general, and policymakers in particular about these needs.

Supplementary Staff

Frequent changes also occur among supplementary staff members. Parents and other volunteers, students, and those from Foster Grandparents, and welfare-to-work programs can contribute greatly to early childhood programs, but they may require special attention by on-site supervisors. Some may work only a few hours per week. Often they have had little or no experience with small children in group settings. In addition, there is great variation in their educational backgrounds and in their motivations for becoming involved in early childhood programs.

These caregivers have specific training needs, and since most of them work in classrooms, much of this responsibility falls on teachers. For some an outside agency may have well-defined training expectations and may provide oversight, including periodic supervisory visits. For others expectations may be vague or generalized, and their supervision is left up to the center or school.

Creating Stability

Many of the factors contributing to turnover can be addressed by supervisors. First, the situation should be analyzed to see what is causing people to leave. As Marcy Whitebook (1997) put it, *"Is* it low pay, or is it that there's only one bathroom?" and then suggests, "Staff are adults: ask them!"

Both permanent and temporary staff members benefit when there is a system for orienting all new personnel, paid or volunteer (see Chapter 14). Support should also be provided for teachers when they take responsibility for supervising temporary staff or for mentoring new teachers. Recognition, along with training in communication and supervisory skills, develops teachers' confidence as well as their competence in carrying out these responsibilities. Extra compensation, if at all possible, increases the status of and the caregiver's sense of responsibility for this work.

Follow-up studies of centers that have received National Association for the Education of Young Children (NAEYC) accreditation indicate that turnover in these programs is considerably lower, and that staff have a greater commitment to their jobs and pride in their programs (Bloom, 1995b). Both the accreditation self-evaluation process and the improved quality that results contribute to this.

Working relationships with programs or agencies from which volunteers and trainees come will be smoother if there are agreements as to the roles and responsibilities of the parties involved. If standards and expectations for the selection of people who will work with children are established, temporary staff can be screened to ascertain whether they are truly interested in and have an aptitude for working with children. Alternative placements can then be arranged when appropriate. These and other policies are recommended by the Center for the Child Care Workforce (From Welfare to Working in Child Care, 1996) for centers that employ welfare recipients fulfilling work requirements. Supervisors may have to take strong stands to accomplish this, but it will strengthen their programs as well as contribute to the development of the individual caregiver.

Written material describing the program's goals, philosophy, and daily schedule also aids in matching resources and needs (see Chapter 15). A contract between the agency and the center is recommended to clarify the commitment and expectations of each, whether or not money is not involved. Such agreements have proven especially useful in Child Development Associate (CDA) training programs, even when the candidate is a regular member of the staff.

Increasingly, resources are becoming available to assist practitioners in developing skills for negotiating with boards and for advocating for better salaries and benefits. The Center for the Child Care Workforce (see Appendix B) has become a major national voice for the empowerment of early childhood staff in their own behalf. Associations of child care directors and providers and public policy committees of state and local affiliates of NAEYC are becoming skilled at publicizing the issue of salaries, including lobbying state legislators. Some directors have found that one sympathetic board member may be willing to help interpret staff needs to others, to assist in developing strategies, and to become an advocate for center and staff concerns. Meetings of supervisor support groups are good places to explore and share these and other strategies.

It is sometimes the efforts of teachers themselves—especially when supported by supervisors—that have the greatest impact. A determined group of Colorado providers (Colorado State Board of Education, 1973) discovered that persistence and patience can have results:

> You can call Welfare Department people a lot of dirty names, and that is exactly what we were doing at that time, but the political reality is that they need the community pressure . . . because any kind of increase in their budget needs to be justified. (p. 12)

It should be said that there can be positive aspects to staff turnover. Supervisors, especially in programs employing low-income staff, can be proud if they have supported the personal and professional growth of caregivers so that they continue their education, take advantage of promotions in the early childhood field, or even move on to new careers in other fields. The involvement of parents, senior citizens, high school students, and volunteers brings diversity to the lives of both children and permanent staff. When a program has contributed to the training of student teachers and job trainees, it has contributed to the profession and to a better life for young children. What we do not want is for skilled and promising practitioners to leave the field because of low pay, poor working conditions, and lack of support and appreciation.

STAFF AND CHILD DIVERSITY

"Cultural diversity means that the hopes and expectations that adults have for young children, as well as how they interact with young children—from comforting to disciplining to teaching—differ, sometimes dramatically" (Cohen & Pompa, 1996, p. 81). For supervisors this has implications in two areas: in their own relationships with teachers, and in their work with teachers as they interact with children and parents. While we have discussed these issues to some extent in previous chapters, this section examines their implications in greater depth.

Culture, Race, and Class

The revision of NAEYC's *Developmentally Appropriate Practice in Early Childhood Programs* (DAP) (Bredekamp & Copple, 1997) has made some major changes that acknowledge the importance of culture in early care and education. Instead of looking at practitioners' work with children in only two major dimensions—knowledge of development and knowledge of individual children—it has added a third—knowledge of social and cultural context. Where in the earlier version of DAP, culture was seen only as a variation of individuality, the revised work recognizes that an understanding of culture has as much of an effect on how caregivers work with children as does their awareness of children's development and individual differences.

We all carry preconceived ideas about members of particular groups, which although often unconscious, can nevertheless affect our work. We tend to make assumptions about people based on their color, class, gender, religion, sexual orientation, or other identities. Gordon Allport (1958), one of the pioneers in examining prejudice, called this "the normality of prejudgment," stemming from the human need to mentally group things in order to make sense of them.

Talking about differences, however, usually makes us uncomfortable. To say that someone is different seems to imply inferiority. This stems from perceptions of social status that have become attached to various ethnic, religious, or racial groups. The term *class* itself is one that Americans do not like much, but classes do exist and do affect people's views of one another. Differences are not deficits, though, and denying their existence does not make them or their effect on our own and others' lives go away.

It often seems safer to rely on a basic sense of fairness and good will, to say, "I don't see color," than to attend to differences and to examine their implications, especially when it seems that to do so may offend someone. But understanding and communication do not happen automatically. A true atmosphere of openness and trust is based on knowledge of another's life experiences and values and a sensitivity to the ways one is perceived. A middle-class Anglo-American head teacher, for example, may have developed a good understanding of Mexican-American culture and have been able to communicate well with her Latino staff, but a new low-income Mexican-American aide who has experienced much discrimination has no way of knowing this. This aide's emotional survival *requires* that she proceed cautiously and perhaps defensively in her relationship with her supervisor. This head teacher must proceed from an awareness not only that the aide might have such feelings, but also that, because of her role and because she is a member of the majority culture, she possesses power and authority that affect their relationship (Delpit, 1995). In fact, class and cultural stereotypes are often reinforced when a supervisor or director is of the dominant culture or from a middle-income background and staff members, especially those in lower-status jobs, are people of color or from low-income families, not an uncommon situation.

The most difficult task is to accept and understand differences when they conflict with personal and professional values. The values of the mainstream culture are generally reinforced in schools, so those who are born or socialized into the mainstream culture may have had no opportunity to question them. They may assume that others have the same values, or perhaps that if they differ they should be corrected. This can lead to the values of teachers and parents from African-American, Native-American, Asian, and Latino cultures, and those of the poor, being devalued or stereotyped (King, Chipman, & Cruz-Jazen, 1994).

Powell (1994) notes that what has been considered developmentally appropriate practice in child care and education is in "stark contrast with the images of appropriate settings for young children generally held by lower income and ethnic minority parents" (p. 171). They are likely to believe that adults should act as limit-setting authorities and should direct and guide children. Middle-class parents, on the other hand, tend to feel they should help the child to become self-disciplined and autonomous. Since the goals of a developmental early childhood program include autonomy and independence, along with nondirective adult/child interactions, middle-class, and especially white, supervisors and caregivers are more likely to be comfortable with these goals because they do not conflict with their values. On the other hand, they may find that their own indirect style leaves children and even adults from other ethnic and income groups confused as to what is expected.

We need, then, to acknowledge that people's differing ways of interacting with one another are not necessarily wrong, even when they seem to be at odds with developmentally appropriate practice. Lisa Delpit (1995) shows, with numerous examples, that teachers of color often feel that their experiences are discounted in discussions of ways to work with children. An African-American teacher's or aide's reluctance to follow a recommended way of working with children, for example, may represent a legitimate concern about the children based on personal knowledge of their cultural or family expectations. In such an instance, a supervisor's role is to do lots of listening, allowing "the realities of others to edge themselves into her consciousness" (p. 47), and thus learn, and consider changes in program implementation. To have a goal of actively affirming the cultures of both school and home without devaluing either means that supervisors must become aware of others' views and be willing to negotiate or come to an accommodation with teachers or parents where behavior expectations are in conflict. (See Gonzalez-Mena, 1992, for a helpful discussion.)

Language

The supervisory issues involved when even one child speaks a language other than English can become dauntingly complex when several home languages are present in the same classroom. The issues are important whether the children are recent arrivals or members of long-established Spanish-speaking, Native-American, or other communities who see their native language as an important part of their culture.

Teachers and parents often have strong feelings about encouraging the use of a child's first language in school. Many fear that it will interfere with the learning of English. Or they may believe that speaking English is a symbol of being, or wanting to be, truly American and that the use of another language emphasizes what is different about each child and leads to divisiveness rather than unity. Others may feel equally strongly that children should begin school entirely in their first language, gradually moving into English, or that both languages should be used equally.

Supervisors have to acknowledge the highly personal and emotional meaning that language has in people's lives, while also becoming knowledgeable about second-language acquisition. There is considerable evidence, for example, from several countries, that a second language is learned best when students are both literate and fluent in their first language (Cazden, 1995). Garcia (1997) reports that successful teachers of second-language learners understand and value the home language, culture, and values; recognize that children come to school with some knowledge about language and how it works; and understand that children develop higher language skills through socially meaningful activities and that development and learning occur in the "interaction of linguistic, sociocultural, and cognitive knowledge and experiences" (p. 12).

We support the view stated in the NAEYC (1996) *Position Statement* on cultural and linguistic diversity that "because knowing more than one language is a cognitive asset, early education programs should encourage the development of children's home language while fostering the acquisition of English" (p. 5).

Building a Culturally Responsive Program

A supervisor's attitudes and willingness to deal openly with the issues of race, class, language, and culture are crucial to the creation of an atmosphere of understanding, trust, and responsiveness to children's needs. Only by bringing these "tender topics" (status and other inequities) to the surface, Elizabeth Jones (1994) cautions, can we "open the way for those with less power but greater understanding to speak out with authority about their personal experiences with inequity" (p. 30). This is by no means an easy task, especially as we are all at different stages in awareness of and openness to issues of culture, race, and language.

The first step toward intercultural competence is to create the time and space to find out who *we* are, how we feel about it, and "how we are connected and disconnected to one another" (Delpit, 1995, p. xv). "We" means *all* staff, including supervisors. Connie Sturm (1997) started a group for this purpose when she and other teachers realized that some of their parents were approaching child rearing very differently from the ways that they considered developmentally appropriate. After exploring their own previously unexamined values, they began a series of parent-teacher dialogues, structured so as to be open to mutual sharing by parents and teachers. Through these experiences they gained new insights about commonalities as well as differences, and began to develop the intercultural communication skills that carried over to their classroom interactions.

Valuing the recruitment of a diverse staff, especially for teacher or supervisory positions, even if your program is relatively monocultural, is another way that you as a supervisor can address issues of culture, race, and class. Become committed to the education, mentoring, and promotion of people in lower-status positions, while allowing for flexibility regarding credentials and English proficiency when looking for staff who speak the children's home languages. Use caregivers', parents', and volunteers' knowledge as a resource for others and as a connecting link between home and school, especially if the administration and/or staff of your program are not from the same background as the families.

We suggest that the following guidelines, provided by Janet Gonzalez-Mena (1992), for teacher-parent relationships, can apply equally to supervisor-caregiver relations:

- Know what each teacher in your program wants for his or her children.
- Become clear about your own values and goals; have a bottom line, but leave room for flexibility.
- Become sensitive to your own discomfort; don't ignore it; try to identify exactly what it is.
- Build relationships; be patient, it takes time.
- Become effective cross-cultural communicators; learn about styles different from your own; don't make assumptions.
- Learn how to create dialogues; how to open up dialogue and to recognize what closes it down; listen as much as you talk.

- Use *problem-solving* rather than a *power* approach.
- Commit yourself to education, your own and teachers'.

We encourage supervisors to build programs where diversity in race, culture, and language is honored. Even when children and staff are relatively homogeneous, this can be an exciting way to begin to initiate them into a world of diversity. Three books that can be very useful in this process are: Chang, Muckelroy, and Pulido-Tobiassen, *Looking In, Looking Out: Redefining Child Care and Early Education in a Diverse Society* (1996), Derman-Sparks and the A.B.C. Task Force, *Anti-Bias Curriculum: Tools for Empowering Young Children* (1989), and Kendall, *Diversity in the Classroom* (1996).

It may help to keep in mind Jim Greenman's (1989) aphorism: "Diversity is the spice of life. It also makes us sneeze a lot" (p. 13).

CONCLUSION

The issues discussed in this chapter present challenges to supervisors and staff alike, but thoughtful supervisory and staff development practices, those we have described and others, can have an impact. It will also take concerted, long-term efforts by professional groups and individuals to have an impact on the views of the public at large about the value of well-trained and adequately compensated early childhood staff. As research about the importance of children's early years continues to be publicized in the popular press, the public at large will become better informed, and early childhood professionals will be better able to interpret to them how training and improved compensation of caregivers contributes to quality care and education for young children. Closer to home, parents can be educated through involvement in classrooms, by getting to know and respect staff members through a variety of means. As a supervisor in a program with a strong multicultural emphasis said, "So *many* things are solved by including parents."

Staff meetings and staff development are essential elements of the supervisory process not only for improving staff skills but also for their positive effect on morale. The community building that results can be especially important where the staff and the children served are from diverse backgrounds. In the next two chapters we explore these issues further, including some specific suggestions for implementation.

PROGRAM ACCREDITATION

Directors who would like to obtain NAEYC (*Guide to Accreditation*, 1998) accreditation must show evidence of meeting the following criteria:

E-1b.   The annual program evaluation examines the adequacy of staff com-
        pensation and benefits and rate of staff turnover, and a plan is devel-
        oped to increase salaries and benefits to ensure recruitment and reten-
        tion of qualified staff and continuity of relationships (p. 66).
E-10a. Staff and administrators plan and consult together frequently about
        the program, children, and families.
E-10b. Staff plan and consult together.
E-10c. Regular staff meetings are held for staff to consult on program plan-
        ning, to plan for implementing and attaining goals, to plan for indi-
        vidual children, and to discuss program and working conditions (may
        be meetings of small group of or full staff).
E-10d. Teachers are provided paid planning time, away from responsibilities
        for children.
E-11.   Staff are provided space and time away from children during the day.
        (When staff work directly with children for more than 4 hours, they are
        provided breaks of at least 15 minutes in each 4-hour period) (p. 69).
F-2b.   Substitutes are provided to maintain staff-child ratios when regular staff
        are absent. Substitutes for infants and toddlers are familiar with chil-
        dren and oriented to children's schedules and individual differences
        in a systematic way before assignment. Volunteers who work with
        children complete a pre-assignment orientation and participate in
        ongoing training (p. 71).
J-2a.   At least annually, administrators, families, staff, school-age children, and
        other routinely participating adults are involved in evaluating the pro-
        gram's effectiveness in meeting the needs of children and families (p. 79).
J-2b.   The program regularly establishes goals for continuous improvement
        and innovation (p. 80).

Reprinted with permission from the National Association for the Education of Young Children

EXERCISES

1. As a new supervisor, you discover that there has been a lot of staff turnover
   in your center in the past few years. Using the information presented in
   this chapter as a beginning, how would you analyze this problem, and how
   would you work with staff to develop a strategy for combating it?
2. Use some of the activities suggested in Chapter 12 of the *Anti-Bias Curriculum* (Derman-Sparks et al., 1989) or those in *Teaching/Learning Anti-
   Racism* (Derman-Sparks & Phillips, 1997) to help explore the intercultural
   issues people encounter in their own lives as well as in their programs.
3. Brainstorm strategies for advocating higher pay, increased benefits, or other
   quality issues, such as lower staff-to-child ratios, with the person or group

that has control over funds for your program. Sort these through and try out the most promising.

4. *A Problem for Discussion:* (Note: You may wish to substitute an actual example that deals with the same kinds of issues.) Rosa is a new aide in the child care program of which you are the director. It has a high percentage of Portuguese children. She is a Portuguese immigrant who has been in this country for about 3 years and speaks English fairly well, although she has an accent and her speech is not always grammatically correct. She has had no previous experience in group care, although she has two children of her own.

Elaine, the teacher in whose room Rosa works, has come to you with concerns about Rosa's interaction with children, which she finds overly directive. She thinks that Rosa speaks too much Portuguese with the children and that her "broken" English presents a poor model for them.

How do you feel about Elaine's concerns? What supervisory issues are apparent? What do you need to know? How would you approach these issues with each caregiver individually and what kinds of supervision or training might you plan in response for (1) Elaine, (2) Rosa, and (3) the staff as a whole?

14

A Framework for Staff Development and Training

Staff development is a term that can be applied to all experiences that aid staff in improving their work with children. It is a growth-oriented concept, based on the assumption that the quality of early childhood programs can be maintained and improved only through a well-planned and continuing program of experiences designed to foster practitioners' personal and professional development. Elizabeth Jones (1993) calls it "growing teachers."

All staff, including administrators and highly competent teachers, can benefit from staff development opportunities. However, because of the many different paths through which early childhood practitioners come to their work, it is a challenge to find ways to serve all of their professional development needs. We suggest that you keep in mind the concept of a career ladder, as described in Chapter 3, as you plan staff development, training, and education experiences. This ladder can provide a framework for planning as you think about and discuss with staff members where each fits within it, and what her or his next step might be.

Staff training—that is, experiences designed to help staff develop the knowledge, skills, and attitudes needed for teaching and caring for young children—is one dimension of staff development. We are aware that *training* is a term that some readers may find offensive, feeling that it connotes limited goals, rote learning, or emphasis on skills and methods alone without an understanding of the reasons behind what is done. However, we view the term, as does Milly Almy (1975), as one that is useful in describing a concentration on the particular skills needed to fit a person for a specified role:

> As trainer the early childhood educator assumes responsibility for the preparation of competent workers for early childhood programs. . . . The trainer role does not exclude approaches that are broadly educative as compared with those that are more narrowly focused. (p. 196)

The discussion that follows is divided into descriptions of four areas of focus: *orientation* for new staff; *on-the-job training* for those with little or no training in early care and education; *career development and CDA training* available to but not required for all staff; and *fine tuning* for those with considerable experience and a high level of skills. In the next chapter, we will describe the tools that can be put to use in these areas.

ORIENTATION FOR NEW STAFF

Many a supervisor has had the experience of accepting with eagerness parent volunteers, students, or extra staff from funded programs, only to find after a few weeks or months that these individuals have misperceptions about their place in the program or that they act inappropriately with children or parents. Trained and experienced staff members, too, bring with them expectations and preconceptions from their previous experience that affect their adjustment to a new setting.

Many problems, misunderstandings, and disruptions of well-established child care practices can be avoided by having an effective set of orientation experiences. The quality of an individual's first few days on the job can have a lasting effect on the program, the children, and the staff. The advantages to both the individual and the center of using this initial period to set the stage for a new person's involvement cannot be overestimated.

Content and Structure

The orientation need not be elaborate. The goal is that a new person will feel welcome and will develop a sense of the structure and goals of the program and his or her place within it. Much of this knowledge is needed by all new people, but flexibility in design allows the special needs of volunteers and other untrained staff to be attended to along with those of personnel with greater training and experience.

The manner in which this information is conveyed, with respect for what each new person brings to the program, will set the tone for future staff relations. A handbook (see Chapter 15) can be an especially valuable supplementary tool for presenting organizational information that is uninteresting or hard to retain, or requires special emphasis.

An overview of the goals and philosophy, what is unique about the program, briefly and simply addressed, sets the context within which the new person will be working. This introduction might include a review of some foundations of a good developmental program for young children as well as certain key ideas that require continued emphasis and reinforcement—for example, the place of play in young children's lives, policies concerning speakers of other languages, respect for children, the importance of discovering the views of and communicating positively with parents, and the need for objectivity and confidentiality.

Basic information regarding organizational aspects of the program is also valuable. For example:

- Daily schedules for children with the times for arrival and departure, meals and snacks, naps, and so forth
- Locations of rooms, personnel, and supplies
- Descriptions of the administrative structure and the names of staff and their roles
- Ground rules for children and adults about use of space, outdoor procedures, field trips, nonsleepers at nap-time, toileting, rules for parent pickup, and so forth
- Hours of work, including break and lunch, along with other expectations of staff or volunteers (e.g., punctuality, what to do in case of illness)
- Safety precautions and health rules, including risk-management policies, such as what forms of physical contact are encouraged or discouraged (Nurturing Green Staff from Day One, 1993)
- Information about the community
- Personnel policies for permanent employees

It is also advantageous to set forth clearly and simply the program's point of view about discipline right from the start. For staff with little training, very specific examples—even explicit dos and don'ts—are more effective than general statements that can be misinterpreted. The reasons behind these procedures can be explored when the new person has had a variety of experiences to build on.

Volunteers, students, and job trainees who work only a few hours a week are often not aware that their roles in the classroom are important and affect other members of the staff as well as the children. Clarification of responsibilities, presented in a positive way, enhances the person's role, while at the same time making clear that the expectations are real.

New staff members or volunteers do not always begin their employment at the start of the school year. It can be most useful, therefore, to design a set of individual and group experiences that can be put into place for any new person at any time.

Developing Relationships with Staff

A major objective of the orientation period is to help each new person feel comfortable as a member of the staff. Dorothy Sciarra and A. G. Dorsey (1990) suggest that all staff members should see themselves as having "an obligation to become involved with making the new employee's transition to the staff position as smooth and satisfying as possible" (p. 181). Introductions to all staff, including secretaries and custodians, should not be overlooked. The staff member assigned to do this becomes a key person in facilitating the new person's transition to becoming a member of the staff. If there are trained mentors on the staff, this would be a time for them to initiate their relationship.

An introduction to parents can take place informally, when they leave their children and pick them up, and through a newsletter or announcement on a bulletin board. Notices can include brief background information about the new caregiver and his or her special interests and role at the center. Supplemental staff members such as job trainees, students, and foster grandparents should also be introduced. Parents can be given a list of their names, the times they will be working, and the rooms to which they are assigned, along with some information about how their presence helps the program.

If possible, have new people take part in setting up the rooms and in planning at the beginning of the school year. This gives them a stake in what will be happening with children and helps them understand what is needed to make it work.

Other Activities

Having new caregivers, especially those with little early childhood background, observe in classrooms before they begin to work is an especially effective means for helping them understand what a program for young children is all about. At this stage, observations can focus on such things as becoming familiar with children's names, identifying areas of the room and what goes on in each, and noting some aspects of the roles of the teaching staff. Allowing time for observation also helps more experienced teachers to get to know children and staff, and the "personality" of the particular program.

Group sessions provide opportunities for sharing perceptions and for becoming acquainted with others with whom they will be working. When more formal workshops are held for volunteers and trainees, information should not be far removed from the experiences the new people will be involved in during their first few weeks at the center, and active learning techniques should be used.

When orientation is designed so that it can be carried out on an individualized basis, it can combine independent experiences with supervisory conferences. Figure 14.1 illustrates a sequence of activities used in a small program to which student volunteers are regularly assigned.

Supervisors often become aware of particular areas that cause problems for new staff members. One Head Start supervisor, who noticed that the paperwork in her program can be confusing, has developed a packet of forms she finds useful in orienting new staff members. As she "walks through" each form

Figure 14.1 Orientation for Student Volunteers

1. The student reads the handbook from cover to cover.

2. The supervisor discusses the information in the handbook with the student.

3. The student independently watches a slide/tape of the center and students at work in it.

4. The student observes the program. The assignment is to watch one learning center and learn the children's names.

5. The student discusses what was observed.

Used with permission of Elsa S. Grieder, Director, Barrington College Early Childhood Center, Barrington, RI.

with the staff member, different facets of Head Start's components and regulations and their implications for children and staff are revealed. Such creative solutions to specific problems can make the supervisor's job more interesting and provide important learning for new staff members.

There is sometimes a temptation to teach everything at orientation time. The purpose of an orientation, however, is to lay the foundation for a continuing process that builds as it goes on. It is usually most effective, therefore, to be very specific and present the most basic ideas, using examples wherever possible, even with sophisticated people if they are beginners. The general tone of this initial training period and the use of active learning principles can make it a model of the kinds of attitudes, and to some extent the techniques, that are to be used with children.

Taking time to orient new staff pays off, even if it places a burden on other staff members for a while.

ON-THE-JOB TRAINING

On-the-job training is targeted toward those with little training in early care and education or experience with young children in a group setting. It is more intensive than the ongoing staff development designed for all personnel. For the most part, those participating in this phase of training will be people who do not have the major responsibility for a group of children. However, head teachers whose background in early childhood education is weak may also need some training.

For staff members for whom on-the-job training is intended, learning about children and teaching begins with their experience in the classroom. The supervisor's role as teacher of these staff members is to make use of this experience not only to help them learn the skills of caregiving but also to become self-directed learners—to help them learn how to learn about children and teaching.

Volunteers, student teachers, and newly hired staff members alike come to their jobs with images of what it is they will be doing, but these views may or may not reflect the reality of a new situation. Nor may regular staff members have thought about how new volunteers or trainees will fit into the existing pattern of responsibilities. Added to this is the fact that those who are taking part in on-the-job training really have two roles: They are workers who are expected to carry out their jobs responsibly and with skill, but they are also learners who have imperfect skills but who are open to change.

Clarification of roles and expectations for the training participants, the supervisor, and the classroom staff sets the stage for positive staff relations. Knowledge of what the training consists of, the extent of the head teacher's and any other supervisor's training responsibilities, and the roles of the trainee as worker and learner is useful to everyone in a program. Most participants will welcome the opportunity for training, though perhaps with some apprehension. An emphasis on its supportive nature helps to alleviate some of their concerns.

Training objectives and methodology can be planned more effectively if the participants' strengths and needs are assessed at an early stage in the training. This should be done in the context of their jobs and in the light of adult developmental issues. For example, a Foster Grandfather who has spent most of his life working as an accountant and whose assignment is to give one or two children special attention and love will have very different needs from a parent volunteer who eventually wants to move into a paid job in the program. Similarly, a student teacher who is familiar with child development theory but lacks experience will come with skills and needs different from those of a teenage high school student who is not even sure she or he wants to work with children. Such assessments make it possible to identify strengths and abilities so that caregivers can be involved in classroom activities in meaningful ways. They are then able to see themselves as necessary and competent staff members right from the beginning.

Content

There are many sources for the content of on-the-job training. In addition to the goals of the individual early childhood program itself, a strong basis for training can be provided by the Head Start Performance Standards (U.S. Department of Health and Human Services, 1996); the National Association for the Education of Young Children's (NAEYC) *Developmentally Appropriate Practice* (Bredekamp & Copple, 1997); the High/Scope Key Experiences (Hohmann & Weikart, 1995); and the Child Development Associate (CDA) Competencies, discussed later in this chapter.

Since the purposes of on-the-job training are to equip caregivers with basic skills and to help them *learn how to learn* about children and teaching, we suggest that five processes or skills be emphasized:

1. Learning to see
2. Learning to listen
3. Learning to communicate
4. Understanding and carrying out group and individual activities with children
5. Becoming knowledgeable about and sensitive to cultural and linguistic differences

Learning to see is probably one of the most valuable abilities that can be developed by anyone working with children. So much of good teaching and caregiving comes from being able to understand the subtle meanings of what children do and say—to see that for a 4-year-old play is more than aimless activity or "merely" a time for fun; or to see what an 8–month-old is learning from crawling around the floor that she would not be learning in a play pen. As Alice Honig (1983) has put it, "Infants are the caregivers' teachers. Informed caregivers pace their teachings and their interactions depending on the responses of infants" (p. 131). It is not easy to discern many of the small but important things that a good teacher does that make each day a positive one for children: to see how he or she responds to a child's individuality or culture, or to see how the arrangement of the learning environment can affect life for children and adults in a classroom or child care home. It takes time and training to learn how to make sense of such things.

A skill that parallels learning to see is *learning to listen.* As teachers learn to listen to children during play—as the children talk to adults, to other children, to themselves, and even as they quarrel—they can understand the child's view of the world at a particular time. Caregivers can also learn to hear the underlying as well as surface messages of parents as they talk about their children and about their own concerns.

Caregivers can build on the above skills by *learning to communicate* appropriately with both children and adults in many kinds of situations. They can begin to understand the role of the teacher in enhancing a child's self-directed learning by learning to use effective language with children, including at least some of the home language if it is other than English. Caregivers can become conscious of and begin to use open-ended questions and non-directive statements where appropriate, and they discover ways that help rather than hinder the explorations of children. They can begin to develop a repertoire of positive ways to respond when children misbehave and to develop flexibility in their use and can learn to use cues from their observations to help them decide how to respond.

New teachers can now also begin to acquire skills in communicating with parents, listening as well as talking, so they can share the child's daily joys and sorrows in informal contacts. Teachers need to understand what is appropriate to discuss at such times and what should be saved for a parent conference. In all child care and education programs, but especially those for infants and toddlers and in family child care, it is critical that caregivers build close and positive relationships with parents right from the beginning.

This is also a time to begin developing skills for *carrying out group activities* and for *facilitating individual learning*. Caregivers can learn to view both group experiences and "free" play activities as means for developing children's confidence in themselves as individuals, along with their ability to solve problems, to express themselves, to negotiate with their peers, and to practice skills in their own ways. For many caregivers, learning to allow children to make decisions and to use their own means of expression requires an entirely new way of viewing the teaching/learning process. Time as well as a variety of training approaches may be needed to help them feel comfortable with these teaching modes.

Finally, trainees can begin to use both seeing and listening to develop an understanding of the *role of culture and language* in the lives of children and their families. These issues have been discussed at length in previous chapters.

Structure

It is both practical and effective to take advantage of the classroom setting as much as possible for on-the-job training. Through observations of teachers and children, caregivers can now begin to examine the teaching/learning process in more varied ways. A focus on children enables them to see the marvelous capacity that children have for self-initiated learning. An examination of the learning environment reveals the ways that arrangement of space affects children's ability to be independent and to control their own behavior. Observations of teachers, either in everyday or planned situations, provide opportunities to study the way disciplinary incidents are handled and the teacher's role in play, transitions, and group situations. Visiting other programs in the area gives experienced as well as beginning caregivers a different perspective. Not only can it serve as a source of new ideas, but it can also provide reinforcement for what they are already doing.

A series of group meetings provides a setting for introducing trainees to or reviewing basic child development principles, tying them in with the participants' observations and classroom experiences. Some time should also be made available to discuss concerns that a group of trainees may have in common.

Foster grandparents, for example, may need to talk about transportation to work and maintaining energy when working with active children. They may also need help in understanding "modern" methods of discipline. On the other hand, they can contribute to a supervisor's understanding of community life from a variety of cultural perspectives. Of course, many in-service training activities planned for the staff as a whole are equally valuable for volunteers and teachers-in-training, giving them an opportunity to become part of the program.

CAREER DEVELOPMENT AND CDA TRAINING

The NAEYC Position Statement on Professional Development (Willer, 1994) states: "To attract and retain qualified adults to work in early childhood programs, there must be viable career options that provide opportunities for continued professional development and increased compensation" (p. 10). We would add that in any program where there is concern for adults as well as children, career or professional development should be one of the training options for staff.

Career development can be described simply as a planned program designed to provide opportunities for upward mobility within an early childhood program and perhaps beyond. Opportunities for staff to obtain credentials that verify their acquired knowledge and skills are important elements of such programs. It is here that the career-ladder concept can be especially useful.

Career-development efforts are often focused on staff members who are at the lower job levels and who do not have degrees. These are the people who traditionally have the fewest options and can benefit most from credit-bearing course work or recognized credentials. The provision of such opportunities is especially important in programs that employ or serve people from low-income families or where licensing requirements for staff qualifications are minimal, and is a major goal in Head Start and a number of other government-funded programs.

The career-development concept is not limited to such individuals, however. In any program, even staff members with degrees may be interested in preparing for a role such as educational coordinator or director, in changing direction from preschool to infant care, or toward social services, parent education, or special-needs education.

Career-development Assistance

There is a considerable range in the extent of involvement of supervisors in career development. In a large program with a commitment toward such training, it is best to have someone on the staff who has the major responsibility for coordinating contacts with educational institutions and keeping up with staff members who are taking part. Problems with finding transportation or baby sitters, choosing appropriate courses, or working through a college bureaucracy can quickly discourage a staff member whose self-confidence is low. The coordinator can field such problems and help trainees find ways to solve them.

In smaller programs, the involvement will be more informal, with supervisors acting as encouragers and facilitators for staff who wish to pursue professional goals. A third role for supervisors is to act as a field adviser or trainer for CDA candidates, which could include supervising field experiences and taking part in the assessment process.

It is discouraging for staff members to put extra time and effort into taking courses or preparing for a CDA assessment only to find that they can receive no recognition until they obtain a degree or must wait until there is a job opening at a higher level. Any organization that has a commitment to career development should make an effort to couple it with job advancement and pay increases based on training. Formalizing this process through a career ladder or lattice, as described in Chapter 3, that provides salary increments for blocks of courses as well as for credentials or degrees is a way to indicate that the program values professional growth.

Training Institutions

The simplest and most helpful part supervisors can play in encouraging formal study is to gather and disseminate information about colleges that have early childhood courses, CDA training, and/or degree programs that are appropriate to the needs of their staff. A college or university that has provided CDA and other training for Head Start staff may also be able to serve staff from other early childhood programs. Institutions that show an understanding of the special strengths and needs of adult learners are preferable. Since it is not unusual for staff members to have training from a variety of nontraditional sources or courses from several institutions, supervisors should also search out programs that assess previous work or life experience for credit. This is especially important for family child care providers (Fyfe, 1994). External degree programs, which provide course work off campus or through independent studies or distance learning, are becoming more available. The latter two should be undertaken only when the caregiver has developed both the skills and the confidence to work on her or his own.

It is often possible to negotiate for courses on special topics and even for new degree programs if sufficient numbers of students can be guaranteed. On-site courses are also sometimes an option. Working together with other early care and education programs or public schools helps develop evidence that there will be a continued market for such courses or programs in that location. Resource and referral (see Appendix B) and other early childhood training agencies can be very helpful in these efforts.

So that formal study programs will affect more than a few highly motivated staff members with enough money to pay for their own courses, every effort should be made to provide or seek out some kind of tuition subsidy.

The CDA Credential

The Child Development Associate credential has a number of advantages as a career-development goal. This system allows people with varying amounts of formal or informal education, with or without degrees, to focus on the same goals and reach them at their own pace and in a way that is most appropriate for them. The requirements are flexible, both in time and in the type of training needed. And, because the CDA competencies are based on sound child development principles and the credential is awarded on the basis of a caregiver's actual work with children, there is a direct relationship with the quality of teaching and care of children.

The CDA assessment and credentialing system was developed in the early 1970s to provide a nationally recognized, validated standard of competence for early childhood practitioners. It is administered by the Council for Early Childhood Professional Recognition, a nonprofit corporation in Washington, D.C. (see Appendix B).

At the heart of the CDA system are the six major competencies, which are subdivided into 13 functional areas (see Appendix C). These define the standards by which the individual is assessed and the credential awarded. There are some variations based on where the candidate for the credential works; that is, in a center-based preschool, center-based infant/toddler program, family child care home, or bilingual or special-needs setting, or as a home visitor. CDA is an especially attractive alternative for those who do not feel ready to pursue a degree and to those with degrees but without early childhood course work.

Candidates for the CDA must have had, within the past 5 years, the equivalent of about a year's experience and 120 clock hours of formal child care education in eight specific areas related to the age group and setting of the credential for which they are applying. They must be observed by their adviser using an instrument supplied by the CDA, and distribute and collect Parent Opinion Questionnaires. They must also prepare a professional resource file, which includes an autobiographical statement, written examples of competence in each of the six areas, and a collection of resource materials. Finally, there is a verification visit, during which the candidate is observed working in the role of lead caregiver (Council, 1996).

All CDA training, which is administered separately from the assessment and credentialing system, is really preparation for the assessment, focusing on the 13 functional areas. Candidates who are competent in many areas when they begin may require little further training; preparation for their assessment may take only a few months of intensive work. For others it can take 2 years or more, with credit or noncredit courses or seminars, self-directed learning modules, in-service training, and field supervision. Field-based training may be conducted by an individual program, independent consultants, colleges, universities, or training agencies. The council also administers a one-year program, the CDA Professional Preparation Program (CDA P_3).

As a supervisor, you may be asked or wish to volunteer to be an adviser for CDA candidates, to help them prepare for the assessment. Or you may become a training supervisor over a longer period of time. Either of these roles is significant. Trainers must be both advocates and critics for candidates, helping them see what areas need improvement and supporting their efforts to change. Much of the work involves helping candidates learn to assess their own competence and then finding ways to help them develop understandings and skills in the areas that need improvement. With those who need a longer period of training, the process is similar to the kind of on the-job training we described earlier, with, if anything, a greater amount of in-classroom support. The clinical supervision model works very well for this process.

Preparation for a CDA assessment, whether in a formal training program or not, takes a strong commitment of time and energy on the part of the candidate. The support and encouragement of a supervisor, even one who is not serving as an adviser, can contribute immeasurably to the staff member's experience with CDA. At its best, the process is one of self-affirmation, confidence building, and growth for the candidate—and often for others in the center as well.

Detailed information about the CDA assessment and credential system can be obtained from the council.

Staff Resistance to Career-development Opportunities

It is often surprising to find that there are staff members who do not take advantage of, and even resist, professional development opportunities. This can be discouraging for supervisors who have scrounged for training or tuition money or have offered their services as CDA advisers. A number of factors contribute to this reluctance.

First, for many people, especially those from low-income backgrounds or people of color, formal schooling has meant negative experiences with teachers, lack of relevance to their lives, and even academic failure. Further schooling is often seen as a chore at best, and can easily be feared as a repetition of a painful experience. Those with poor language or literacy skills may have very real obstacles to overcome.

Some of these caregivers come from backgrounds that are quite different culturally from the setting in which they are asked to take part. They may have spent most of their lives in isolated rural or inner-city communities, or may have English as their second language. Some may have great potential as teachers, but as "received learners" have never developed a sense of the power of words or of reflective thought (Belenky et al., 1997). Having little or no sense that they can shape their own world without an authority to tell them how, they need time and sensitive support to become involved and make progress in formal education.

Peer pressure not to become involved in anything beyond what is required can also deter people. This may come from those who feel they cannot or do not want to take part themselves or who see courses as an added burden when they are receiving very low pay. They often do not understand how career development can benefit them or the children they teach.

Factors related to a staff member's personal life can also be a deterrent. Women who are working and caring for a family, whether single or married, may just not have the energy to do more or may not want to spend any more time away from their families. Husbands are not always supportive of having their wives further their education, especially as they become more independent or assertive. Even if supportive, they may not be willing or able to help out with housework or babysitting or the caregiver may not feel comfortable asking her husband to do so.

Developmental issues, including life transitions, strongly affect a person's readiness for professional development experiences. For example, young single adults might seem to be obvious candidates for career development, but if they did not finish high school or chose not to go to college, they may be too close to the school experience to want to begin again. Developmentally, their main interest outside of work is likely to be centered on their social life rather than on work or school. Older staff members may feel that it's too late for them to start anew, although frequently people in middle or later years turn out to be the most successful students.

It is important to remember that those who do not respond to opportunities at one time may be candidates at another. Changes in their lives or a new comfort with their jobs may allow staff members to take on the challenge of one course, and this may be enough to start them on a path to a degree or a CDA credential.

As a supervisor, if you have a watchful eye for staff with potential, are sensitive to the factors that affect readiness to become involved, and are able to find ways to help staff realize the advantages of career development, you will discover that many staff members blossom once they begin. The kinds of learning experiences described in the next chapter, which include observations of children and teachers, chances to reflect and figure things out for themselves, and events that make connections to teachers' own experience, often move them to surprising levels.

FINE TUNING

The professional growth of experienced and highly competent staff members and those who have degrees or advanced training in early childhood should not come to a halt simply because they are already skilled or because they are "old-timers." These teachers, who are generally at the higher levels as described in Chapter 5, are, potentially or actually, the backbone of a program, but can seldom be financially rewarded to the extent that they deserve.

Tuning is a term that Bruce Joyce and Beverly Showers (1980) use to describe the act of working on the craft of teaching. Teachers at this stage are ready to fine tune their skills, to be challenged by new ideas, and to have their expertise and experience put to use in new ways. In identifying these practitioners, one should not overlook those who have nontraditional educational backgrounds.

These teachers may be interested in doing classroom "action research" on an area of classroom life that is of special concern to them or to their teaching team, such as the facilitation of language development or play. They may want to learn more about and then implement aspects of program models such as Reggio Emilia, High/Scope, or Montessori. Or they might be willing, with the support of administrators, to take on the challenge of such projects as examining ways to help their program become more family-centered or to better respond to the needs of children whose first language is not English.

Leading workshops within or outside of the program for peers or parents in areas in which they have particular strengths or interests gives skilled staff members a chance to receive recognition for their expertise. It also challenges them to develop the new skills necessary to make a presentation to a group of adults. Although some teachers may at first be reluctant to set themselves up as "experts" before their peers or may lack confidence in their ability to make effective presentations, supervisors can provide support by sharing in the planning or co-leading the session. Acceptance by fellow teachers is more assured if workshop leaders are asked to present in an area in which they are generally recognized as having skill, in which they have recently received training, or in which others admit that they do not feel very competent.

The strategies described below can also be motivating for highly competent teachers while providing the stimulation that helps prevent them from stagnating, becoming burned-out, or leaving.

- Forming a study group around professional readings, perhaps with practitioners from other early childhood programs, or attending seminars that explore issues in depth and over a period of time.

- Having opportunities to be trained and serve as mentors for less trained or experienced teachers. This helps the program as well as the individuals involved. (See Chapter 15 for discussion of mentoring.)
- Taking responsibility for a group developing curriculum, a parent or teacher handbook, a newsletter, or training materials.
- Taking leadership roles in local, regional, and national early childhood organizations. This helps teachers retain a sense of professionalism and receive stimulation, support, and recognition from colleagues beyond their own program or even region.
- Becoming an accreditation validator or CDA adviser. These roles require the flexibility to be released from their work for several days at a time.

In general, fine-tuning activities should recognize staff members' experience and training and, by putting them in new roles, stimulate them to continue to learn and grow as professionals. When there is supervisory support for risk-taking and the flexibility to make changes, the benefits may extend well beyond what the individual accomplishes.

BRINGING THE STAFF TOGETHER

In all well-functioning early childhood programs, time is made available for staff to work together in a variety of ways: in teaching teams, staff meetings, and other working groups. These settings, in which practitioners work with each other across roles, years of experience, and skills and abilities, present especially good opportunities for staff growth.

Teaching Teams

The teaching team of teacher and assistant, which often incorporates other full- and part-time staff, is the fundamental unit of most early childhood centers. At its best, a teaching team is able to plan collaboratively for implementing long- and short-term goals for the classroom; plan day-to-day curriculum and activities; discuss concerns about children and come to agreement on expectations of them as individuals and in groups; and develop a consensus about expectations of one another.

Teamwork does not happen automatically, however. As part of an individualistic society, Americans have few experiences with the give-and-take of a working group. There are all kinds of stumbling blocks: differences in values, unclear educational goals or expectations of children, differences in personality and style, and lack of confidence in resolving differences while trying to come to a consensus.

Staff development at the team level strengthens the team as a unit and helps team members develop or improve collaborative skills. Supervisors may find it beneficial to act as consultants to teams at times, assisting them in planning a new approach to curriculum, changing the room environment, or reflecting on a specific problem. A team's autonomy and growth is enhanced when a supervisor is able to facilitate its efforts to assess its present situation, work through issues, and develop strategies for change.

A social worker, psychologist, parent worker, or special needs coordinator can also contribute to a team's functioning. As a temporary member of the team, he or she can bring valuable expertise, background information, and an outside perspective. Through this process staff members develop skills and knowledge that they can use on their own in the future.

Staff Meetings

Staff meetings that reach beyond the classroom team level are an essential means of communicating with the staff as a whole. They are an important element in combatting burnout, because they are the setting for two-way communication, increased participation in decisions by staff at all levels, developing goal consensus, and the chance for social interaction and professional growth (Boyd & Schneider, 1997; Seiderman, 1978). Meetings can become support systems for teachers when agendas include time for sharing information and feelings about current classroom projects, individual or team progress in putting to work something from the latest workshop, or problems on which staff members would like feedback and ideas.

When shared decision making, goal consensus, and team building are priorities, supervisors can use staff meetings to develop a common vision about goals for children and families. They can discuss in behavioral terms what these goals might look like at the classroom level, and practice decision-making and consensus-building processes as models for using these skills in team meetings (Bloom et al., 1991). At meetings where center-wide matters are discussed and decisions made, staff at all levels should usually be involved—including maintenance workers, cooks, or bus drivers if they are affected.

Other Working Groups

Different groupings of staff within as well as across roles from time to time can also be productive. For example, when lead teachers meet without their assistants, they can share feelings about their role, work on leadership skills, and deal with administrative issues. Aides and assistants too gain from meeting on their own. They may need to discuss concerns about their roles within a team and professional development toward new roles, and to develop skills in communicating their ideas and feelings in a safe atmosphere. Staff cohesion and morale are also increased when small work groups are formed that cut across teams and roles. Curriculum development, revising an evaluation system, or planning workshops, parent meetings, or parties are among the purposes for convening such groups.

Meetings that include variety, stimulation, and fun and that show concern for the group as well as each staff member as an individual and a person contribute to high morale in the work of teaching and caring for children.

CONCLUSION

When staff development is viewed as a means for stimulating the continuing growth of all personnel, its dimensions are boundless. Growth-oriented staff development can take place through planned, ongoing, face-to-face supervision as well as through small-group, large-group, and other enriching experiences that occur on a regular basis. Programs that focus on the specific needs of staff members at different phases of their professional development will challenge them without being overwhelming. And when focused training is balanced with experiences that bring all staff together, supervisors can build relationships among individuals, increase communication, work on common problems and issues, and maintain high spirit and morale in a program.

PROGRAM ACCREDITATION

Directors who would like to obtain NAEYC program accreditation must show evidence of meeting the following criteria (*Guide to Accreditation*, 1998). In addition, the criteria in sections A: "Interactions among Teachers and Children"; B: "Curriculum"; C: "Relationships among Teachers and Families"; and H: "Health and Safety" provide sources for assessing staff competencies when planning the content of staff training and education.

D-1e. Volunteers receive orientation and ongoing professional development and only work with children under supervision of qualified staff members (p. 64).

D-3. New staff, volunteers, and substitutes are adequately oriented about the goals and philosophy of the program, emergency health and safety procedures, individual needs of children assigned to the staff member's care, guidance and classroom management techniques, planned daily activities of the center, and expectations for ethical conduct.

D-4a. The program provides regular training opportunities for staff to participate in ongoing professional development to improve skills in working with children and families or to prepare them to assume more responsible positions.

D-4b. Ongoing professional development provides continuing education and other opportunities for staff to keep abreast of the latest developments in the field, including new programs and practices and pending policy, legislation, or regulatory changes. The amount and kind of continuing education provided varies, depending on the needs of the program, the pre-service qualifications of the staff, and the number of staff pursuing higher education (p. 65).

Reprinted with permission from the National Association for the Education of Young Children

EXERCISES

1. What problems are often encountered in your program when new staff or volunteers first begin? Plan a series of activities to deal with these concerns.

2. Discuss staff development experiences that you could create to help a staff "stay alive" and not get bogged down by the routines of child care or overwhelmed when working conditions are not ideal.

3. If you are presently working in child care and education, identify staff members who could benefit from on-the-job training, career development, or fine tuning. Explore ways to accommodate their individual needs.

4. Are there reasons, other than those covered in this chapter, that explain why staff members might resist taking advantage of career-development opportunities, especially formal course work? How could you work to overcome these or those mentioned in the chapter?

15

Tools for Staff Development and Training

The strategies and techniques described in this chapter are among those that we believe are especially effective as elements of a staff development program. Handbooks, observations of teachers and children, professional reading, workshops and classroom follow-up, mentoring, and accreditation are described in the following pages. Any of these, along with teacher research and individual and group supervision, can be put to use within the framework described in Chapter 14.

Probably the most important factor in planning for the use of these strategies is that they be tied to the overall goals of the center or program in which the teacher, administrator, or provider works. As supervisors and teachers work together to develop goal consensus for their program, they can also plan together both the content and the methods for the training and other experiences that will help them reach these goals. While it is very important to consider individual staff needs and start professional development from where staff members are, the direction this training takes must lead toward the accomplishment of the goals of the organization as a whole (Sparks & Hirsh, 1997).

Most of these methods can be used in more than one phase of training and for more than one purpose. As a supervisor, your decisions about the timing or about content and form of training should be considered in the context of how they can be combined to enhance and reinforce each other so as to provide a coherent staff development plan, and how they can be used for different stages or types of training (orientation through fine tuning). Also keep in mind the special attributes or needs of the participants as a particular group (e.g., total staff, volunteers) and the levels of professional and personal development of the individuals with whom you will be working.

Whatever the tool, ways of connecting training and professional development experiences with children's development and learning must always be a goal. Through discussions with others, whether peers, mentors, or supervisors, and through other reflective practices such as journal writing, caregivers become better able to construct their own knowledge and create meaning from their experiences.

HANDBOOKS

Written material in handbook form can be one of the most practical training tools, especially when used as part of the orientation of new staff or volunteers. It can also be used as a reference in other phases of training.

A handbook should include enough information so that the reader is able to obtain some understanding of the program's purposes and goals, and of the expectations for children, staff, and parents. A word of welcome and a statement about the philosophy of the program sets the tone. The kinds of information listed in the "Orientation for New Staff" section of Chapter 14 are also an important part of this manual.

An expanded version of the daily schedule is a useful way of presenting what goes on during each part of the day and the purposes of each period for the child. Some centers include a description of the learning areas typically found in preschools and the kinds of things children can learn in each. One program uses the daily schedule as a framework for illustrating all aspects of its goals and activities for parent volunteers (see Figure 15.1).

When a handbook is to be used with volunteers, or others with little or no background in early care and education, the most valuable section can be one that contains guidelines and suggestions—even dos and don'ts—for the adult's role with children. Headings like "Why Preschool?" "How Children Learn Best," or "Why So Much Play?" can stimulate interest in important goals such as the primacy of a child's self-esteem, policies about children's home language, and the need for active learning and making choices. It is best to avoid statements that are too general or words and phrases that have meaning mainly to professionals. Wording such as "respect for the child" or "positive ways of changing behavior" are not much help for a person who has had little experience with young children in a group setting. One program with many student volunteers begins a handbook section with "Students frequently ask WHAT DO I DO WHEN . . . ?" followed by simple statements and drawings illustrating ways of handling specific situations, and even words and phrases that can be used with children (Barrington College, n.d.).

A handbook for family child care training might include a greater emphasis on relationships with parents, suggestions for meal planning including sample menus, and information on representative fees, attendance policies, and accounting procedures.

The material in a handbook is most effective when it is direct, positive, and written in simple language without talking down to the reader. An attractive and lively format and a personal style make it easier to read and to absorb. Simple drawings, some blank space on the pages, and different colored paper for different sections can immeasurably enhance the readability and usefulness of such a booklet. A group of teachers who frequently work with students or volunteers might be interested in developing this material.

Figure 15.1 Daily Schedule

8:30 A.M.–9:00 A.M.

Before the children arrive teachers are busy setting up the classroom; tables are set up for breakfast, and materials and supplies are gathered for the day's activities. You can help by

 Setting the tables

 Asking the teachers if they need help preparing the activities they have planned

 Cleaning the classroom, being sure that materials and supplies are in their proper place and look neat—ask a teacher if you need suggestions

9:00 A.M.–9:15 A.M. Headstarters Arrive

Five to ten minutes each day is devoted to a family meeting to discuss the day's activities and share experiences. This is the time where all children, teachers, and volunteers are informed of the day's activities. If you are interested in a special activity and would like to be involved, please inform a teacher. Also, if you have any questions, please feel free to ask. During this time you can help by

 Greeting the children as they arrive at the center

 Helping each child feel important by noticing something special about him/her (e.g., "Jane, I love the flowers on your pants, they're beautiful!", "Can you run fast, John, in those new green sneakers?")

 Encouraging the children to hang their outerwear on the hooks (All cubbies and hooks are labeled with the children's names and a picture they have chosen)

 Participating freely in the family meeting

 Encouraging children to select a mat and sit on it in the large group discussion area

 Sitting with the children in the large group area (a loving arm around a restless child is always helpful)

Reprinted with permission from Woonsocket Head Start, *Let Us Tell You About Head Start* (Woonsocket, RI, no date).

A handbook must not merely be given out with the expectation that it will be read and understood. Rather it should be considered as an adjunct to and reinforcement for other aspects of training. Its greatest advantages are that it provides the same information to all readers and can be referred to whenever necessary to refresh the memories of both supervisor and staff member. The written words provide a degree of objectivity that is sometimes obscured in person-to-person interchanges.

OBSERVING TEACHING

Two observational techniques can help both new and experienced caregivers *learn to see* what teachers do to create an environment where children can grow and learn. The first takes advantage of the incidental, day-to-day experiences of the classroom as they happen. For the second, a supervisor and an individual or a group plan what is to be observed with specific goals in mind.

Informal Modeling

Modeling goes on all the time when there are two or more people working together in the same space with the same children. Sciarra and Dorsey (1990) emphasize that directors model behavior beginning with their first encounter with a new staff member. An attitude of trust and mutual respect for adults and children communicated at this early phase sets the stage for the way staff members are expected to interact with children, families, and colleagues.

Caregivers are most likely to learn from the modeling of teaching behaviors when they are helped to focus on significant aspects of what is taking place. It is not easy to recognize, for example, the importance of the ways in which a teacher reacts to small incidents during the day, spontaneously picking up on what a child says or does, preventing trouble by anticipating problems, and then keeping activities moving or changing pace.

One preschool director/teacher models reflective teaching by thinking out loud, describing what she is doing as she does it. She might say, "It's beginning to cloud up outside. The children seem to be getting restless. Let's go sit with them for a minute." Or (to illustrate that few decisions are clear cut) "Activity in the house corner seems to be beginning to break down. I wonder, shall we wait a little to see if it will work out, or take a group and read a story?"

Nonteaching supervisors who visit a classroom during a free-play period can model appropriate behaviors in the role of a temporary assistant on the classroom team. This technique, which Virginia Hatch (1979) calls "participatory supervision," is especially effective when the lead teacher or the classroom team as a whole is the focus of training.

Lenore McCarthy and Elizabeth Landerholm (1978) used a similar method in their work as consultants to day care centers. They found that participating in planning and acting as a backup for "first-time activities" were especially effective. They had particular success with initiating staff to field trips, both local walks and more extensive excursions. Teachers became eager to try trips on their own, as they were able to see the positive effects of planning.

Trainees also benefit when teachers or supervisors talk about children—their styles, likes and dislikes, and skills—as they work together in the classroom. This helps caregivers see the individuality of each child and to understand teachers' actions in relation to specific child behaviors. This can be especially useful when a class includes children with special needs or those from a variety of cultural or linguistic backgrounds.

Commenting when a child is misbehaving (or seems to be) can be especially instructive, since views about discipline are so bound by one's own experiences. The supervisor might say, "We're letting Tommy stay out of the group for the time being, since he becomes overwhelmed by sitting with so many people." Or "I wasn't sure whether to intervene in that little squabble or not. I'm glad to see they've worked it out themselves. It can be valuable when they do, but I try to keep an eye out."

These situations become a rich source of material for individual or group conferences, which should follow important incidents as closely as possible. They can be discussed and related to other experiences, to readings, or to other kinds of training in which caregivers have taken part, and trainees can be encouraged to try out effective techniques themselves.

There are some cautions about modeling by supervisors, especially if they are not members of the classroom team. Sensitivity to the roles of other adults in the classroom, particularly in participant supervision situations, is essential. It is helpful to make clear to all members of the team, especially the lead teacher, that your role is to fit in with the ongoing program, not to take over responsibilities that teachers, assistants, or volunteers see as their own. The message "You're really not doing it right; super-teacher will show you how" is less likely to be conveyed when supervisors respond in a natural way to children's real needs within the context of the particular activity.

Taking advantage of informal modeling opportunities helps new staff and volunteers to see that "teaching" includes everything that goes on in the classroom. These built-in strategies can in themselves make the difference between a person's passively accepting what goes on in the classroom and discovering that teaching involves an attitude of continually questioning and learning from one's experiences.

Planned Observations

Planned observations of other caregivers provide a different kind of learning opportunity. These observations work especially well when based on a specific need identified by the supervisor or the supervisee. A particular setting, behavioral focus, or time of day can then be selected to best accomplish that purpose. The caregiver thus takes part in the decision about what to observe and why.

Beginning Teachers

During orientation or on-the-job training, trainees can be assigned to observe teachers during different parts of the day, especially times such as free play or transitions when the teaching role is not so clearly identifiable. A discussion beforehand about what to look for or an observation sheet with focus questions narrows what is to be examined to manageable proportions. For example, instead of suggesting that a caregiver "observe transitions," a series of observations might be set up. One could focus on how teachers prepare children for a change (say, going from free play to snack), another on what they do to make it easier for children who don't function well during transitions, and a third on how teachers work together to take care of stragglers. An observation sheet for free play/choice time might include this series of questions:

How do teachers help children make choices?
What do they do when a child seems to be wandering around?
What seems to help children learn from their play?
What seems to interfere?

Eventually, as caregivers develop their observation skills, they will be able to function with much more open-ended guidelines.

Experienced Teachers

More experienced caregivers may respond better to ideas for changes in teaching strategies when they can examine alternatives to help them determine what method would work best for them. For example, in a supervisory conference a concern may be raised about keeping the children's attention while reading aloud. Through a problem-solving process, the teacher may be able to come up with some causes for their inattentiveness but still be unsure of what to do about it. It could then be suggested that she observe several other teachers as they read to children and identify some alternative strategies for keeping the children involved.

Frequently teachers are stimulated by workshops to try new teaching techniques or activities but do not feel confident enough to actually attempt them. In such situations, the supervisor or a skilled teacher can demonstrate the technique in the classroom. Art, cooking, and creative movement are types of experiences that lend themselves well to this type of demonstration, since they are more easily shown than explained. If at all appropriate to the activity, classroom team members should take some part in it. These observations are most effective when they begin with a planning session in which all participants are actively involved and when they are followed by an evaluation session during which perceptions, questions, and opinions are shared.

Other Observation Strategies

When opportunities for conferences are limited, an interactive journal can be an effective means of structuring observations. Journals also help caregivers to begin the process of reflection and to gain insight into their own work. A supervisor's response to an entry about a disruptive child might be:

> I see Joey's difficulties in coping with change made the transition from snack very difficult the other day. Ms. R. has some effective ways of working with a similar child. See if you can arrange to observe her this week as she interacts with him. Keep notes in your journal, adding your own thoughts, and we can discuss it next week.

Peer support, sharing, and a sense of community can be engendered when staff members are encouraged to observe each other. One supervisor started a regular series of observations in which every staff member visited at least one other classroom in the center over a period of several weeks. There was preparation beforehand and an observation sheet. Although the purpose was to find new ideas and to gain perspective on their own teaching, the teachers were asked to give some kind of feedback to the other teachers they observed. Not only did the project serve the purpose it was designed for, but because the teachers each received nonjudgmental, mostly positive feedback and had seen their colleagues' teaching, they became more confident in sharing and in working together without the reluctance they had previously shown.

The benefits of group observations, which can take place in staff members' own or other programs, have been noted in the discussions of group clinical supervision in Chapters 10 and 11. Groups can be composed of staff from similar or different roles and backgrounds, depending on the purpose. The discussions before and after the observations, with or without a supervisor's assistance, allow for sharing multiple views of the same situation, which adds immeasurably to the kinds of insights obtained from the observations.

Even when models are less than ideal, there are likely to be some teaching techniques worth examining. A highly structured experienced teacher may have excellent ways of planning for or handling routines, while a teacher whose room seems somewhat chaotic may have interpersonal or creative skills worth observing. Learning also occurs from negative role models: "The process of comparing and contrasting philosophies and practices gives a stronger sense of what one's own program is like. Essentially, it defines it and increases the staff member's sense of identity with the program" (Willis & Ricciuti, 1975, p. 119).

The advantages of using observation of teaching as a training tool are many. It is easily arranged and has a base in the reality of the classroom. The consciousness-raising that occurs during its use, when combined with other training and staff development experiences, results in real learning for staff members.

OBSERVING CHILDREN

When teachers—whether they are new to the job or have been teaching for years—really begin to look at children, new worlds open up to them. Observing increases caregivers' understanding of developmental age/stage characteristics and of how children construct learning through their play. They gain insight into some of the very real differences children show in their interactions with adults, with other children, and with equipment and materials. And they develop an awareness of changes in individual children over time, an ability especially important for those who work with infants, speakers of other languages, or special-needs children. Objective observation of children is also, of course, a skill in itself that should be acquired and used by anyone who works with young children.

The specific techniques for observing explained below are especially appropriate for on-the-job trainees and experienced teachers, as they take some time to learn. As suggested in Chapter 14, observations during the orientation phase of training are better developed around aspects of the classroom or the children that will help the new staff person understand the immediate setting. In addition to the following, the methods described in Chapter 11 may also be helpful.

Anecdotal records of one or two children over a period of several weeks help caregivers gain an understanding of children's behavior over time. These brief notes of events during the day can be recorded on cards when teachers get a chance, or during rest periods and at the end of the day. They should be reviewed periodically to look for patterns of behavior that give clues for various aspects of classroom planning. Many programs require that these be done on a regular basis.

Ten-minute time samples (Rowen, 1973) provide different kinds of information. They are direct "running records" of everything that happens during a 10-minute period and are made on the spot, when the observer is not interacting with children. The technique is especially valuable in revealing children's ability to be self-directing, to explore and learn from their explorations, and to learn through their play. With the use of a format that separates objective observations and comments (see Chapter 11), practitioners become aware of the difference between *describing* exactly what they hear and see and *interpreting* that behavior, and they learn to eliminate judgmental statements.

Time samples are especially effective for those working with infants. Someone with little experience with babies may see little more than flailing limbs, smiles, and crying, or sleeping and eating. Direct observations often result in surprising insights when caregivers see that every gesture provides information about a child's development and personality.

Elizabeth Jones and Margie Carter (1991) ask teachers to look for the kinds of play they would like to see, looking for "master players." They ask them to represent what they see, by sketching children's constructions or writing down what children say about their play. They then have them "broadcast" this information throughout the center, perhaps on a bulletin board. Both teachers and children are thrilled to see these representations of their work. Teachers using the Reggio Emilia approach gather information from listening to and observing children to help in planning next steps in projects from day to day. They extensively document these projects and post them for children and parents to see (Vecchi, 1993).

Observations of individual children have an added advantage in that they can be used as a working tool for the classroom team. When care is taken that records are descriptive and not judgmental, they can be shared among staff members and even with parents to assist in making decisions about a child or the program. Assignment of any observations of children, of course, must be accompanied by a discussion of professionalism and confidentiality.

There are many sources for tools and methods for observing young children. Among these are Cohen, Stern, and Balaban's classic book, *Observing and Recording the Behavior of Young Children* (1997), which provides guidelines and questions for looking at classroom behavior in a variety of settings, and the *High/Scope Child Observation Record (COR) for Ages 2½–6* (1992).

Because young children's behavior reveals so much about their abilities and about how they learn, observation is an especially valuable tool for training. It makes available a reality base that is hard to find in any other way.

PROFESSIONAL READING

A well-stocked library of professional materials has an essential place in any child care setting. Finding ways to encourage its use, however, can sometimes be a challenge. Although books and magazines with specific project ideas are usually quite popular, it may be more difficult to stimulate other professional reading by staff members. There are, however, both direct and indirect ways of working on this goal.

Polly Greenberg, in *Day Care Do-It-Yourself Staff Growth Program* (1975), takes the direct approach. She suggests that staff be given a new recommended reading assignment every 2 weeks, with specified times during the day when staff members are *expected* to read. In Greenberg's program some of the times regularly scheduled for staff meetings were designated for reading, along with one or two nap-times and "light hours" when volunteers and other staff could cover. She provided specific guidelines for reading and for discussing the material. On certain days, staff meetings were used for "imaginative problem solving" based on the readings. Greenberg's feeling about the importance of reading is so strong that she lists "Finding Time for Professional Reading" as one of the specific skills for staff members.

Other, less direct methods can also be used to encourage staff in this most important medium for growth. A place should be found in which books, magazines, and photocopied articles can be informally displayed. Teachers are much more likely to leaf through such material if it is in a place that they gather frequently and if it is changed periodically so as not to get stale. Books and articles related to current in-service topics or background information on classroom themes are among those that can be highlighted. Workshop leaders can sometimes provide copies of readings ahead of time to provide background for the topic to be presented, and even allow a brief time for the readings to be reported on and discussed at the workshop. Even though not all participants will read them, this encourages more interest in the topic.

Supervisors serve as models when they share their own reading experiences in staff meetings on a regular basis and by making the reading materials available afterward. Staff members too can be invited to share books or articles they have recently read. Individual conferences and meetings with classroom teams also provide opportunities for supervisors to suggest readings related to a specific area of concern. In any of the above settings, the greatest value will come when staff have opportunities to discuss with each other ideas from their reading in terms of their relevance to their work with children and families or with each other.

Some staff members may be interested in researching books, articles, or magazines to recommend to parents; writing short reviews for the center newsletter; or creating a special book-sharing area on the parent bulletin board.

Supervisors are sometimes surprised to discover that some members of their staff are not proficient readers. For these caregivers, seen more frequently in programs in low-income areas, materials that are both appropriate and not too difficult must be searched out. For those for whom English is a second language, readings in appropriate languages can be made available. Connecting staff members with courses in reading and writing improvement can make a great difference in enabling all to become full participants in the field. An awareness of the readiness levels of all staff members and a sensitivity to differences in ability to read English are important factors in making reading a successful training tool. When encouraged through enthusiasm and low-key persistence, staff may gradually become comfortable with the idea of doing regular reading and discover its relevance to their day-to-day work.

WORKSHOPS AND RELATED ACTIVITIES

We expect a lot from workshops. In one or a few sessions, participants are supposed to develop new skills or understandings, or to change attitudes toward children and parents. They are then presumed to be ready to demonstrate what they have learned on their return to the classroom. It's no wonder the results are often disappointing.

What is it that makes workshops "take"? A survey of participants in staff development in Head Start found that follow-up activities were among the highest rated training components both in promoting change and in helping participants to transfer their learning to the classroom (Wolfe, 1994). In particular, follow-up job assistance, opportunities to observe, opportunities to practice, and handouts were especially helpful. Among other factors that have been found to be effective are clear objectives, staff readiness and motivation, and matching workshops to staff needs and interests, including allowance for choice.

We need to be clear that the purpose of having staff take part in such training, as in all staff development experiences, is to create change. Change is a highly personal experience and is dependent on the feelings of those involved (Bloom et al., 1991). It takes place in three areas: knowledge, skills or behaviors, and attitudes. Change in knowledge tends to be the easiest to obtain, but does not always carry over into new practices, thus follow-up activities (discussed below) are an important factor in translating knowledge into skills. When carried out in ways that encourage discussion and reflection on implications, in group or one-to-one situations, this follow-up assistance can lead to attitude change as well. A change in attitude is an especially important consideration when staff members are confronted with new approaches that impact on value systems and long-held ideas about how children learn.

Ideally, staff members should be able to avail themselves of both outside and "in-house" workshops. Those that take place outside the program make it possible for teachers to choose sessions that meet their needs and interests, and give them opportunities to interact with staff from other centers or day care homes. On-site meetings are especially relevant when they are planned as a result of discussions of overall center goals or from the self-evaluation process for accreditation or Child Development Associate (CDA).

All programs should have a budget line for staff development, including funds for paying presenters and fees for workshop and courses. Parent fundraisers and small grants can also be tapped, a process that helps to educate parents and business leaders about the need for better-educated early childhood personnel.

Becoming involved with the organizations that sponsor training in your area helps to ensure that the topics and the presenters represent the values and approaches you want for your staff. Consideration of adult learning principles, including active learning and links to real life and work, are especially important. As a supervisor, you also may find it a good policy to lead some workshop sessions and to encourage teachers to do so. The process of preparation, though time-consuming, is a way of keeping up-to-date in the field and adds to your credibility with staff.

The following points may be helpful in incorporating workshops into your overall plan for staff development:

- You can identify the needs and interests of staff through a variety of methods. Discussing plans for specific workshops or courses with individuals during evaluation conferences allows them to express special interests and gives them a stake in their choices. Individual or team interviews about workshop interests make it possible to clarify and explore issues in depth.
- A more thorough understanding of any topic is developed if you schedule a series of workshops over several weeks. This allows between-session assignments such as trying out certain behaviors or activities, or observing a child or a classroom situation. There is a motivation to try these activities when participants know that they will be able to discuss them and receive feedback on their efforts. This design is also helpful for staff members who are uneasy about taking college courses, giving them opportunities to begin to gain confidence through multisession training.
- To further the likelihood that workshop participants will put new ideas or skills to work, you can ask them to write down at least one thing they will do to try out a new technique or put new knowledge to use, and to check off which of several kinds of assistance they would like to have. Arrangements can then be made for you or mentor teachers to help or for teams or study groups to plan together about changes they would like to make.
- You can provide effective follow-up assistance by seeing that materials and resources are available; physically helping to rearrange a room; and being available to assist in planning and trouble shooting, demonstrate new techniques, join in as a colleague when new methods are first being tried, and observe and give feedback to staff as they try them out.
- By inviting staff members to share their experiences at staff meetings, you can give added encouragement and support and help to reinforce and maintain continued growth.

MENTORING

The use of mentors for beginning teachers or family home providers offers an added dimension to the individual assistance available to them. At the same time, the mentors themselves are able to grow in their own professionalism.

Mentors are skilled and experienced teachers or providers who serve as guides or coaches for novice teachers. They may work in the same program as their "protégés" (or "mentees") or in a different one. Their role differs from that of a supervisor in two ways: They are peers of the people they guide, and while they support, give feedback, and counsel them, they do not formally evaluate them.

Many knowledgeable and skilled caregivers could find this role fulfilling. It provides opportunities for new challenges and learning, both through formal training in such areas as communication skills and adult learning, and through opportunities to learn from their less experienced protégés. Not all advanced teachers, however, would make good mentors. They should be people who are interested in helping adults as well as children to learn and grow; who see themselves as learners; who are creative, flexible, and reflective; and who have good interpersonal skills with adults and a respect for diversity (Bellm, Whitebook, & Hnatiuk, 1997).

The training that is required for mentors would include many of the approaches described in this book. There are a number of formal training programs, the oldest of which is the state-supported California Early Childhood Mentor Program. The Early Childhood Mentoring Alliance at the Center for the Child Care Workforce (see Appendix B) can provide information on many aspects of mentoring.

ACCREDITATION AS A STAFF DEVELOPMENT STRATEGY

The self-study process for the National Association for the Education of Young Children (NAEYC) and other accreditation systems (see Chapter 2) can become a highly effective context for staff development. The decision to work toward accreditation is a statement of a commitment to quality, and thus to the examination—and improvement where needed—of all aspects of the program. Because all staff members are working toward the same goal, and using the same criteria as they work through the self-study, they gain a sense of community and ownership of their program.

The self-study criteria provide concrete outside standards against which staff members can measure their work. Like the CDA, the process is self-affirming when strengths are validated, which helps caregivers to feel more comfortable in pinpointing areas of concern. When supervisors build training around these identified areas, staff members have a strong incentive to apply the newly acquired information and skills. As a consequence, they often find that their jobs are made easier, because their new knowledge and skills support their everyday work (S. Connor, personal communication, April 2, 1998).

The accreditation process takes a strong, significant, and sustained commitment from administration and staff. Studies have indicated that centers that have intensive on-site assistance are much more likely to complete their self-study. This assistance includes regular mentoring, paid staff release time for training, and support groups for administrators ("What Centers Need," 1997). State and other funds can often be obtained to support training and fees.

KEEPING THE JOY IN EARLY CARE AND EDUCATION

Because we believe that an early childhood program should be an enjoyable place for both staff and children, we conclude this book with a few suggestions from many people in the field for experiences designed with these goals in mind.

- Promote caring and sharing, Clare Cherry (1980) suggests. At the first staff meeting of each new school year, she challenges each staff member to "see to it that each of the other teachers has the best year teaching they've ever had" (p. 27). Cherry has found that teachers who previously hoarded their ideas behind closed doors now get excited about sharing new ideas, resources, and materials.
- Highlight staff accomplishments through the newsletter and bulletin boards. Have a "photo gallery" to celebrate "who we are as a center." Include places for this and for the exchange of staff ideas in the teachers' room as well (Bloom, 1995a).
- "Make teaching fun," one supervisor suggests. Plan center-wide special days for the children built around a theme, a special guest, or a puppet show. Do it so it's fun for the *teachers* as well as the children, *not* so that it's so much work that the enjoyment is lost.
- Have social events periodically in which staff have a chance just to get to know each other as people. When people discover or rediscover that they can have fun together, tensions can be relieved and even dissipated. Include families and friends in some events. Plan them with sensitivity for financial and family needs, and help staff to accept individual lack of participation without resentment.
- Add food to a work session or a staff meeting. It is a catalyst for informal talk and relaxation. If done only occasionally, it gives a meeting a bit of a party atmosphere. One staff found that getting together to make cookies and wrap presents for the holidays was fun in itself and also provided an opportunity to share perceptions of children on a professional level while enjoying the holiday spirit. Including parents adds to creating a community around the program.
- Once in a while, vary the place where meetings are held. This creates a change of pace for a regular staff meeting but is especially effective if you must hold an extra one. Sometimes issues arise that the staff themselves feel cannot be resolved during the regular course of the day. Perhaps tensions have developed, or time is needed just to think about a problem in a different way. A meeting at someone's house for pizza, for example, can supply the time and the atmosphere to permit staff to look at an issue as a problem to be solved rather than as a difficulty that creates hard feelings.

- Have "catch-up days" or "curriculum refreshers." Find blocks of uninter-rupted time when the staff can work on renewing skills, rearranging the learning environment, or discussing special curriculum topics. Even full-day programs can sometimes close down for one or two days, perhaps in late August, if parents know ahead of time that they will have to make other arrangements. In the summer, when there are fewer children in attendance, several days to a week of full afternoons might also be arranged. Hire sub-stitutes and use job trainees and supplementary staff where needed.
- Encourage teachers to try out things that are related to their special inter-ests and provide personal and material support for them. Help them to use these areas as a focus within the overall goals of the center and classroom.
- Build a personal day or flexible time off into personnel policies. A half-day off on a staggered basis for holiday shopping can make a huge difference to staff who work long hours, as can pay or at least "comp time" to make up for an evening meeting.
- Finally, and perhaps most important, be an advocate for better pay and working conditions for early childhood staff, to parents and to the public at large, both in your own program and in the profession as a whole.

EXERCISES

1. Design a handbook for new staff and volunteers at your center or form a committee of staff members for this purpose. Serve as a facilitator as needed.
2. Develop ways to assess the needs and interests of staff members as a basis for planning staff development activities. Use a combination of means. Develop a plan for addressing one of those needs/interests through an integrated set of experiences.
3. You are relatively new to your supervisory job at the Sunny Brook Child Care Center. In a recent evaluation you noted that Josh, a new teacher, has been giving an excessive number of time outs to children in his kindergar-ten class. In discussing this with him, he indicates that the children are being disrespectful and need to be held accountable. Your observations indicate that other methods of handling these situations would be more appropriate and effective. Using any three or more of the methods discussed in this chapter, describe how you and Josh could make a staff development plan to help him understand this issue and change his approach.

Appendix A: Responding to Linguistic and Cultural Diversity: Recommendations for Effective Early Childhood Education

(Excerpted from the NAEYC Position Statement, 1996)

For the optimal development and learning of all children, educators must *accept* the legitimacy of children's home language, *respect* (hold in high regard) and *value* (esteem, appreciate) the home culture, and *promote* and *encourage* the active involvement and support of all families, including extended and nontraditional family units.

A. Recommendations for working with children

- Recognize that all children are cognitively, linguistically, and emotionally connected to the language and culture of their home.
- Acknowledge that children can demonstrate their knowledge and capabilities in many ways.
- Understand that without comprehensible input, second-languaage learning can be difficult.

B. Recommendations for working with families

- Actively involve parents and families in the early learning program and setting.
- Encourage and assist all parents in becoming knowledgeable about the cognitive value for children of knowing more than one language, and provide them with strategies to support, maintain, and preserve home-language learning.
- Recognize that parents and families must rely on caregivers and educators to honor and support their children in the cultural values and norms of the home.

C. Recommendations for professional preparation

- Provide early childhood educators with professional preparation and development in the areas of culture, language, and diversity.
- Recruit and support early childhood educators who are trained in languages other than English.

D. Recommendations for programs and practice

- Recognize that children can and will acquire the use of English even when their home language is used and respected.
- Support and preserve home-language usage.
- Develop and provide alternative and creative strategies for young children's learning.

Source: Young Children, 51 (2): 4–12. Excerpted by permission of the National Association for the Education of Young Children.

Appendix B:
Organizational Resources

Center for Career Development in Early Care and Education
Wheelock College
200 The Riverway
Boston, MA 02215
617-734-5200
Helps states and localities bring about systematic change, replacing fragmented systems of training. Publications, seminars.

Center for the Child Care Workforce
735 15th Street, NW, Suite 1037
Washington, DC 20005-2112
202-737-7700
www.ccw.org
Compensation, working conditions, training, publications. Worthy Wage Campaign, Early Childhood Mentoring Alliance.

Council for Early Childhood Professional Recognition
1341 G Street, NW, Suite 400
Washington, DC 20005-3015
800-424-4310
Child Development Associate (CDA) competency standards, assessment, and training.
www.cdacouncil.org

National Association for Family Child Care
206 Sixth Avenue, Midland Bldg., Suite 900
Des Moines, IA 50309
515-282-8192
Affiliates; newsletter, publications, insurance, accreditation.
www.nafcc.org

National Association for the Education of Young Children
1509 16th Street, NW
Washington, DC 20036-1426
800-424-2460; 202-232-8777
www.naeyc.org/naeyc
Also state, regional, and local affiliates; accreditation, conferences, journals, publications, position statements.

National Association of Child Care Resource and Referral Agencies
1319 F Street, NW, Suite 810
Washington, DC 20004
202-393-5501
www.childcarerr.org
A membership organization for community-based child care resource and referral agencies; publications, technical assistance, training, advocacy.

National Black Child Development
Institute
1023 15th Street, NW, Suite 600
Washington, DC 20005
202-387-1281
www.nbcdi.org
Publications, affiliates, direct services,
newsletters, conferences.

National Institute on Out-of-School
Time
(Formerly School-Age Child Care
Project)
Wellesley College
106 Central Street
Wellesley, MA 02181-8259
781-283-2547
www.wellesley.edu/WCW/CRW/
SAC/

Research, education and training,
consultation, and program development. Publications, self-study process
(ASQ); accreditation system being
developed.

National Latino Children's Institute
142 West Sixth Street
Austin, TX 78703-5139
512-472-9971
www.nlci.org
A national network of endorsers,
supporters, and experts on Latino
children's issues; promotes the National
Latino Children's Agenda; clearing-
house/resource center; training and
technical assistance; special events.

Appendix C: CDA Competency Goals and Functional Areas

CDA COMPETENCY GOALS	FUNCTIONAL AREAS
I. To establish and maintain a safe, healthy learning environment.	1. *Safe:* Candidate provides a safe environment to prevent and reduce injuries.
	2. *Healthy:* Candidate promotes good health and nutrition and provides an environment that contributes to the prevention of illness.
	3. *Learning Environment:* Candidate uses space, relationships, materials, and routines as resources for constructing an interesting, secure, and enjoyable environment that encourages play, exploration, and learning.
II. To advance physical and intellectual competence.	4. *Physical:* Candidate provides a variety of equipment, activities, and opportunities to promote the physical development of children.
	5. *Cognitive:* Candidate provides activities and opportunities that encourage curiosity, exploration, and problem solving appropriate to the developmental levels and learning styles of children.
	6. *Communication:* Candidate actively communicates with children and provides opportunities and support for children to understand, acquire, and use verbal and nonverbal means of communicating thoughts and feelings.

continued

CDA COMPETENCY GOALS	FUNCTIONAL AREAS
III. To support social and emotional development and to provide positive guidance.	7. *Creative:* Candidate provides opportunities that stimulate children to play with sound, rhythm, language, materials, space, and ideas in individual ways and to express their creative abilities.
	8. *Self:* Candidate provides physical and emotional security for each child and helps each child to know, accept, and take pride in himself or herself and to develop a sense of independence.
	9. *Social:* Candidate helps each child feel accepted in the group, helps children learn to communicate and get along with others, and encourages feelings of empathy and mutual respect among children and adults.
	10. *Guidance:* Candidate provides a supportive environment in which children can begin to learn and practice appropriate and acceptable behaviors as individuals and as a group.
IV. To establish positive and productive relationships with families.	11. *Families:* Candidate maintains an open, friendly, and cooperative relationship with each child's family, encourages their involvement in the program, and support the child's relationship with his or her family.
V. To ensure a well-run, purposeful program responsive to participant needs.	12. *Program Management:* Candidate is a manager who uses all available resources to ensure an effective operation. The Candidate is a competent organizer, planner, record keeper, communicator, and a cooperative co-worker.
VI. To maintain a commitment to professionalism.	13. *Professionalism:* Candidate makes decisions based on knowledge of early childhood theories and practices. Candidate promotes quality in child care services. Candidate takes advantage of opportunities to improve competence, both for personal and professional growth and for the benefit of children and families.

Source: The Child Development Associate Assessment System and Competency Standards: Preschool Caregivers in Center-Based Programs (1996). Washington, DC: Council for Early Childhood Professional Recognition. Reprinted by permission.

References

Acheson, K. A., & Gall, M. D. (1980). *Techniques in the clinical supervision of teachers: Preservice and inservice applications.* New York: Longman.

Allport, G. W. (1958). *The nature of prejudice.* Garden City, NY: Doubleday Anchor Books.

Almy, M. (1975). *The early childhood educator at work.* New York: Teachers College Press.

Arin-Krupp, J. (1981). *Adult development: Implications for staff development.* Manchester, CT: Adult Development and Learning.

Arredondo, D. E. (1998, April). *Enhancing cognitive complexity through collegial supervision.* Paper presented at the annual meeting of the American Educational Research Association, San Diego.

Baker, A. C. (1997). Provider-led training: A new model of development for low-income providers. *Young Children, 52*(7), 4–7.

Barrington College Early Childhood Center (n.d.). *Student handbook.* Barrington, RI: Author.

Beers, C. D. (1993). Telling our stories: The CDA process in Native American Head Start. In E. Jones (Ed.), *Growing teachers: Partnerships in staff development* (pp. 2–19). Washington, DC: National Association for the Education of Young Children.

Belenky, M. F., Clinchy, B. M., Goldberger, N. R., & Tarule, J. M. (1997). *Women's ways of knowing: The development of self, voice, and mind.* New York: Basic Books. (Original work published 1986)

Bellm, D., Whitebook, M., & Hnatiuk, P. (1997). *The early childhood mentoring curriculum: A handbook for mentors.* Washington, DC: Center for the Child Care Workforce.

Bents, R. H., & Howey, K. R. (1981). Staff development—change in the individual. In B. Dillon-Peterson (Ed.), *Staff development: Organization development* (pp. 11–36). Alexandria, VA: Association for Supervision and Curriculum Development.

Binh, D. T. (1975). *A handbook for teachers of Vietnamese students.* Arlington, VA: Center for Applied Linguistics.

Blanchard, K. H., & Johnson, S. (1982). *The one-minute manager.* New York: William Morrow.

Bloom, P. J. (1989, March). *The qualifications of child care center directors.* Paper presented at the annual meeting of the American Educational Research Association, San Francisco.

231

Bloom, P. J. (1995a). Building a sense of community: A broader view. *Child Care Information Exchange, 101*, 47–50.

Bloom, P. J. (1995b). The quality of worklife in early childhood programs. In S. Bredekamp & B. Willer (Eds.), *NAEYC accreditation: A decade of learning and the years ahead* (pp. 13–24). Washington, DC: National Association or the Education of Young Children.

Bloom, P. J. (1997). Decision-making influence: Who has it? Who wants it? *Child Care Information Exchange, 114*, 7–14.

Bloom, P. J., Sheerer, M., & Britz, J. (1991). *Blueprint for action: Achieving center-based change through staff development.* Lake Forest, IL: New Horizons.

Bowers, C. A., & Flinders, D. J. (1990). *Responsive teaching: An ecological approach to classroom patterns of language, culture, and thought.* New York: Teachers College Press.

Bowers, C. A., & Flinders, D. J. (1991). *Culturally responsive teaching and supervision: A handbook for staff development.* New York: Teachers College Press.

Boyd, B. J., & Schneider, N. I. (1997). Perceptions of the work environment and burnout in Canadian child care providers. *Journal of Research in Childhood Education, 11*, 171–180.

Brandt, R. (1996). On a new direction for teacher evaluation: A conversation with Tom McGreal. *Educational Leadership, 53*(6): 30–33.

Bredekamp, S., & Copple, C. (Eds.). (1997). *Developmentally appropriate practice in early childhood programs* (rev. ed.). Washington, DC: National Association for the Education of Young Children.

Bredekamp, S., & Willer, B. (1992). Of ladders and lattices, cores and cones: Conceptualizing an early childhood professional development system. *Young Children, 47*(3), 47–50.

Brundage, D. H., & Mackeracher, D. (1980). *Adult learning principles and their application to program planning.* Toronto: Ontario Institute for Studies in Education.

Bruner, J. (1996). *The culture of education.* Cambridge, MA: Harvard University Press.

Cadwell, L. B. (1997). *Bringing Reggio Emelia home: An innovative approach to early childhood education.* New York: Teachers College Press.

Carnegie Task Force on Meeting the Needs of Young Children. (1994). *Starting points: Meeting the needs of our youngest children.* New York: Carnegie Corporation of New York.

Carter, M. (1995). Building a community among teachers. *Child Care Information Exchange, 101*, 52–54.

Caruso, J., & Graham, C. (1994). *Collaborative supervision handbook.* Unpublished. Framingham State College, Framingham, MA.

Cazden, C. L. (1979). *Language in education: Variation in the teacher-talk register.* Paper presented at the 30th Annual Georgetown University Round Table on Languages and Linguistics, *Language in Public Life.*

Cazden, C. L. (1995). A different road to English. *Harvard Graduate School of Education Bulletin, 39*, 12.

Center for the Child Care Workforce. (1998). *Current data on child care salaries and benefits in the United States.* Washington, DC: Author.

Chang, H. N-L., Muckelroy, A., & Pulido-Tobiassen, D. (1996). *Looking in, look-*

ing out: Redefining child care and early education in a diverse society. San Francisco: California Tomorrow.

Cherry, C. (1980, July). Promoting harmonious staff relationships. *Child Care Information Exchange,* pp. 25–28.

Cochran-Smith, M., & Lytle, S. L. (1993). *Inside/outside: Teacher research and knowledge.* New York: Teachers College Press.

Cogan, M. L. (1973). *Clinical supervision.* Boston: Houghton Mifflin.

Cohen, D., Stern, V., & Balaban, N. (1997). *Observing and recording the behavior of young children* (4th ed.). New York: Teachers College Press.

Cohen, N. E., & Pompa, D. (1996). Multicultural perspectives on quality. In S. L. Kagan & N. E. Cohen (Eds.), *Reinventing early care and education: A vision for a quality system* (pp. 81–98). San Francisco: Jossey-Bass.

Colorado State Board of Education. (1973). *Developing training support systems for home day care.* Denver, CO: Author.

Cost, Quality, and Child Outcomes Study Team. (1995). *Cost, quality, and child outcomes in child care centers: Technical report.* Denver, CO: Economics Department, University of Colorado at Denver.

Council for Early Childhood Professional Recognition. (1996). *The Child Development Associate assessment system and competency standards: Preschool caregivers in center-based programs.* Washington, DC: Author.

Deal, T. E., & Kennedy, A. A. (1982). *Corporate cultures: The rites and rituals of corporate life.* Reading, MA: Addison-Wesley.

Delpit, L. (1995). *Other people's children: Cultural conflict in the classroom.* New York: New Press.

Derman-Sparks, L., & the A.B.C. Task Force. (1989). *Anti-bias curriculum: Tools for empowering young children.* Washington, DC: National Association for the Education of Young Children.

Derman-Sparks, L. & Phillips, C. B. (1997). *Teaching/learning anti-racism: A developmental approach.* New York: Teachers College Press.

Dodge, D. T., & Colker, L. J. (1992). *The creative curriculum for early childhood* (3rd ed.). Washington, DC: Teaching Stategies, Inc.

Duff, E. R., Brown, Mac H., & Van Scoy, J. (1995). Reflection and self-evaluation: Keys to professional development. *Young Children, 50*(4), 81–86.

Dunne, F., & Honts, F. (1998, April). *"This group really makes me think!" Critical Friends groups and the development of reflective practitioners.* Paper presented at the annual meeting of the American Educational Research Association, San Diego, CA.

Egan, K. (1987). Literacy and the oral foundations of education. *Harvard Educational Review, 57*(4), 445–472.

Eisner, E. (1982). An artistic approach to supervision. In T. J. Sergiovanni (Ed.), *Supervision of teaching* (pp. 60–65). Alexandria, VA: Association for Supervision and Curriculum Development.

Erikson, E. H. (1980). *Identity and the life cycle.* New York: Norton.

Erikson, E. H. (1982). *The life cycle completed.* New York: Norton.

Foster, M. (1987). "It's cookin now": An ethnographic study of the teaching style of a successful black teacher in a white community college. In L. Delpit (Ed.),

Other people's children: Cultural conflict in the classroom (pp. 135–151). New York: The New Press.

Fraser, R. C. (1982). *Practical and legal aspects of teacher evaluation.* Unpublished paper.

Freire, P. (1972). *Pedagogy of the oppressed.* New York: Herder and Herder.

From Welfare to Working in Child Care: Possibilities and Pitfalls. (1996). *Rights raises respect: News and issues for the child care workforce, 1,* 1, 3.

Fuller, F. (1969). Concerns of teachers: A developmental conceptualization. *American Education Research Journal, 6*(2), 207–226.

Fuller, F., & Bown, O. H. (1975). Becoming a teacher. In K. Ryan (Ed.), *The 74th yearbook of the National Society for the Study of Education* (Part 2, pp. 25–52). Chicago: University of Chicago Press.

Fyfe, B. (1994). Assessing experiential learning for college credit. In J. Johnson & J. B. McCracken, *The early childhood career lattice: Perspectives on professional development* (pp. 153–156). Washington, DC: National Association for the Education of Young Children.

Gallas, K. (1998). *Sometimes I can be anything.* New York: Teachers College Press.

Galloway, C. M. (1974). Nonverbal communication in teaching. In R. T. Hyman (Ed.), *Teaching: Vantage points for study* (2nd ed.; pp. 395–406). Philadelphia: Lippincott.

Garcia, E. (1997). The education of Hispanics in early childhood: Of roots and wings. *Young Children, 52*(3), 5–14.

Gardner, H. (1983). *Frames of mind: The theory of multiple intelligences.* New York: Basic Books.

Garman, N. B. (1982). The clinical approach to supervision. In T. J. Sergiovanni (Ed.), *Supervision of teaching* (pp. 35–52). Alexandria, VA: Association for Supervision and Curriculum Development.

Genser, A., & Baden, C. (Eds.). (1983). *School-age child care: Programs and issues. Papers from a conference at Wheelock College.* Urbana, IL: ERIC Clearinghouse on Elementary and Early Childhood Education.

Gilligan, C. (1982). *In a different voice: Psychological theory of women's development.* Cambridge, MA: Harvard University Press.

Glassberg, S. (1980, April). *A view of the beginning teacher from a developmental perspective.* Paper presented at the annual meeting of the American Educational Research Association, Boston.

Glickman, C. D., Gordon, S. P., & Ross-Gordon, J. M. (1998). *Supervison of instruction: A developmental approach* (4th ed.). Boston: Allyn and Bacon.

Goldhammer, R. (1969). *Clinical supervision: Special methods for the supervision of teachers.* New York: Holt, Rinehart and Winston.

Goleman, D. (1995). *Emotional intelligence.* New York: Bantam Books.

Gonzalez-Mena, J. (1992). Taking a culturally sensitive approach in infant/toddler programs. *Young Children, 47*(2), 4–9.

Gould, R. L. (1978). *Transformations: Growth and change in adult life.* New York: Simon and Schuster.

Gratz, R. R., & Boulton, P. J. (1996). Erikson and early childhood educators: Looking at ourselves and our profession developmentally. *Young Children, 51*(5), 74–78.

Greenberg, H. M. (1969). *Teaching with feeling*. New York: Pegasus.

Greenberg, P. (1975). *Day care do-it-yourself staff growth program*. Winston-Salem, NC: Kaplan Press.

Greene, M. (1988). What happened to imagination? In K. Egan & D. Nadaner (Eds.), *Imagination and education* (pp. 45–56). New York: Teachers College Press.

Greene, M. (1995). *Releasing the imagination: Essays on education, the arts, and social change*. San Francisco: Jossey-Bass.

Greenman, J. (1989). Diversity and conflict: The whole world will never sing in perfect harmony. *Child Care Information Exchange, 69,* 11–13.

Greenough, K. (1993). Moving out of silence: The CDA process with Alaska native teachers. In E. Jones (Ed.), *Growing teachers: Partnerships in staff development* (pp. 21–35). Washington, DC: National Association for the Education of Young Children.

Grimmett, P. (1983, April). *Effective clinical supervision conference interventions: A preliminary investigation of participants' conceptual functioning*. Paper presented at the annual meeting of the American Educational Research Association, Montreal, Canada.

Guba E. G., & Lincoln, Y. S. (1981). *Effective evaluation*. San Francisco: Jossey-Bass.

Guide to accreditation by the National Academy of Early Childhood Programs. (1998). Washington, DC: National Association for the Education of Young Children.

Hall, E. T. (1973). *The silent language*. New York: Anchor Press/Doubleday.

Harms, T., & Clifford, R. M. (1989). *Family day care rating scale*. New York: Teachers College Press.

Harms, T., Clifford, R. M., & Cryer, D. (1998). *Early childhood environment rating scale, revised edition*. New York: Teachers College Press.

Harms, T., Cryer, D., & Clifford, R. M. (1990). *Infant/toddler environment rating scale*. New York: Teachers College Press.

Harms, T., Jacobs, E. V., & White, D. R. (1995). *School-age care environment rating scale*. New York: Teachers College Press.

Harris, P. R., & Moran, R. T. (1991). *Managing cultural differences* (3rd ed.). Houston: Gulf Publishing.

Hatch, V. B. (1979). Creative supervision of Head Start centers. In D. W. Hewes (Ed.), *Administration: Making programs work for children and families* (pp. 141–146). Washington, DC: National Association for the Education of Young Children.

High/Scope child observation record (COR) for ages 2½–6. (1992). Ypsilanti, MI: High/Scope Press.

Hilliard, A. G., III (1974). Moving from abstract to functional teacher education: Pruning and planting. In B. Spodek (Ed.), *Teacher education: Of the teacher, by the teacher, for the child* (pp. 7–23). Washington, DC: National Association for the Education of Young Children.

Hirsh, E. (1984). *The block book* (2nd ed.). Washington, DC: National Association for the Education of Young Children.

Hohmann, M., & Weikart, D. (1995). *Educating young children: Active learning practices for preschool and child care programs*. Ypsilanti, MI: High/Scope Press.

Honig, A. S. (1983). Quality training for infant caregivers. *Child Care Quarterly, 12*(2), 121–135.

Hubbard, R. S., & Power, B. M. (1993). *The art of classroom inquiry: A handbook for teacher researchers.* Portsmouth, NH: Heinemann.

Hunt, D. E. (1971). *Matching models in education.* Toronto: Ontario Institute for Studies in Education.

Irvine, J. J. (1991, November). *A response to David Flinders: Implications for culturally diverse schools.* Paper presented at the annual fall conference of the Council of Professors of Instructional Supervision, University of Houston, Houston, TX.

Johnson, R. G. (1979). *The appraisal interview guide.* New York: Alpine Press.

Johnson, S. M. (1990). *Teachers at work: Achieving success in our schools.* New York: Basic Books.

Jones, E. (Ed.). (1993). *Growing teachers: Partnerships in staff development.* Washington, DC: National Association for the Education of Young Children.

Jones, E. (1994). Breaking the ice: Confronting status differences among professionals. In J. Johnson & J. B. McCracken (Eds.), *The early childhood career lattice: Perspectives on professional development* (pp. 27–30). Washington, DC: National Association for the Education of Young Children.

Jones, E., & Carter, M. (1991). Teacher as scribe and broadcaster: Using observation to communicate—Part 2. *Child Care Information Exchange, 77,* 35–38.

Joyce, B., & Showers, B. (1980). Improving in-service training: The messages of research. *Educational Leadership, 37,* 379–385.

Kagan, S. L., & Neuman, M. J. (1996, January). The relationship between staff education and training and quality in child care programs. *Child Care Information Exchange,* pp. 65–70.

Katz, D., & Kahn, R. L. (1966). *The social psychology of organizations.* New York: John Wiley & Sons.

Katz, L. G. (1977). Teachers developmental stages. In L. G. Katz, *Talks with teachers: Reflections on early childhood education* (pp. 7–13). Washington, DC: National Association for the Education of Young Children.

Kendall, F. (1996). *Diversity in the classroom: New approaches to the education of young children* (2nd ed.). New York: Teachers College Press.

King, E. W., Chipman, M., & Cruz-Jazen, M. (1994). *Educating young children in a diverse society.* Needham Heights, MA: Allyn & Bacon.

Kisker, E. E., Hofferth, S. L., Phillips, D. A., & Farquhar, E. (1991). *A profile of child care settings: Early education and care in 1990.* Vol. 1. (MPR Reference No.: 7828–970). Princeton, NJ: Mathematica Policy Research.

Kleinfeld, J. (1988, June). *Learning to think like a teacher: The study of cases.* Fairbanks: Center for Cross-Cultural Studies, University of Alaska.

Kohlberg, L. (1984). *The psychology of moral development.* San Francisco: Harper and Row.

Kontos, S. (1992). *Family day care: Out of the shadows and into the limelight.* Washington, DC: National Association for the Education of Young Children.

Kontos, S., Howes, C., Shinn, M., & Galinsky, E. (1995). *Quality in family child care and relative care.* New York: Teachers College Press.

Kostelnik, M. J. (1982, September/October). How to mediate staff conflict. *Child Care Information Exchange,* pp. 1–5.

Lally, J. R., Young-Holt, C. L., & Mangione, P. (1994). Preparing caregivers for quality infant and toddler child care. In J. Johnson & J. B. McCracken (Eds.), *The early childhood career lattice: Perspectives on professional development* (pp. 100–105). Washington, DC: National Association for the Education of Young Children.

Levine, S. L. (1989). *Promoting adult growth in schools: The promise of professional development.* Boston: Allyn & Bacon.

Levinson, D. (1978). *The seasons of a man's life.* New York: Ballentine.

Levinson, D. (1996). *The seasons of a woman's life.* New York: Ballentine.

Lieberman, A., & Miller, L. (1992). *Teachers, their world, and their work: Implications for school improvement.* New York: Teachers College Press.

Little, J. W. (1982). Norms of collegiality and experimentation: Workplace conditions of school success. *American Education Research Journal, 19,* 325–340.

Little, J. W. (1990). The persistence of privacy: Autonomy and initiative in teachers' professional relations. *Teachers College Record, 91*(4), 509–536.

Loevinger, J. (1976). *Ego development: Conception and theories.* San Francisco: Jossey-Bass.

Marsh, K. J. (1998, April). *Classroom relationships: The narratives of a Lakota high school teacher.* Paper presented at the annual meeting of the American Educational Research Association, San Diego.

Mayeroff, M. (1971). *On caring.* New York: Harper and Row.

McCarthy, L. B., & Landerholm, E. (1978). Classroom interaction: A field-based model for improving teaching in the day care center. *Child Care Quarterly, 7,* 35–44.

McLaughlin, M. W., & Pfeifer, R. S. (1988). *Teacher evaluation: Improvement, accountability, and effective learning.* New York: Teachers College Press.

Meyer, T., & Achinstein, B. (1998, April). *Collaborative inquiry among novice teachers as professional development: Sustaining habits of heart and mind.* Paper presented at the annual meeting of the American Educational Research Association, San Diego.

Mitchell, A., & Modigliani, K. (1989). Young children in public schools? The "only ifs" reconsidered. *Young Children, 44*(6), 56–61.

Morgan, G. (1997). *Taking the lead: Director credentialing info packet.* Boston: Wheelock College, Center for Career Development in Early Care and Education.

Morgan, G., Azer, S. L., Costley, J. B., Genser, A., Goodman, I. F., Lombardi, J., & McGimsey, B. (1993). *Making a career of it: The state of the states report on career development in early care and education.* Boston: Wheelock College, Center for Career Development in Early Care and Education.

Morimoto, K. (1973). Notes on the context of learning. *Harvard Educational Review, 43,* 247–249.

National Association for the Education of Young Children. (1998). *Accreditation criteria and procedures of the National Academy of Early Childhood Programs* (rev. ed). Washington, DC: Author.

NAEYC Position Statement: Responding to linguistic and cultural diversity—Recommendations for effective early childhood education. (1996). *Young Children*, *51*(2), 4–12.

Neugebauer, R. (1980). Techniques for avoiding director burn-out. *Child Care Information Exchange*, pp. 9–15.

Neugebauer, R. (1993). Status report #1 on school-age child care. *Child Care Information Exchange*, *89*, 11–15.

Newberger, J. J. (1997). New brain development research—a wonderful window of opportunity to build public support for early childhood education. *Young Children*, *52*(4), 4–9.

Noddings, N. (1984). *Caring: A feminine approach to ethics and moral education*. Berkeley: University of California Press.

Noddings, N. (1992). *The challenge to care in schools: An alternative approach to education*. New York: Teachers College Press.

Nurturing green staff from day one: Ideas from directors. (1993). *Child Care Information Exchange*, *90*, 5–10.

O'Connor, S. (1994). Professional development for school-age child care. In J. Johnson & J. B. McCracken (Eds.), *The early childhood career lattice: Perspectives on professional development* (pp. 121–125). Washington, DC: National Association for the Education of Young Children.

Oja, S. N. (1981, April). *Deriving teacher educational objectives from cognitive-developmental theories and applying them to the practice of teacher education*. Paper presented at the annual meeting of the American Education Research Association, Los Angeles.

Paley, V. (1986). *Mollie is three: Growing up in school*. Chicago: The University of Chicago Press.

Perry, W. G. (1969). *Forms of intellectual and ethical development during the college years*. New York: Holt, Rinehart and Winston.

Peterson, K. D. (1995). *Teacher evaluation: A comprehensive guide to new directions and practices*. Thousand Oaks, CA: Corwin Press.

Piaget, J. (1961). The genetic approach to the psychology of thought. *Journal of Educational Psychology*, *52*, 275–281.

Pickhardt, C. E. (1981). Supervisors and the power of help. *Educational Leadership*, *38*, 530–533.

Powell, D. R. (1994). Parents, pluralism and the NAEYC statement on developmentally appropriate practice. In B. L. Mallory & R. S. New (Eds.), *Diversity and developmentally appropriate practices: Challenges for early childhood education* (pp. 166–182). New York: Teachers College Press.

Rogers, C. E. (1962). The interpersonal relationship: The core of guidance. *Harvard Educational Review*, *32*, 416–429.

Rothenberg, D. (1995, May). *Full-day kindergarten programs*. ERIC Digest. (Eric Document Reproduction Service No. ED 382 410).

Rowen, B. (1973). *The children we see: An observational approach to child study*. New York: Holt, Rinehart and Winston.

Ruopp, R., Travers, J., Glantz, F., & Coelen, C. (1979). *Final report of the national day care study: Vol. 1. Children at the center*. Cambridge, MA: Abt Associates.

Schein, E. H. (1985). *Organizational culture and leadership*. San Francisco: Jossey-Bass.

Schön, D. A. (1987). *Educating the reflective practitioner: Toward a new design for teaching and learning in the professions*. San Francisco: Jossey-Bass.

Sciarra, D. J., & Dorsey, A. G. (1990). *Developing and administering a child care center* (2nd ed.). Boston: Houghton Mifflin.

Seidel, S. (1998). Learning from looking. In N. Lyons (Ed.), *With portfolio in hand: Validating the new teacher professionalism* (pp. 65–89). New York: Teachers College Press.

Seiderman, S. (1978). Combatting staff burn-out. *Day Care and Early Education, 5*, 6–8.

Seppanen, P. S., deVries, D. K., & Seligson, M. (1993). *National study of before- and after-school programs: Executive summary*. Washington, DC: U.S. Department of Education.

Sheehy, G. (1976). *Passages: Predictable crises of adult life*. New York: E. P. Dutton.

Sheehy, G. (1998). *Understanding men's passages: Discovering the new map of men's lives*. New York: Random House.

Shore, R. (1997). *Rethinking the brain: New insights into early development*. New York: Families and Work Institute.

Shulman, J. H., & Colbert, J. A. (Eds.). (1987). *The mentor teacher casebook*. San Francisco: Far West Laboratory for Educational Research and Development.

Sparks, D., & Hirsh, S. (1997). *A new vision for staff development*. Alexandria, VA: Association for Supervision and Curriculum Development.

Spodek, B., & Saracho, O. N. (1982). The preparation and certification of early childhood personnel. In B. Spodek (Ed.), *Handbook of research in early childhood education* (pp. 399–425). New York: Macmillan.

Steinmetz, L. (1969). *Managing the marginal and unsatisfactory performer*. Reading, MA: Addison-Wesley.

Sturm, C. (1997). Creating parent-teacher dialogue: Intercultural communication in child care. *Young Children, 52*(5), 34–38.

Thies-Sprinthall, L. (1980). Supervision: An educative or mis-educative process? *Journal of Teacher Education, 31*(4), 17–20.

U.S. Department of Education. (1990). *A profile of child care settings: Early education and care in 1990, executive summary* (ED/OUSs/91-44). Washington, DC: Author.

U.S. Department of Health & Human Services. (n.d.) *National Head Start Bulletin*, Issue No. 60. Washington, DC: Author.

U.S. Department of Health and Human Services. (1996). *Head Start program performance standards* (ACYF-IM-HS 96-23). Washington, DC: Author.

Vander Ven, K. (1988). Pathways for professional effectiveness for early childhood educators. In B. Spodek, O. N. Saracho, & D. L. Peters (Eds.), *Professionalism and the early childhood practitioner* (pp. 137–160). New York: Teachers College Press.

Vartuli, S., & Fyfe, B. (1993). Teachers need developmentally appropriate practices too. *Young Children, 48*(4), 36–42.

Vecchi, V. (1993). The role of the Atelierista. In C. Edwards, L. Gandini, & G. Forman

(Eds.), *The hundred languages of children: The Reggio Emilia approach to early childhood education* (pp. 119–127). Norwood, NJ: Ablex.

Vecchi, V. (1997, January). *The hundred languages of children: Children and art.* Paper presented at the Winter Institute, Reggio Emilia, Italy.

Wessen, P. D. (1981, November). Off-site stress and the disadvantaged caregiver: A neglected factor. *Child Care Information Exchange*, pp. 10–12.

What centers need to succeed at accreditation. (1997). *Rights Raises Respect: News and Issues for the Child Care Work Force, 2, 7*.

Whitebook, M. (1997, November). *Managing staff turnover in child care centers: Best practices for the field.* Paper presented at the annual meeting of the National Association for the Education of Young Children, Anaheim, CA.

Whitebook, M., Howes, C., Darrah, R., & Friedman, J. (1982). Caring for the caregivers: Staff burn-out in child care. In L. Katz (Ed.), *Current topics in early childhood education* (Vol. 4; pp. 211–235). Norwood, NJ: Ablex.

Whitebook, M., Howes, C., & Phillips, D. (1989). *Who cares? Child care teachers and the quality of care in America.* Final Report, National Child Care Staffing Study. Oakland, CA: Child Care Employee Project.

Whitebook, M., Phillips, D., & Howes, C. (1993). *The national child care staffing study revisited: Four years in the life of center-based child care.* Oakland, CA: Center for the Child Care Workforce.

Willer, B. (Ed.). (1994). A conceptual framework for early childhood professional development: NAEYC Position Statement, adopted November 1993. In J. Johnson & J. B. McCraken (Eds), *The early childhood career lattice: Perspectives on professional development* (pp. 4–21). Washington, DC: National Association for the Education of Young Children.

Willis, A., & Ricciuti, H. (1975). *A good beginning for babies: Guidelines for group care.* Washington, DC: National Association for the Education of Young Children.

Wolf, K. (1991). The schoolteacher's portfolio: Issues in the design, implementation, and evaluation. *Phi Delta Kappan, 73*(2), 129–136.

Wolfe, B. L. (1994). Effective practices in staff development: Head Start experiences. In J. Johnson & J. B. McCracken (Eds.), *The early childhood career lattice: Perspectives on professional development* (pp. 111–114). Washington, DC: National Association for the Education of Young Children.

Woonsocket Head Start. (n.d.). *Let us tell you about Head Start.* Woonsocket, RI: Author.

Index

About the Authors

Joseph J. Caruso is Professor of Education and Chair, Education Department, at Framingham State College, Framingham, Massachusetts. He has also taught at Wheelock College and at Fairfield University. He received his bachelor's degree from Boston University, and his master's and doctorate from Teachers College, Columbia University. He has published articles in various educational journals. His major research and writing interests are in the fields of supervision and teacher education.

M. Temple Fawcett is Professor Emeritas of Early Childhood and Elementary Education at Roger Williams University in Bristol, Rhode Island. She received her B.A. in music from Brown University and her M.Ed. from the Harvard Graduate School of Education in Elementary Education. She was director of the CDA pilot training program in Fall River, Massachusetts, has been a teacher and teacher educator in a variety of settings, and has been active in National Association for the Education of Young Children activities at the local, state, and regional levels.